Jossey-Bass Teacher

Jossey-Bass Teacher provides educators with practical knowledge and tools to create a positive and lifelong impact on student learning. We offer classroom-tested and research-based teaching resources for a variety of grade levels and subject areas. Whether you are an aspiring, new, or veteran teacher, we want to help you make every teaching day your best.

From ready-to-use classroom activities to the latest teaching framework, our value-packed books provide insightful, practical, and comprehensive materials on the topics that matter most to K–12 teachers. We hope to become your trusted source for the best ideas from the most experienced and respected experts in the field.

The ESL/ELL Teacher's Survival Guide

Ready-to-Use Strategies, Tools, and Activities for Teaching English Language Learners of All Levels

LARRY FERLAZZO AND KATIE HULL SYPNIESKI

JOSSEY-BASS
A Wiley Imprint
www.josseybass.com

Published by Jossey-Bass
A Wiley Imprint

One Montgomery Street, Suite 1200, San Francisco, CA 94104-4594—www.josseybass.com

Jossey-Bass books and products are available through most bookstores. To contact Jossey-Bass directly call our Customer Care Department within the U.S. at 800-956-7739, outside the U.S. at 317-572-3986, or fax 317-572-4002.

Wiley publishes in a variety of print and electronic formats and by print-on-demand. Some material included with standard print versions of this book may not be included in e-books or in print-on-demand. If this book refers to media such as a CD or DVD that is not included in the version you purchased, you may download this material at **http://booksupport.wiley.com**. For more information about Wiley products, visit **www.wiley.com**.

Library of Congress Cataloging-in-Publication Data
Ferlazzo, Larry.
   The ESL/ELL teacher's survival guide : ready-to-use strategies, tools, and activities for teaching English language learners of all levels / Larry Ferlazzo, Katie Hull-Sypnieski.
        p. cm. — (Jossey-Bass teacher)
   Includes bibliographical references and index.
   ISBN 978-1-118-09567-6 (pbk.), ISBN 978-1-118-22359-8 (ebk.), ISBN 978-1-118-23697-0 (ebk.), ISBN 978-1-118-26191-0 (ebk.)
   1. English language—Study and teaching—Foreign speakers. I. Hull-Sypnieski, Katie, 1974- II. Title.
   PE1128.A2F455 2012
   428.0071—dc23

                                                                                        2012011534

Printed in the United States of America
FIRST EDITION

PB Printing V10009364_041219

About the Authors

Larry Ferlazzo teaches English and social studies to English language learners and mainstream students at Luther Burbank High School in Sacramento, California. He has written three previous books: *Helping Students Motivate Themselves: Practical Answers to Classroom Challenges; English Language Learners: Teaching Strategies That Work;* and *Building Parent Engagement in Schools* (with co-author Lorie Hammond).

He has won numerous awards, including the Leadership for a Changing World Award from the Ford Foundation, and was the grand prize winner of the International Reading Association Award for Technology and Reading.

He writes a popular education blog at http://larryferlazzo.edublogs.org and writes a weekly teacher advice column for *Education Week Teacher.* His articles on education policy regularly appear in the *Washington Post* and the *Huffington Post.* In addition, his work has appeared in publications such as *The New York Times, ASCD Educational Leadership, Social Policy,* and *Language Magazine.*

Ferlazzo was a community organizer for nineteen years prior to becoming a public school teacher. He is married and has three children and two grandchildren.

Katie Hull Sypnieski has taught English learners of all levels for fifteen years in the Sacramento City Unified School District. She has served as a teaching consultant with the Area 3 Writing Project at UC Davis for the past ten years and as a district lead trainer for the WRITE Institute.

She is a member of the Teacher Leaders Network and has published articles in *Education Week Teacher.*

Sypnieski currently teaches English and ELD at Luther Burbank High School in Sacramento, California. She is married and has three children.

Contents

CONTENTS

Acknowledgments

Larry Ferlazzo. I'd like to thank my family—Stacia, Rich, Shea, Ava, Nik, Karli, and especially, my wife, Jan—for their support. In addition, I need to express appreciation to my co-author, Katie Hull Sypnieski, who has also been a classroom neighbor and co-teacher for eight years. I would like to thank Kelly Young at Pebble Creek Labs and my many colleagues at Luther Burbank High School, including Principal Ted Appel, for their assistance over the years. Thanks also to Dr. Stephen Krashen for his helpful review of the manuscript. And, probably most important, I'd like to thank the many English language learner students who have made me a better teacher—and a better person. Finally, I must offer a big thank-you to Marjorie McAneny and Tracy Gallagher at Jossey-Bass for their patience and guidance in preparing this book.

Katie Hull Sypnieski. I would like to thank all the students I've had over the years for their determination, their creative energy, and for helping me to grow as an educator and as a person. In addition, I am grateful for all of the support I have received from my colleagues at Luther Burbank High School, especially Larry Ferlazzo, my co-author, co-teacher, and friend. I also greatly appreciate the help from Marjorie McAneny and Tracy Gallagher at Jossey-Bass. Finally, to all of my family members, especially my husband, David, and children Drew, Ryan, and Rachel, I want to thank you for supporting me in this process—you are the best!

Introduction

*T*here was a great forest fire—everything was burning and all the animals were scared and didn't know what they could do. A hummingbird, though, went to a lake and got a drop of water. It flew to the fire and dropped the water there, and it kept on going back again. The other animals kept on telling the hummingbird that it was wasting its time, telling it there was no way a little water was going to make a difference. The hummingbird replied, "I'm doing the best I can."

—Japanese folktale[1]

The hummingbird did its best in the face of many challenges and adversity, and nothing could stop it.

While it would have been ideal for the hummingbird to organize all the animals to join it in fighting the fire, always encouraging the use of that kind of strategy is not the main point of the story or this book. This book is primarily designed to help the secondary-level ESL teacher do the best she can in her classroom (though it does also include a chapter on how to help mainstream educators make their content more accessible to English language learners, too). In addition, the majority of approaches and strategies we discuss can be easily modified for younger ELLs.

This book is written by two committed and experienced educators who have a rich family life outside of school, plan on continuing to teach for years to come, and who are always interested in providing high-quality education to their students without requiring enormous extra work for the teacher.

It is not written by or for teachers who lack awareness of their own limitations and what is needed to stay in education for the long haul.

This book is a careful distillation of selected instructional strategies that have been used successfully by us for years in the classroom.

It is not a laundry list of every ELL teaching method that's been discussed in the literature.

In addition to providing a selective review of ELL teaching methods, this book shares highly regarded research supporting just about everything we suggest.

It is not just speaking from our experience and what we think is good.

This book shares numerous specific suggestions about how ESL teachers can use technology to bring a value-added benefit to their language-learning students.

It is not a treatise on how educational technology is the "magic bullet" that is always (or even often) superior to nontech strategies.

This book recognizes that teachers need to deal with standards (we use a simple summary of California State ESL/ELD standards throughout the book that has been developed by the Sacramento City Unified School District—see Exhibit 3.1 in Chapter Three), textbooks, and standardized tests. This book also recognizes that not everything always goes according to plan, and includes a lengthy chapter on how to deal with potential problems. This book understands the realities of what work in the classroom world actually is like.

It does not offer a pie-in-the-sky view assuming we operate in an ideal classroom world all the time.

This book emphasizes the importance of learners being co-creators of their education.

It does not encourage the teacher being the "sage on stage."

The point of this book is not to claim it is the be-all and end-all for ESL teacher professional development. We strongly encourage teachers and their schools to develop ongoing mentor relationships with experienced educator organizations, and we recommend three of them in the Afterword.

This book does not promote the idea that any teacher is an island and only needs a few books and informal professional relationships to reach his full potential.

We hope that you can gain from this guide at least as much as we learned from writing it.

Bonus Web Content

Numerous Tech Tools supporting the lessons and instructional strategies that we discuss are highlighted throughout this book. In addition, we have a lengthy web page listing links to all the tools we cite, as well as to many others that we did not have space to include. All Exhibits in the book can also be downloaded. Readers can access these resources by going to www.josseybass.com/go/eslsurvivalguide. To post messages pertaining to this book or interact with the authors, join the Twitter conversation: #eslsg.

PART ONE

Getting Started with English Language Learners

CHAPTER ONE

ESL Instruction: The Big Picture

Long ago in the southwestern part of the United States an Indian tribe lived near a range of mountains. Climbing the highest of these mountains was considered an important accomplishment, and all the young boys of the village couldn't wait until they were old enough to make the climb on their own.

One night, the Chief gathered the boys together and said to them, "You have reached the age to take on the challenge. Tomorrow you may all go and climb that mountain with my blessings. Go as far as you can, and when you are tired, turn around and come home. Remember to bring back a twig from the place where you turned around."

The next morning, the boys began the long awaited climb. A few hours later, one of the boys returned with a piece of buckthorn. The Chief smiled and said, "I can see you made it to the first rockslide. Wonderful!" Later in the afternoon, another boy arrived with a cedar frond. "You made it halfway up! Well done!" remarked the Chief. An hour later another boy returned with a branch of pine, and the Chief said, "Good job. It looks like you made it three-quarters of the way. If you keep trying, next year you will surely reach the top!"

As the sun began to set, the Chief began to worry about the last boy, who still had not returned. Just when the Chief was about to send out a search party, the boy finally returned. He ran to the Chief and held out his hand. His hand was empty, but his eyes sparkled with happiness as he said, "Chief, there were no trees where I turned around. I saw no twigs, no living things at the very top of the peak, and far away I could see the majestic sun shining off the sea."

The Chief's eyes also sparkled with joy as he proclaimed, "I knew it! When I looked in your eyes I could see that you made it! You have been to the top! It shines in your eyes and sings in your voice! My son, you do not need twigs or branches as prizes of your victory. You have felt the prize in your spirit because you have seen the wonder of the mountain!"[1]

This tale describes the satisfaction and joy felt by the boy who reached the mountain's peak and witnessed the compelling view from the top. He didn't return with any physical "prizes," but instead carried the treasures of his journey within himself. The next time he climbs the mountain, he will be motivated from within, not because there are tokens or prizes to be collected.

As educators, we hope all of our students will "see the view from the peak" and will feel compelled to take on many more journeys as they learn and grow. In a recent paper, Stephen Krashen explains how "compelling input" relates to language learning:

> Compelling means that the input is so interesting you forget that it is in another language. It means you are in a state of "flow."[2] In flow, the concerns of everyday life and even the sense of self disappear—our sense of time is altered and nothing but the activity itself seems to matter.[3]

This idea will be reflected throughout this book as we identify and describe research-based instructional strategies and approaches that "compel" students to want to learn English. Compelling input can help students "reach the peak" of acquiring language without seeking external rewards. However, it is ultimately important for students to come to their own conclusions about the value of "reaching the peak." Once students see the value of language learning and become intrinsically motivated to learn English, they will take the risk and climb that mountain over and over again. Sometimes they will need encouragement and support from us, especially when the peak is obscured by clouds along the way.

This book contains strategies and tools for the English as a second language (ESL) teacher to act as a guide on this trek up the mountain. We hope it will help you feel prepared and excited about this journey. We know that everyone's trail will be different, and we hope this survival guide will serve as a compass rather than a direct map.

In the following subsections we will lay out a big picture of ESL instruction, including statistics on the English language learner (ELL) population, research on language development, and several ESL instructional best practices. Later chapters will go into more detail on how to successfully use the research and practices presented in this big picture in your own classroom.

Some Facts About the ELL Population

It is hard to find a school or district in this country that doesn't have an English learner population. For teachers in states like California, Texas, Florida, and New York it is sometimes hard to find a classroom without any English language learners. In fact, the U.S. Department of Education estimates that approximately 4.5 million English learners are enrolled in public schools across the country—roughly 10 percent of all students enrolled in K–12 schools in the United States.[4] The number of English learners has increased by over 50 percent in the last decade, with some states, like South Carolina and Indiana, experiencing extremely rapid growth of English learner populations (400 to 800 percent increases).[5] The ELL population continues to grow, with some demographers predicting that in twenty years the ratio of ELL students to English-only students could be one in four.[6]

While English learners in this country come from over four hundred different language backgrounds, the majority (80 percent) of the ELL population enrolled in our nation's schools are Spanish speakers.[7] Vietnamese and Chinese are the next two most common first languages spoken among ELLs (accounting for 1.8 percent and 1.4 percent, respectively, of the ELL population).[8]

ELL, ESL, ELD, LEP, EFL: WHAT DO ALL THE LABELS MEAN?

ELL, or English language learner. ELL is the most current term used in the United States to describe students whose native language is not English, who are in various stages of acquiring English, and who require various levels of language support and development in order to become fully proficient in English.

ESL, or English as a second language. The term *ESL* was formerly used as a designation for ELL students, but is more commonly used now to refer to "a program of instruction designed to support ELL students" and is often still used at the postsecondary level to refer to multilingual students.[9]

ELD, or English language development. ELD is often used to describe instruction and programs for ELL students that focus on developing English language proficiency in the domains of reading, writing, listening, and speaking.

LEP, or limited English proficiency. *LEP* is used by the U.S. Department of Education for ELLs who have not yet demonstrated proficiency in English, according to state standards and assessments.[10]

EFL, or English as a foreign language. EFL refers to students who are "nonnative English speakers, but who are learning English in a country where English is not the primary language."[11]

Many educators and researchers, including the authors of this book, prefer the term *ELL* because it emphasizes that students are active *learners* of English, as opposed to being limited or deficient in some way.

ADOLESCENT ELLS AND LONG-TERM ELLS

Adolescent ELL students are a fast-growing population and come from a variety of cultural, linguistic, and educational backgrounds. ELLs in grades seven through twelve increased by approximately 70 percent between 1992 and 2002.[12]

From 9 to 20 percent of students enrolled in middle and high schools are newcomer or refugee students. While some of these students come with high literacy skills and content knowledge, the majority of newcomers are students with interrupted formal education (SIFE) who have had two or more years of interrupted schooling in their home country.[13] These students enter U.S. schools with limited educational experiences and lower levels of literacy in their native languages.

Well over half of ELLs in middle and high schools were born in the United States, are second- or even third-generation immigrants, and have been enrolled in U.S. schools since kindergarten.[14] Researchers have identified these students as long-term English language learners, or LT-ELLs. Typically, these students have high levels of oral English proficiency, but may lack the academic language and skills in reading and writing needed to master subject matter.[15] Many long-term ELLs are stuck at the intermediate level due to their lack of proficiency in academic language and their challenges with reading and writing skills. Many of these students may not have received targeted language development, may have been placed with teachers lacking the professional development needed to meet specific language needs, and may have lived in particularly challenging socioeconomic conditions, including poverty.[16]

With such diversity among adolescent ELLs, it is important for teachers to learn as much as possible about their students and to have knowledge of strategies that directly address the needs of these students. Chapter Two contains ideas for getting to know students and for building relationships of trust with students and their families. It also outlines important resources for working with adolescent ELLs and gives ideas for establishing classroom routines that promote a positive learning environment. Chapters Three and Four present instructional strategies designed for newcomer and beginning students, and Chapters Five and Six offer numerous strategies designed for intermediate-level learners, including long-term ELLs.

While adolescent learners enter our classrooms with diverse needs and challenges, it is important to remember that adolescents also bring creative minds capable of processing higher-order thinking and learning. The general public may often have the impression that language learning is easiest for young children and becomes harder and harder with age. However, recent research has shown that some elements of language acquisition may actually be easier for adolescents than for young children. One study found that young adults who were taught a specific language rule were better than younger children at "recognizing the rule, applying it quickly, and using it in new situations."[17]

A Primer on ESL Research

The following subsections present basic descriptions of research and concepts that are foundational components of ESL instruction. While this is not a comprehensive summary of all the research on language development, it is an introduction to several key concepts that are highly important for teachers of ELLs and can serve as launching points for further study.

L1 AND L2

Researchers and educators commonly use the term *L1* to refer to a student's native language (also called primary language, home language, or heritage language) and *L2* to refer to the language a student is acquiring in addition to their native language, which in the United States is English. The next subsection, on ESL best practices, will discuss the important link between L1 and L2 in language learning.

BICS AND CALP

Jim Cummins, a professor at the University of Toronto, first introduced the distinction between basic interpersonal communicative skills, or BICS, and cognitive academic language proficiency, or CALP,[18] and his research has had a major impact on both policy and practices in second language education.

Basically, BICS, also called *communicative competence,* refer to the listening and speaking skills that students tend to acquire quickly in a new language (within the first couple of years) in order to communicate in social situations. For example, BICS enable one to talk with friends on the soccer field or to ask someone for directions.

CALP refers to the academic language and more cognitively demanding skills that are required for academic success. CALP takes longer for students to develop, often between five to seven years, but can take longer for students with less proficiency in their native language.[19] CALP is required in academic situations such as lectures, class discussions, and research projects, and includes skills such as summarizing, analyzing, extracting and interpreting meaning, evaluating evidence, composing, and editing.[20]

More recent research has extended CALP to include the following three dimensions of academic English: linguistic (knowledge of word forms, functions, grammatical elements, and discourse patterns used in academic settings), cognitive (higher-order thinking involved in academic settings), and sociocultural-psychological (knowledge of social practices involved in academic settings).[21] ESL instruction based on CALP is still widely accepted as best practice,[22] as many researchers agree upon the need to focus on academic language proficiency in order for English learners to succeed in school.

ACQUISITION VERSUS LEARNING

Most researchers acknowledge a distinction between language acquisition and language learning. A simple, rudimentary explanation of the difference is that acquisition involves being able to easily use the language to communicate, while language learning might place more emphasis on filling out grammar worksheets correctly. This does not mean, however, that the two are mutually exclusive.

This distinction has led to much debate over the place of explicit grammar study in language development. Some linguists have argued for a more communicative approach, where the focus is on the message versus the form and fosters language acquisition, while others believe students need direct instruction in grammatical forms of the target language.[23]

Recent research has proposed a more balanced approach—that second language instruction can provide a combination of both *explicit* teaching focused on features of the second language such as grammar, vocabulary, and pronunciation, and *implicit* learning stemming from meaningful communication in the second language.[24] We agree that the best language instruction uses meaningful input and contexts to help students develop their English skills, but we also feel that teaching language features in context is also necessary for students to develop proficiency. Specific strategies for how to employ this kind of balanced approach in the classroom will be described in later chapters.

STAGES OF LANGUAGE DEVELOPMENT

While it is important to note that ELL students come with different cultural and educational experiences that can affect their language development, researchers, beginning with Stephen Krashen and Tracy Terrell,[25] have identified the following *general* stages of second language acquisition that students go through:

Preproduction. Also called the "silent period," when the student is taking in the target language, but not speaking it.

Early production. The student begins to try speaking using short phrases, but the focus is still on listening and absorbing the new language. Many errors occur in this stage.

Speech emergent. Words and sentences are longer, but the student still relies heavily on context clues and familiar topics. Vocabulary increases and errors decrease, especially in common or repeated interactions.

Beginning fluency. In social situations, speech is fairly fluent with minimal errors. New contexts and academic language are challenging due to gaps in vocabulary.

Intermediate fluency. Communicating in the second language is fluent, especially in social language situations. In new situations or in academic areas, speech is approaching fluency, but some gaps in vocabulary knowledge still exist. There are very few errors, and the student is able to demonstrate higher-order thinking skills (such as opinions and analysis) in the second language.

Advanced fluency. Student communicates fluently in all contexts and can maneuver successfully in new contexts and when exposed to new academic information. The student may still have an accent and use idiomatic expressions incorrectly at times, but is essentially fluent and comfortable communicating in the second language.[26]

It is important to remember that not all students' experiences fall neatly into these categories, and that prior educational experiences and literacy in their L1 can have a great impact on students' language acquisition processes. Most researchers believe it takes from five to seven years to reach advanced fluency if a student has strong first language and literacy skills, and that it can take between seven to ten years for students with less language proficiency in their first language.[27]

Knowing students' proficiency levels can help teachers differentiate their instruction and address the language needs of each student. For example, when working with students in preproduction and early production stages, it can be helpful to ask yes-or-no questions. Students at the speech emergent level could be asked questions that require a fairly short, literal answer, and students at the beginning fluency stage could be asked if they agree or disagree with a statement and why.

PROFICIENCY LEVELS

As described earlier, research has found that ELLs progress through several stages of language acquisition. Most states use a model that divides this process into five levels of English proficiency: beginning, early intermediate, intermediate, early advanced, and advanced.

Researchers have also found that students generally progress much more quickly from beginning to intermediate level (often taking two to three years) than from intermediate to advanced (often taking four or more years). This is likely because the lower levels of proficiency require simpler vocabulary and sentence patterns and involve language situations that are highly contextualized (familiar, recurrent, and supported by nonlinguistic clues such as gestures and intonation). Full proficiency, on the other hand, means students must have command of more complex sentence structures and vocabulary. They must have the academic English to function well in less contextualized situations (for example, a classroom discussion or a prompted essay), where they must clearly communicate their ideas on higher-level, more abstract concepts.

This research directly contradicts the argument that students who are immersed in all-English instruction will quickly become fluent, and it challenges the policies proposed and implemented in some states requiring students to move into mainstream classes after just one year of school.[28]

A Quick Tour of ESL Best Practices

Throughout this book we will describe many effective instructional strategies and activities to use with ELL students. The following are a few basic best practices in ESL instruction that will guide the strategies and activities presented in the following chapters. We have found that consistently using these practices makes our lessons more efficient and effective. We also feel it is important to include a few "worst" practices we have witnessed over the years in the hopes that they will not be repeated! The best practices outlined below, as well as others, will be explained in greater detail in subsequent chapters.

MODELING

Do. Model for students what they are expected to do or produce, especially for new skills or activities, by explaining and demonstrating the learning actions, sharing your thinking processes aloud, and showing samples of good teacher and student work. Modeling promotes learning and motivation by developing student self-confidence. It helps them "believe that they, too, will be successful if they follow the same behavioral sequence."[29] Modeling (or demonstrating) is one way for teachers to provide students with "critical input" in order to help students process content more "deeply and comprehensively."[30]

Don't. Just tell students what to do and expect them to do it.

RATE OF SPEECH AND WAIT TIME

Do. Speak slowly and clearly and provide students with enough time to formulate their responses, whether in speaking or in writing. Remember—they are thinking and producing in two or more languages! After asking a question, wait for a few seconds before calling on someone to respond. This wait time provides all students with an opportunity to think and process, and gives ELLs an especially needed period to formulate a response.[31]

Don't. Speak too fast, and if a student tells you they didn't understand what you said, never, ever repeat the same thing in a louder voice!

USE OF NONLINGUISTIC CUES

Do. Use visuals, sketches, gestures, intonation, and other nonverbal cues to make both language and content more accessible to students. Teaching with visual representations of concepts can be hugely helpful to ELLs.[32] Specific suggestions are included throughout this book.

Don't. Stand in front of the class and lecture or rely on a textbook as your only "visual aid."

GIVING INSTRUCTIONS

Do. Give verbal *and* written instructions—this practice can help all learners, especially ELLs. In addition, it is far easier for a teacher to point to the board in response to the inevitable repeated question, "What are we supposed to do?"[33]

Don't. Act surprised if students are lost when you haven't clearly written and explained step-by-step directions.

CHECK FOR UNDERSTANDING

Do. Regularly check that students are understanding the lesson. After an explanation or lesson, a teacher could say, "Please put thumbs up, thumbs down, or sideways to let me know if this is clear, *and it's perfectly fine if you don't understand or are unsure—I just need to know*." This last phrase is essential if you want students to respond honestly. Teachers can also have students quickly answer on a sticky note that they place on their desks. The teacher can then quickly circulate to check responses.

When teachers regularly check for understanding in the classroom, students become increasingly aware of monitoring their own understanding, which serves as a model of good study skills. It also helps ensure that students are learning, thinking, understanding, comprehending, and processing at high levels.[34]

Don't. Simply ask "Are there any questions?" This is not an effective way to gauge what all your students are thinking. Waiting until the end of class to see what people write in their learning log is not going to provide timely feedback. Also, don't assume that students are understanding because they are smiling and nodding their heads—sometimes they are just being polite!

ENCOURAGE DEVELOPMENT OF L1

Do. Encourage students to continue building their literacy skills in their L1. Research has found that learning to read in the home language promotes reading achievement in the second language as "transfer" occurs. These transfers may include phonological awareness, comprehension skills, and background knowledge.[35] It is also recommended as a best practice that teachers validate students' primary languages and encourage them to continue reading and writing in their L1.[36]

While the research on transfer of L1 skills to L2 cannot be denied, it doesn't mean that we should not encourage the use of English in class and outside of the classroom. For ideas on how to balance the use of L1 and L2 in the classroom, see the section on primary language use in the ESL classroom in Chapter Twelve.

Don't. "Ban" students' use of their native language in the classroom. Forbidding students from using their primary languages does not promote a positive learning environment where students feel safe to take risks and make mistakes. This practice can be harmful to the relationships between teachers and students, especially if teachers act more like language "police" than language "coaches."

We hope you will keep this big picture of ESL demographics, research, and best practices in mind as you explore the rest of this book and as you teach in your classroom.

 Additional resources, including ones on current ESL research and instructional strategies by proficiency level, can be found on our book's web site at www.josseybass.com/go/eslsurvivalguide.

CHAPTER TWO

ESL Classroom Basics: Building a Positive and Effective Learning Environment

*L*ong ago there was an old farmer named Pao who was dying. He had two lazy sons and he wanted them to care for the farm after his death. On this farm, they grew grapes. The dying man told his sons that there was gold treasure hidden on the farm.

The two sons spent many days looking for the treasure. They dug up the ground all over the farm, but never found any gold.

However, all the digging helped the grapevines. Many more grapes grew on the vines. Because of their hard work, the farm flourished and the sons were rich.

The two sons had learned a lesson from their father about the importance of hard work. From then on they were no longer lazy and took great care of the farm.[1]

The two sons in this folktale learned that their hard work of turning over the soil resulted in a more fruitful harvest. The same holds true in the classroom. Doing the hard work of "preparing the ground"—developing relationships with students and parents, gathering resources, and establishing routines—will yield a fruitful learning experience for all.

There isn't a perfect formula for being an effective ESL teacher, but for growth to occur, students must feel comfortable taking risks, making mistakes, and taking ownership of their learning. The teacher needs to take the lead in building relationships and fostering this kind of encouraging classroom environment. Teachers can work tirelessly to develop a curriculum with well-thought-out strategies and engaging, relevant topics, but if they don't "prepare the ground" and create an atmosphere that facilitates student engagement and achievement, then the results will not be fruitful.

You will notice this chapter comes prior to our sharing more specific ideas for curriculum, instructional strategies, and assessment. It serves as a foundation upon which to build, mirroring the foundation that must be built in the classroom between teacher and students, students and students, and teacher and parents.

We have found that there are three primary components of creating a positive, effective learning environment. Most people have heard of the traditional three Rs—Reading, wRiting, and aRithmetic—but we will be describing the three Rs of a successful ESL class: relationships, resources, and routines.

The First R: Building *Relationships*

Building relationships with students is vital. Simply put, it is perhaps the most critical factor affecting student motivation and learning. This is especially true for students in an ESL class who are faced each day with the challenging and often scary experience of learning a new language and interacting in a new culture. In order for students to learn and thrive, they must be willing to take risks, make mistakes, and receive feedback. Research and overall human experience have taught us that these behaviors are more likely to occur when one feels safe and supported. A safe, supportive learning environment can be created when teachers build relationships of trust and mutual respect with students and their families. This section presents strategies to promote positive relationships between teachers and students, students and students, and teachers and parents.

Supporting Research. Making relationship building a priority, especially in an ESL classroom, will yield many positive outcomes for both the students and the teacher. Numerous studies have shown the importance of supportive relationships for students, especially immigrants.[2] One recent study conducted by Carola Suarez-Orozco, Allyson Pimentel, and Margary Martin followed over four hundred newcomer immigrant students for five years and examined how school-based relationships affected the engagement and achievement of these students. They concluded that "supportive school-based relationships strongly contribute to both the academic engagement and the school performance of the participants."[3]

Another study conducted with high school students found that teachers using a relational approach of building trust with students had higher levels of student cooperation and fewer behavior problems. The study also found that "students saw *themselves* as cooperative—engaged with the course materials and activities—in classes with teachers who focused on building relationships."[4]

Education researcher Robert J. Marzano also points to relationships as a key ingredient to a successful learning environment when he sums up, "If the relationship between the teacher and the students is good, then everything else that occurs in the classroom seems to be enhanced."[5]

TEACHER-STUDENT RELATIONSHIPS

Positive relationships are the foundation of a successful ESL classroom. Teachers must learn about their students' experiences and backgrounds in order to connect them to new learning. Teachers also need to know what their students are interested in and what their goals are in order to create lessons that engage students and are relevant to their lives. When teachers get to know their students, they can make better decisions about the curriculum, instructional strategies, classroom management, assessment, pacing, and so forth.

The simplest way for teachers to get to know their students is by talking with them on a daily basis. This can easily be done by "checking in" with a few students each day either before class, while students are working at their desks, or after class. Taking this time to ask students about their experiences, both inside and outside of school, helps to build a genuine relationship, one where the students feel that their teacher takes an interest in their lives.

Another simple way for teachers to learn about their students is by reading what students write. Sometimes students feel more comfortable sharing through writing, and a quick note responding to a student can mean a lot. There have been many times we have learned about our students' feelings, problems, and successes by reading their weekly journals (see the homework sections in Chapters Four and Six).

This process can also be reversed and students can read what the teacher has written, especially when this writing is about the class and about the students. In today's world, many teachers already blog and write about their teaching experiences. However, they may not take the extra step of sharing this writing with their students. This can be powerful on a number of levels, but in terms of relationship building, it shows students that the teacher thinks about them outside of the classroom.[6] Taking a few minutes to write about the class (whether it is a simple reflection on how a lesson went, how a student demonstrated an exceptional insight, or sharing a few successes and challenges from the week) and then sharing this writing with the class can increase trust and respect between the teacher and the students.

Supporting Research. When students feel that they matter, their levels of motivation and achievement are more likely to increase. Joanne Yatvin[7] explains this idea in the context of the "Hawthorne effect." This effect was identified in a study that tested whether the level of worker productivity would change when the plant's lighting was dimmed or brightened. Results showed that productivity increased with *any* change in lighting. Yatvin explains that this study is often interpreted as illustrating "the fact that human subjects who know they are part of a scientific experiment may sabotage the study in their eagerness to make it succeed." However, she points out a deeper meaning that reflects the importance of students feeling valued in the classroom: "When people believe they are important in a project, anything works, and, conversely, when they don't believe they are important, nothing works." In other words, when students believe they are an important part of the educational process, then they will act like it! Having students see that teachers are writing about their insights and their successes publicly, whether on blogs or in e-mails to other teachers, is just one more way to show students they are important.[8]

Positive relationships between teachers and students can also be a way to decrease and even prevent behavior problems. Marzano and Marzano conducted a meta-analysis of over one hundred studies on this topic and found that "on average, teachers who had high-quality relationships with their students had 31 percent fewer discipline problems, rule violations, and related problems over a year's time than did teachers who did not have high-quality relationships with their students."[9]

STUDENT-STUDENT RELATIONSHIPS

In an effective ESL class, the students and teacher have developed a positive, trusting relationship. It is also critical that ESL students develop trusting and enriching relationships with each other. One of the best ways to facilitate strong relationships between students in an ESL class is through cooperative learning activities. Students can gain valuable speaking practice while learning from each other and building leadership skills. Cooperative learning activities are a key way to increase student motivation and decrease student anxiety.

However, in order to serve these purposes, cooperative learning must be thoughtfully structured. Simply telling students to work together or assigning them to groups does not always build relationships or constitute effective cooperative learning. The teacher should think carefully about the size and makeup of groups and whether the groups will be created by the teacher or by the students. Specific cooperative learning activities are shared in the next two chapters.

Research indicates that the biggest individual academic gains result from students working in groups of two to four students and that when the group is larger than four, academic *losses* are the result.[10] Specific ESL research recommends that working in pairs is more effective for language activities: "Partner activities maximize the amount of classroom language use because, theoretically, half the students are able to talk simultaneously and all students leave class with more 'miles on the tongue.'"[11]

At times, the teacher may also want to consider grouping students in a way to promote relationship building by pairing students of different language backgrounds and creating different triads each time so students have a chance to work with everyone in the class, being mindful of proficiency levels and trying to evenly distribute students within each group. At other times, it may be more appropriate to group students who speak the same native language for learning support. The teacher should model positive behaviors expected when working in a group, including academic language that promotes interpersonal skills (such as how to respectfully disagree or ask someone to speak up or repeat what they've said).

In addition to cooperative learning as a way to reinforce student relationships, we have students write weekly about two positive events that occurred in their lives and one not-so-positive event (along with what they could have done to make it better or what they learned from it). Students then share what they wrote in small groups. Research has shown that this kind of sharing results in "capitalization"—the building of social capital, also known as strengthening relationships.[12]

Supporting Research. Research on cooperative learning and adolescents has shown the importance of peer relationships in relation to learning and overall well-being. Research has confirmed that "the better a student's relationships with his classmates, the higher the student tended to achieve academically."[13] Using a meta-analysis of thousands of articles on cooperative learning, David W. Johnson, Roger T. Johnson, and Cary Roseth further conclude, "A teacher's secret strategy for increasing student achievement may be building more positive relationships among students. Put very simply, if you want students to increase their academic achievement, give them friends."[14]

TEACHER-PARENT RELATIONSHIPS

Building relationships between teachers and parents is also key to increased student motivation and academic achievement. Extensive evidence points to a link between parental involvement or engagement and a child's educational development. A trusting partnership relationship between teachers and parents can have a major impact on the level of parent participation in their child's academic development.[15]

Taking steps to reach out to parents of ESL students can be more challenging when the parents and teacher don't speak the same language; however, this shouldn't be seen as a barrier. Many schools and districts have bilingual aides or staff members who can translate written communication, make phone calls, and translate during meetings. Students can even translate assignments that require student-parent interaction, a practice that allows both the student and the teacher to learn more about a student's family! However, during more formal meetings or conversations it is usually not a good idea for students to have the responsibility of translating. When students take on this role, especially in high-stakes situations, it is not surprising that they often experience feelings of pressure and anxiety.[16]

Contacting parents on a regular basis to give positive feedback about their child's achievements, behavior, and other areas of improvement serves to build trust between parents and the school. These conversations are opportunities to let parents and students know that positive behaviors and successes are valued and recognized, thus increasing student motivation to reproduce positive outcomes. Of course, this doesn't mean the teacher should never call home to discuss negative behaviors or academic problems, but these conversations will be better received and will be more productive if a genuine relationship has already been formed with both the parents and the student.

Home visits can be a powerful way to connect with parents and students. Some districts provide funding and training for teachers, counselors, and interpreters to conduct visits with families before the school year starts and periodically throughout the year. This is a valuable opportunity to learn more about the student's background experiences and educational strengths and challenges. Parents may share what has and has not worked with their child in the past and what goals they have for themselves and for their child. Many schools across the country work with the Parent-Teacher Home Visit Project (www.pthvp.org), which has developed a highly successful model of training teachers and other school staff to implement home visits as a key strategy in strengthening relationships with families and, in turn, increasing student academic success.

Building positive relationships with parents can also lead to shared learning between students and their families. An example of this is the Family Literacy Project at our school (Luther Burbank High School in Sacramento), which grew out of conversations between parents and teachers during home visits and on-campus meetings. Many new immigrant families faced the challenge of lack of access to technology and little proficiency in English. To address these issues, the Family Literacy Project (funded by a small private grant and then by the school district) distributed free home computers and DSL service to over forty immigrant families who used the technology to read and learn together nightly. This project was powerful for the families and for the students, who showed four times greater improvement in English literacy than a control group without home computers.[17]

Forming these types of links between home and school can lead to stronger relationships between families and educators. These connections can also lead to more learning for students, parents, and teachers. These relationships can be further developed when teachers make an effort to learn about the work, hobbies, and background knowledge of parents. Just as we want to view our ELL students through a lens of assets instead of deficits, it is important to view parents through this same lens. For example, during one home visit, we learned that a student's father was an expert at making and repairing the traditional Hmong flute called the *qeej*. We invited him to visit our beginning ESL class, where he demonstrated how to make one and also performed. He didn't speak English, but we had prepared for his visit by learning new vocabulary, and then wrote and talked about it afterward using the Language Experience Approach (which is explained in full in Chapter Three). He later became one of the leaders of the effort to create the Family Literacy Project we described earlier. When teachers validate the experiences and knowledge of parents, great learning experiences can take place while also strengthening the relationship between students, their families, and school.

Once these kinds of positive relationships have been established, it can be valuable to engage parents in conversations about the important link between primary language proficiency and second language development. Many parents, especially those with fewer formal schooling experiences, are unsure about how to support their children as they are acquiring a new language. It can be extremely helpful to talk about what they should see their children doing at home (such as reading books in their native language and in English and watching English-language movies) and why these activities will help their language development.

Helping parents understand what the research says about the cognitive and financial benefits of being bilingual can also help them feel informed and empowered as they make various parenting decisions and also decisions about their own lives. More and more research is being published highlighting the increased benefits of being bilingual on brain-based activities like problem solving, learning, multitasking, and memory, and on increased earnings in the workplace.[18] A lesson plan highlighting these benefits can be found in Chapter Twelve.

Supporting Research. A common misperception about parents of ELL students is that because they are sometimes less involved in school-based activities, they don't care about their children's education. However, current research has indicated the opposite—that immigrant parents place a high value on education, but also face barriers to being involved in their child's education such as "limited English proficiency, lack of formal education, time constraints (work and family responsibilities), and limited knowledge of mainstream American culture."[19] The suggestions we have shared, including phone calls, home visits, and making efforts to learn about the lives of parents, can all be effective responses to these challenges.

Tech Tool
Online Resources: Translating

It is not always possible to have translators and/or bilingual staff available to translate when needed. While translation technology tools available online and on smartphones aren't always 100 percent accurate and easy to use, they can at least show parents the teacher is making an effort to clearly communicate.

A few of the most useful free online translating tools we've found are

Google Translate: http://translate.google.com

Bing Translator: http://www.microsofttranslator.com

Yahoo Babel Fish: http://babelfish.yahoo.com

Google Translate is widely preferred for translating longer passages, while both Bing Translator and Babel Fish are known for producing better translations of phrases below 140 characters.

A few useful smartphone applications that include "speak-to-translate" and "listen to your translation" features are

Google Translate: http://itunes.apple.com/us/app/google-translate

Jibbigo Voice Translation: http://www.jibbigo.com/website/index.php

Talk to Me—Text to Speech: http://itunes.apple.com/us/app/talk-to-me-text-to -speech

ACTIVITIES TO BUILD AND STRENGTHEN RELATIONSHIPS IN THE ESL CLASSROOM

There are many activities that can be used both as introductory activities and throughout the year to build and maintain positive relationships in the classroom. Some activities that work well to introduce students to each other and to the teacher can be used again at later points in the year as students' interests change and as they gain new life experiences. While this is certainly not an exhaustive list, it contains several activities we have found successful and that can easily be adapted for use with different levels of students.

Introducing Me: Three Objects

This activity is sometimes called a Me Bag or an All About Me Bag. Students choose a few objects that reveal things about themselves or are special in some way and bring them in to share with the class. The teacher models this activity first by bringing in items special in her life (for example, a photograph, a piece of sports equipment, or a paintbrush) and describing what the object is and what it represents or why it is important. Then the teacher can take a few minutes to answer any questions from students. Students can share their items in various ways—a few students can share each day or students can share in small groups or with a partner and take turns asking each other questions. Question frames can be helpful for lower-level students (Why did you pick _____?). It may also be helpful for the teacher to remind students not to bring very valuable items to school, but they can instead draw or take a picture of the item to share.

I Am Project

There are many variations of the I Am activity. Students can create a poster, a poem, a slide show, a Top Ten list, or other item to describe themselves. It can be helpful to give students sentence starters to spur their thinking and writing. There are endless possibilities, but here are a few examples:[20]

I love _____ because _____.

I wonder _____.

I am happy when _____.

I am scared when _____.

I worry about _____ because _____.

I hope to _____.

I am sad when _____.

In the future, I will _____.

Students can share their projects with the entire class or in small groups.

Teacher-Student Letter Exchange

A good way for teachers to introduce themselves to students is by writing a brief letter to share during the first week. This letter can serve as a model for students to follow as they write back to the teacher. The teacher's letter can be simplified depending upon the level of the class, and the teacher can give beginning students sentence frames to scaffold their letter. (My name is _____. I am _____ years old. I was born in _____.) This activity helps teachers learn more about their students and also provides a quick sample of each student's writing. It can be helpful to keep copies of both the teacher letter and the instructions for the student letter on hand to give to new students as they enter the class later in the year. See Exhibit 2.1 for a sample of a teacher letter.

EXHIBIT 2.1. Teacher Letter Sample

September 7, 2010

Dear Students,

Welcome back to school! I always feel nervous and excited about the first day of school. It is fun to see everyone and get back into a routine, but I will miss being able to stay up late and sleep in (when my kids let me)!

I've been teaching at Burbank for awhile and I <u>love</u> this school! Most of the teachers are caring and funny, and the students are even smarter, kinder, and funnier than the teachers! Here are some things I love about school: students, lunch with my friends, good books, and clean floors. Here are some things I don't love about school: meetings at lunch, boring books, and dirty floors. What do you like about school? What don't you like about school?

My family is very important to me. I like them most of the time and I love them all of the time. I live near downtown Sacramento with my husband and our three kids. When you visit our house there is a good chance you might step on a Lego piece, a Star Wars action figure, a Hot Wheels car, a Barbie shoe, or a Dora necklace. You also might see lots of sports equipment because we like to play soccer, baseball, football, and golf. We are San Francisco Giants fans and we root for the 49ers. We also read books together, go on hikes, and play at the park. What is your family like? What do you like to do when you are not at school?

I am looking forward to our school year together. We will get to know each other better and will learn from each other. I expect you to try your best and be willing to make some mistakes because that is how we learn. What do you expect from me?

Here's to an awesome year together!!

Sincerely,

Ms. Hull

"Find Someone in This Class Who . . ." Scavenger Hunt

A scavenger hunt is an easy way to get students out of their seats, talking, and interacting within minutes. The teacher can easily create a sheet (there are many variations on the Web) listing several categories with a line next to each one. Then students circulate and must find someone who has experienced each category (for example, "Has been to the ocean," "Has a brother and a sister," or "Has broken a bone"). The student must ask for his classmate's name and write it on the line next to the category. The teacher can collect the sheets, choose different items to share, and, depending upon the class and comfort level, ask students to share more details about a specific experience.

Four Squares

The Four Squares activity helps students get to know each other better, while getting both writing and speaking practice. The teacher models how to fold a piece of paper into four boxes and numbers them 1, 2, 3, and 4. Students then write a different category or topic next to the number at the top of each box. The categories could include family, what I like about school, what I don't like about school, places I've lived, my favorite movie (and why), and so forth. Students are given time to write about each category and then asked to stand up. The teacher then instructs students to share their Box Ones with a partner, their Box Twos with a different partner, and so on. This activity can be varied in multiple ways—different topics to write about, the number of boxes, how they are shared, and so on. It can also be used at any point during the year. For example, it can be used at the end of the semester with a box for the student's biggest accomplishment, one for the biggest challenge, and one for goals for the next semester. See Figure 2.1 for one example of how to use the Four Squares activity.

Two Truths and a Lie

This activity is commonly used as an icebreaker and works great with students who don't know a lot about each other. The teacher first models the activity by writing down three statements about herself on an index card and explaining that two of the statements are true, but one is a lie (for example, "I can play the guitar" or "I was born in New York City"). Students can talk in pairs and guess which statement is the lie. Then each student writes two truths and one lie on an index card. Students can share their statements in pairs, small groups, or to the entire class and take turns guessing each other's lies. The teacher can facilitate a follow-up discussion by asking students to share more about their truths, either by speaking or in writing.

Weekly Reflections

One way for teachers to stay connected to students is by having them write a weekly reflection. This reflection can simply be a journal or responses to questions. The teacher can structure the journal prompt or questions to invite students to share their feelings, concerns, and questions about the class and about their lives outside the classroom (What classroom activity did they like the best this week and why? What are their weekend plans?). Reading student reflections can help teachers take the pulse of the class—which activities are being enjoyed, areas of confusion, pacing issues, and so forth. Teachers can immediately make adjustments, offer feedback,

My family:	What I like about school:
What I don't like about school:	**My favorites:** Food: Movie: Music: After-school activity: Place:

Figure 2.1. Four Squares

and address any student concerns. Teachers also gain important information about what is going on in their students' lives and can use this information as talking points when they speak one-on-one with students. These reflections can also function as a formative assessment. See the sections on reflection in Chapters Four and Six for more ideas on incorporating reflection into the ESL classroom.

Evaluations

A teacher can build trust with students by asking them to anonymously evaluate her teaching and use the results to reflect on her practice. This can be done by distributing a quick survey or set of questions for students to answer about class activities, the teacher's style, the pace of the class, and so forth. See Exhibit 2.2 for an example of a teacher, class, or student evaluation.

EXHIBIT 2.2. End-of-Quarter Evaluation

Please read the sentences and circle the answer that best describes your feelings.

1. In this class this quarter I learned   *a lot   some   a little.*
2. My teacher talked   *too fast   just right   too slow.*
3. The work in this class was   *too hard   just right   too easy.*
4. My teacher cares about what is happening in my life   *a lot   some   a little.*
5. This quarter I tried my best   *all of the time   some of the time   not a lot.*

Please write your answers in the space below each question.

6. Which activities *helped you* learn English the most this quarter?
   _____

   _____

7. Which activities *did not really help you* learn English this quarter?
   _____

   _____

8. Which activities did you enjoy *the most* this quarter?
   _____

   _____

9. Which activities did you enjoy *the least* this quarter?
   _____

   _____

10. What could *your teacher* do differently or better to help you in this class?
    _____

    _____

11. What could *you* do differently or better to help yourself in this class?
    _____

    _____

12. What else would you like your teacher to know?
    _____

    _____

Source: Adapted from L. Ferlazzo, *Helping Students Motivate Themselves: Practical Answers to Classroom Challenges* (Larchmont, NY: Eye on Education, 2011), p. 99.

Talking and Walking

Having one-on-one conversations with students about their goals, interests, struggles, and the like can be difficult to do during class time. One way to quickly connect with students is to take a brief walk around the school campus. This five-minute conversation can take place before or after school, or even during a teacher's prep period (if you make prior arrangements with the student's teacher for that time). These talks can strengthen the teacher-student relationship and can also be helpful when getting to know new students or when dealing with students who are having behavior challenges.

The Second R: *Resources* in the ESL Classroom

Resources are highly important to effective instruction in any classroom. The following are several resources we have found vital to structuring an ESL class where students feel comfortable, challenged, and confident.

BASIC ART SUPPLIES

Having basic supplies like pens, pencils, markers, construction paper, glue, scissors, and highlighters can be useful for many different projects and activities. Having supplies on hand that are easily accessible also allows students to immediately focus on the content of the lesson and to immediately get to work.

While this book includes many ideas for using technology with ESL students to increase motivation and enhance language development, it is important to remember that paper, pens, and pencils still matter!

Recent research on the brain, learning, and handwriting shows that putting a pen or pencil to paper is important for new learning to occur, especially when learning a language. Some studies have shown that children write more words, faster, and express more ideas when writing essays by hand as opposed to typing on a keyboard, and that adults learning a foreign language retained more when writing by hand.[21]

BINDERS AND FOLDERS

The age-old debate of whether students should take their materials home every day or leave them in the classroom goes on in many schools. While it may be necessary for students to take some items home (such as a reading book or homework papers), it can be helpful to have a binder or folder for each student to leave in the classroom. A binder can be divided into sections (for example, homework, current unit, and reflections) and can easily be passed out and collected by students. Another option is to give each student a hanging file folder (with a name label) that can be stored in a file cabinet or a plastic file crate. This folder can hold other folders (such as a current unit folder, student portfolio, and homework folder) and can also easily be distributed or picked up by students as they enter the classroom.

Having students keep their materials in the classroom helps students and teachers keep track of papers and makes it easier for students to get to work immediately. To help with organization, students can keep a Table of Contents in the front of their folder or binder section with a running list of materials. Teachers may find this helpful because they can keep track of which activities they did and in what order—always helpful for the next school year!

BILINGUAL DICTIONARIES

Bilingual dictionaries are an important tool in an ESL classroom, and having dictionaries available in the languages spoken by students is obviously a good idea. However, many schools have bilingual dictionaries only in the most common languages. We have found bilingual dictionaries in many languages available for purchase online.

Bilingual and English picture dictionaries are also a great tool, especially for beginning and early intermediate students. Bilingual glossaries (which only offer a word-for-word translation and not a definition) can be useful for students when reading or writing. Many states even allow ELL students to use glossaries when taking standardized tests.

There has been much discussion over the use of dictionaries and direct translation in the ESL classroom. Some have argued that direct translation (from L1 to L2 or vice versa), especially when reading, should be avoided because it can interrupt and slow down the reading process. However, more recent research has found bilingual dictionaries to be an important component of language learning.[22] As Professor Jim Cummins explains, there must be a balanced approach to direct translation—using context clues to decipher meaning should be encouraged, and "bilingual dictionary use can provide rapid access to the meaning of target language text and eliminate the frustration that derives from attempting unsuccessfully to infer meanings from context."[23] Our experience is aligned with Cummins's findings. Of course, it is counterproductive for a student to look up every unfamiliar word or to directly translate their writing word for word. However, bilingual dictionaries can be very helpful, especially for assisting students to understand more complex words and concepts.

It is also important for the teacher to *model* when and how students can best use dictionaries to increase language development. For example, the teacher can demonstrate trying to figure out the meaning of a word by "thinking aloud" as she looks for context clues in a piece of text. The teacher can then show students what to do if they can't figure out the meaning based on context by modeling how to look up the word in the dictionary.

CLASSROOM LIBRARY

As you will see in later chapters, research clearly supports the practice of Free Voluntary Reading, which involves letting students choose reading materials based on their own interests. Having a well-stocked, well-organized library is a key way to build motivation for this kind of reading practice. Some schools provide books for classroom libraries in English classes, but this isn't always the case. Teachers can build a library over time on their own—used book stores, garage sales, and the local library are great places to find low-cost or free books. However, building a classroom library is not a matter of filling the shelves with just anything. Books should be age-appropriate, of high interest, and in good condition. It has been our experience that students won't check out books with torn covers and tattered pages. While some high-quality children's books can be accessible for beginning-level students, there are also plenty of high-interest, low-level books geared toward older ELL students.

It is helpful if the classroom library is organized for accessibility, but not exclusivity. Organizing books by level (placing lower-level books in one area and higher-level ones in another) can be helpful; however, it is important that students not feel restricted when choosing books.

There is much debate about the effects of controlling the books that students are allowed to read. While some studies have found that student test scores increased after using an "accelerated reading" program,[24] some researchers question the validity of these studies. They claim that these "accelerated reader" programs, which are incentive-based and require that students read books only within their level until they "test out," can actually decrease motivation for reading in the long-term.[25] In our experience we have found that it is best *not* to restrict student choice. However, we also guide students toward choosing books at the appropriate level and that match their interests. See Chapter Twelve on for more ideas on helping students find books.

Along with being divided by level, books can also be shelved according to genre or by simply dividing them into fiction and nonfiction. Some teachers have used colored stickers to indicate different types of books.

Because it is important for students to take books home to read (especially ELL students who may not have many English-language books at home), a checkout system can help keep track of books and prevent loss. Keeping a binder or clipboard near the classroom library makes it easy for students to "check out" a book by writing down their name, the title of the book, and the date checked out. Upon returning the book, students can cross off their name or enter the date the book was returned. It can be useful to stamp or label books with the teacher's name so they can be returned if left somewhere else on campus.

It is also important to help students build their own libraries at home. Research has shown that children with more books at home go further in their education, even if their parents aren't highly literate.[26] Many libraries have auxiliary groups that collect donations of books and sell them at a minimal cost. Some even distribute free books to teachers. For example, the Friends of the Library Program in Davis, California, has donated thousands of books to distribute to our students over the years. Taking a field trip to the local library and helping students to get a library card is another way to promote reading at home.

PEER TUTORS

Peer tutors can be a very valuable resource in an ESL class, especially in a large class or a class with a range of proficiency levels. Many secondary schools give students the opportunity to take a period as a Teacher's Assistant. These are usually older students with good grades who have already met many of their graduation requirements. At diverse schools, many of these students are bilingual and can serve as excellent role models, translators, and classroom helpers. Patient English-only students can also do a great job as peer tutors. At our school, students receive credits for serving as peer tutors in ESL classes. They help our ELL students with assignments, offer advice, and even attend field trips with our class. See Chapter Four for ideas on pairing ESL classes with mainstream English classes.

Supporting Research. Recent research on the effects of peer tutoring on English language learners indicates a positive impact on learning for these students: "When peer tutors are used, the tutees have a live example to emulate and behavior to observe which helps to understand the language and culture more so than a textbook could display."[27] It has also been found that pairing younger arriving ELLs with older ELLs can enhance language development in both their native language and in their second language. [28]

CLASSROOM WALLS

The walls of the classroom can be another important resource for ELL students. Word walls, concept maps, academic sentence frames, posted classroom routines, and schedules are tools that become more accessible to students when posted on the classroom walls.

During a thematic unit, posting a word wall with key vocabulary words along with their meanings and/or pictures allows students to easily access the spelling and meaning of the words as they read, write, and talk.

By taking words from the word wall and expanding the visual representation to show how they relate to one another and to key concepts, you can create a *concept map*.

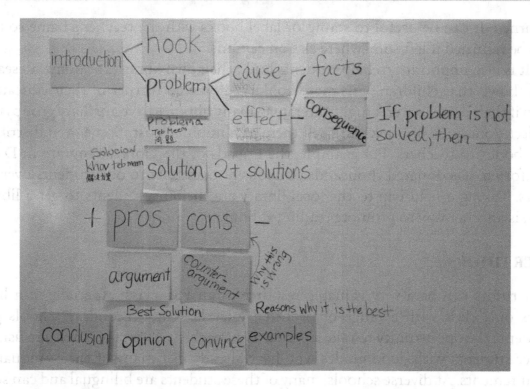

Figure 2.2. Sample Concept Map

For example, "by hanging a set of posters that support a unit, your walls can become like an image-based concept map, useful to help students see how individual ideas form a larger whole. Similar to the way a road map shows various roads connecting various towns, concept maps indicate a connection between concepts."[29] For an example of a concept map used when teaching an essay in an intermediate class, see Figure 2.2.

Academic sentence frames are also valuable to display on the classroom walls so that students can access them when writing and speaking—such as, "I agree (or disagree) because_____." It can be helpful to rotate different sentence frame posters that are based on the unit of study.

When creating posters for the walls, teachers should pay attention to size (large enough for students to see from their desks) and amount of text (not too much). Involving students in the process can be fun, can reinforce learning, and can save teacher energy!

Of course, classroom walls are also a place to publish student work. Students often enjoy seeing their own work and their classmates' work displayed on the walls. Teachers can incorporate displayed student work into a lesson by conducting "gallery walks" where students can read, evaluate, and even add to student work posted on the wall. See Chapter Six for more ideas on gallery walks.

TECHNOLOGY BASICS

Document cameras, computer projectors, and having access to a computer lab and to the Internet can greatly enhance learning in an ESL class.

Document cameras open up many possibilities in the classroom. As opposed to an overhead projector, which requires transparencies, a document camera (attached to a computer projector) simply projects whatever you place underneath it onto a screen. It facilitates teacher modeling and makes it easy for teachers to show good student models, or even better, for students to come up and show the whole class. It also makes it possible for students to create a "poster" to share with the class on a regular piece of paper because it can easily be projected for all to see.

Using a computer projector allows you to project images from your computer onto a screen. This can be extremely useful for showing video clips, playing computer games as a class (see Chapter Eleven), and student-generated computer projects (Chapters Three and Five give specific ideas for using video with ELL students). An advantage of using a computer projector instead of a DVD player is that it gives the teacher access to countless online resources to use with students.

This book will present many ideas for using technology to enhance student learning and that don't require a lot of work to use. Of course, incorporating many of these activities requires student access to computers and to the Internet—in other words, a one-on-one computer laptop program or computer lab. See Chapter Twelve for specific ways to maximize the use of technology when computer access is limited. Also see the upcoming Computer Routines section in this chapter for tips on effectively using time in the computer lab.

Supporting Research. As previously mentioned, students at our school who participated in a Family Literacy Project with home computers showed great improvements in their reading scores. We further found that students who participated in an after-school computer lab program, where they spent an hour on sites accessible to English learners in a variety of content areas, scored a 50 percent greater gain on reading comprehension assessments than ELLs who did not come to the lab.[30]

Another study on the use of audio blogs with teacher feedback (students recording oral assignments and the teacher responding to them) found that students enjoyed the learning process more and also met their learning goals. Other benefits included "ease of use" because the technology was easy to learn, "affordability" because students could use their cell phones to record, and "organizational" benefits such as assignments being easily archived.[31]

Tech Tool
Classroom Blogs

In recent years, the Internet and related technology have become increasingly easy to use. You don't have to be very proficient to use a variety of applications that can increase student motivation and enhance learning. Creating and using a classroom blog where students contribute and respond to each other by leaving comments is one easy way to incorporate technology into the ESL classroom. While some teachers have students create their own individual blogs, we have found that single classroom blogs are easier to manage. The teacher can post an assignment on the blog and students can either write or paste the URL address of the completed project into the Comments section of the blog. Students can then view their classmates' projects on the classroom blog and offer feedback. For examples of online student projects and examples of student feedback, see two ESL class blogs at http://sacschoolblogs.org/eld2 and http://sacschoolblogs.org/larryferlazzo.

Blogs are a great online resource because they are easy, interactive, motivating, involve reading and writing practice, and create an authentic audience for student writing. A recent study found that if students are writing for an online audience such as Wikipedia, they are more concerned with the accuracy of their research.[32] We have observed a similar pattern with our ELL students. They tend to be more focused on the quality of their ideas and the accuracy of their grammar when they know their writing will be posted on our classroom blog.

We've found that Edublogs (http://edublogs.org) is one of the easiest tools to use for creating and maintaining classroom blogs. In addition, since Edublogs is dedicated only to education-related blogs, it is less likely to be blocked by school Internet content filters.

For more tips on creating and using blogs in the classroom, see "A Collection of 'The Best . . . ' Lists on Blogs and Blogging" at http://larryferlazzo.edublogs.org.

The Third R: Establishing *Routines*

Establishing routines is highly important in structuring a positive and effective learning experience for all students. Having a system of procedures not only benefits the students, but preserves teacher sanity as well. For ELL students in particular, having routines frees them up to learn new concepts. Being consistently exposed to new routines *and* new concepts can be overwhelming, frustrating, and detrimental to the learning process. Students can put their focus on learning activities when they know what to expect and are familiar with classroom routines.

This section will present several routines we have found successful. While these routines are crucial for creating an optimal learning environment for ELL students, it is also important to balance routines with novelty. In other words, procedures and routines are valuable for structuring and managing the time spent with students, but what the teacher does *within* this time is hugely important. Learning should never be routine, and in order to keep students engaged, learning activities must be presented in different ways.

OPENING AND ENDING PROCEDURES

Having a walk-in procedure like Free Voluntary Reading, a warm-up question, or a journal topic is a good way to get students focused and learning from the minute they walk in—even if the bell has not yet rung.

Using the last few minutes of class to do a brief closure activity each day is a routine that can serve many purposes. Teachers can quickly assess student learning by having students respond in writing to a question related to the lesson. Students can use this time to reflect on their learning, ask questions about something that is unclear, or set goals for themselves based on the day's lesson. The possibilities are endless, and it is important to keep "mixing it up" so students stay engaged. See the sections on Reflection in Chapters Four and Six for detailed suggestions.

PROCEDURES FOR DISTRIBUTING MATERIALS

Having procedures for distributing and collecting materials can reduce teacher stress and create smoother transitions from one activity to another. These procedures can simply consist of assigning "student jobs" for passing out binders, art supplies, collecting assignments, and so forth. In order to allow for a smooth distribution and collection process, classroom supplies need to be well organized and easy for students to access. Labeling plastic bins or trays is a way to keep supplies like glue, scissors, markers, and colored pencils organized. Binders can be stacked on bookshelves or stored in plastic crates. Some teachers have found it helpful to have a table dedicated solely to supplies that students can easily access. If students are seated at tables or grouped in pods, it can be helpful for each table to have a plastic pencil box that contains supplies like markers, highlighters, sticky notes, and such.

POSTING AGENDAS AND SCHEDULES

It is helpful to post the day's schedule on the board or document camera. Students can easily spend a couple of minutes copying the homework or day's activities. This helps familiarize students with classroom routines and following written directions. Posting basic information like the school bell schedule and classroom protocols (for example, how to check out a book) reinforces for students that the walls of the classroom are important resources.

MODELING ROUTINES AND MAKING MODELING A ROUTINE

Not only is it important to model routines for students so they know what is expected, but it is critical for the teacher to make modeling a part of his daily routine in order to make input more comprehensible for students.

COMPUTER ROUTINES

Introducing new routines in a language classroom on a regular basis can be confusing and frustrating for students. The same holds true for technology—introducing new web sites or applications too often does not build success. When considering how to structure time in the computer lab, keeping it simple *does* build success. Following are a few guidelines that can be used to make time in the computer lab more successful for students:

- Go over directions in the classroom first using a computer projector and have students write down the directions and bring them to the computer lab. Model each step of the process that students will be replicating on their own in the computer lab.
- Use computers more to reinforce key concepts, and less to teach them.
- Students can be producers of online content and not just consumers.
- Computers can be used to help students develop and deepen relationships with each other, not just with the computer screen.
- Use time in the computer lab to help develop leadership among students, and not just have them be your followers.
- Spend less time being the controller and more time helping students develop self-control.

    Source: Adapted from L. Ferlazzo, "What Are You Doing in That Computer Lab?" *Tech & Learning,* Feb. 1, 2008. Retrieved from http://www.techlearning.com/article/8410.

Supporting Research. In the article "Teaching English Language Learners: What the Research Does—and Does Not—Say," Claude Goldenberg explores extensive research on ESL instruction. He points to establishing routines as an effective learning support for all students in any classroom and explains "predictable and consistent classroom management routines, aided by diagrams, lists, and easy to read schedules on the board or on charts, to which the teacher refers frequently" are a particularly important scaffold for English learners.[33]

It is also important to remember that research shows not only that routines and procedures can have a positive impact on student behavior and learning, but that involving *students* in the creation of these routines and procedures helps students feel empowered and more likely to follow them. As Robert Marzano (2005) states, "Effective teachers take the time to explain the reasons behind particular rules and procedures, involve students in creating them, and seek their input as much as appropriate."[34]

By fostering relationships with students and parents, collecting and organizing resources, and establishing routines, teachers can lay the groundwork for powerful teaching and learning to occur. The following chapters contain instructional strategies and curriculum ideas that build upon this foundation of a positive and effective learning environment.

Additional resources, including ones on building positive relationships with students and parents, research on the advantages of being bilingual, and successfully using blogs and other technology with ELLs, can be found on our book's web site at www.josseybass.com/go/eslsurvivalguide.

PART TWO

Teaching Beginning English Language Learners

CHAPTER THREE

Key Elements of a Curriculum for Beginning ELLs

A traveling wise man and his friends passed through a town and asked to speak to a local scholar. He was brought to Nasreddin Hodja. The traveler didn't speak Turkish, and Hodja didn't speak any other languages, so they decided to communicate through signs.

The traveler used a stick to draw a large circle in the dirt. Hodja then divided the circle in two with his stick. The traveler followed by drawing a perpendicular line that divided the circle into four quarters and then pointed at the first three quarters and then lastly pointed to the fourth quarter. Hodja then swirled the stick on all four quarters. The traveler used his hands to make a bowl shape with his hands up and wiggled his fingers. Hodja then made a bowl shape with his hands down and wiggled his fingers.

When the meeting was over, the traveler's friends asked him what they had discussed. "Hodja is very intelligent," he said. "I showed him that the earth was round, and he said that there was an equator in the middle of it. I told him that three-quarters of the earth was water and one quarter of it was land. He said that there were undercurrents and winds. I told him that the waters warm up, vaporize, and move toward the sky. He said that they cool off and come down as rain." The townspeople surrounded Hodja and asked him the same thing.

"This stranger is hungry," Hodja started to explain. "He said that he hoped to have a large tray of baklava. I said that he could only have half of it. He said that the syrup should be made with three parts sugar and one part honey. I agreed, and said that they had to mix well. He then suggested that we should cook it on a blazing fire. I suggested that we should pour crushed nuts on top of it."[1]

Nasreddin Hodja was a Middle Eastern storyteller who lived in the thirteenth century. In this tale, we see both participants entirely focused on what they want to communicate, and absolutely convinced that they are communicating effectively. These assumptions lead to completely different understandings.

Perhaps we educators should be more concerned with what students hear and learn, and less focused on what we believe we are teaching. It could also be framed as the difference between being effective and being "right." The more we view learning as a process of guided self-discovery and less one of a "sage on stage"—more of a two-way conversation instead of a one-way communication—the better teachers we might be for our students. The activities described in our book use this perspective as a guide.

Each instructional strategy and lesson in Parts Two and Three indicate where it fits into the six standards domains the state of California mandates for its English language development (ELD, also known as ESL) classes. Similar standards exist in most other states. To make these standards more easily understandable, a one-sentence description developed for each domain by the Sacramento City Unified School District will be used, and its appropriate numbers will be cited throughout this chapter. The full one-sentence summary of each domain can be found in Exhibit 3.1.

EXHIBIT 3.1. English Language Development Standards

California ELD Domains

1. Students use English for everyday communication in socially and culturally appropriate ways and apply listening and speaking skills and strategies in the classroom.
2. Students apply word analysis skills and knowledge of vocabulary to read fluently.
3. Students will read and understand a range of challenging narrative and expository text materials.
4. Students will read and respond to literature.
5. Students will write well-organized, clear, and coherent text in a variety of academic genres.
6. Students will apply the conventions of standard English usage orally and in writing.

Source: "Course of Study for English Language Development," Sacramento City Unified School District, 2005, pp. 7–12.

Key Elements of a Curriculum

In this section we present key learning and teaching activities that we regularly use in a beginning ESL classroom. Though they are divided into two sections for organization purposes—"Reading and Writing" and "Speaking and Listening"—you will find that many of the activities incorporate all four of these language domains.

READING AND WRITING

The Picture Word Inductive Model

The Picture Word Inductive Model (PWIM) uses an inductive process (in which students seek patterns and use them to identify their broader meanings and significance), as opposed to a deductive process (where meanings or rules are given, and students have to then apply them). In the PWIM, an enlarged photo with white space around it (ideally laminated so it can be used again) is first placed in the classroom (see Figure 3.1); students and the teacher together label objects in the picture; students categorize and add words to their categories; students use the words in sentences that are provided as clozes (fill-in-the-blank exercises; see Exhibit 3.2), which are then categorized and combined into paragraphs; and, finally, a title is chosen.

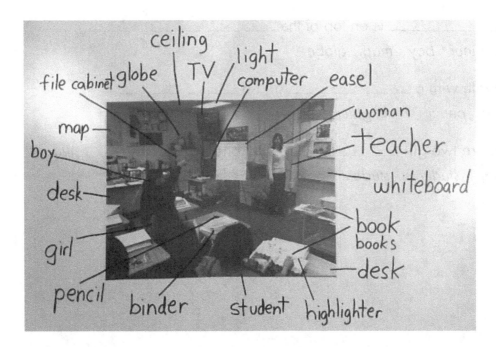

Figure 3.1. Example of Photo Used in the Picture Word Inductive Model

EXHIBIT 3.2. Classroom Picture Sentences

1. The _____ stands in _____ of the room.
back   front   teacher   student

2. Three _____ sit at _____.
teacher   student   students   desks

3. There is a _____ near the _____.
highlighter   globe   map   woman

4. The _____ is black and the _____ is yellow.
highlighter   ceiling   map   computer

5. The _____ points to a picture on the _____.
book   computer   whiteboard   teacher

6. There are _____ and _____ on the desks.
map   binders   books   easel

7. The _____ is on the _____.
student   desk   ceiling   light

8. A _____ is on top of the _____.
file cabinet   boy   map   globe

9. We write with a _____ and a _____.
binder   pencil   highlighter   girl

10. There are two girl _____ and one _____ student.
woman   students   student   boy

The PWIM process can easily be used as the centerpiece for many classroom activities during the year. Each week, a different photo can be connected to an appropriate theme (food, sports, house, and so on), and the instructional process can be made increasingly sophisticated and challenging for students—for example, later the cloze sentences can have two blanks in each and not have words written below them for students to choose. The pictures themselves can be personalized. Local images and ones featuring students could be used. For example, in addition to using a house as the central photo for the class, each student can bring a picture of their own house that they can use for supplementary vocabulary instruction. Students can snap the photos with their cell phone for the teacher to print out, or, with advanced planning, an inexpensive disposable camera can be used by the entire class. Photos can also easily be found on the Web. The best pictures to use in this activity contain one scene with many different objects and generally include people. Occasionally, though, there might be exceptions to these criteria, which are highlighted in the "Year-Long Schedule" section in Chapter Four.

Of course, some themes will take more than one week and/or will require more than one picture. A unit on food, for example, could include separate subunits on healthy eating, eating at a restaurant, shopping at a store, farm life (both as a grower and as a laborer), fruit, vegetables, meat, and dairy.

A Picture Word Inductive Unit Plan describing in detail how to apply the PWIM can be found in Chapter Four. The "Sample Week Schedule" in Chapter Four demonstrates how the PWIM might fit in with other class activities.

Using the PWIM correlates with California ELD domains 1, 2, 5 and 6.

Supporting Research. The PWIM is a literacy instructional strategy that was designed for early literacy instruction and has also been found to be exceptionally effective with both younger and older second-language learners.[2] It was developed by Emily Calhoun,[3] and some studies have found its use resulting in literacy gains of twice the average student, and as great as eight times the average gain for previously low-performing students.[4] It takes advantage of student prior knowledge and visual clues and builds on the key strength of inductive learning—the brain's natural desire to seek out and remember patterns.[5]

A recent study also reinforced the importance of having students repeat aloud new vocabulary, as is done using the PWIM. Researchers found that saying the word aloud helped learners develop an "encoding record" of the new word.[6]

Text Data Sets

Text Data Sets are very similar to the PWIM cloze sentences, and students use the same kind of categorization process done in that activity. Text Data Sets, however, are composed of sentences or short paragraphs. See Exhibit 3.3 for a Text Data Set that is appropriate for beginners. See Chapters Six and Eight for examples of more advanced Text Data Sets. Students first classify them (individually or with partners),

Tech Tool

Photos on the Web

There are vast numbers of resources on the Web to support the use of photos with students. These sites include places where photos specifically designed for use with the PWIM can be seen and purchased, resources that have other lesson ideas and online literacy exercises connected to images, and sources of millions of photos that can be used in the classroom with few, if any, restrictions. You can find a regularly updated list of these links in "The Best Ways to Use Photos in Lessons" at http://larryferlazzo.edublogs.org. (Remember that direct links to all cited resources can be found on our book's web site at www.josseybass.com/go/eslsurvivalguide.)

In addition, a related reinforcing lesson to the PWIM is having students create Picture Data Sets online. Using the categories they have chosen for that week's classroom picture, students can grab images from the Web or upload their own photos of items that fit into those same categories (for example, "words that begin with r," "vegetables," or "transportation"). These photos can either illustrate words they have already identified in class or new ones, and then students can label them with words or sentences. They can also mix up their images, list the names of categories, and challenge other students to organize them correctly. Several easy and free online tools allow students to easily mix and match images for these kinds of activities, including

Corkboard Me: http://corkboard.me

ThingLink (http://www.thinglink.com/) is a web tool that lets students annotate any image on the web similar to how we label photos in the Picture Word Inductive Model. Students can reinforce learned vocabulary by posting pictures they choose from the Internet on class blogs.

Wallwisher: http://www.wallwisher.com

Linoit: https://linoit.com

being sure to highlight or underline their evidence for determining that the example belonged in that specific category. They might use categories given to them by the teacher or ones they determine themselves. Then they might add new pieces of data they find and/or they may convert their categories into paragraphs and a simple essay. They might also just stop at the categorization process. These data sets are another scaffolding tool in the inductive teaching and learning process that can be used by students to develop increasingly sophisticated writing skills.

Using Text Data Sets correlates with California ELD domains 1, 2, 3, 5 and 6.

EXHIBIT 3.3. "Describing Things" Data Set

Categories: Numbers, Colors, Size, Age, Weather, and Temperature

1. There are twenty-two students in class.
2. Choua is wearing a black shirt.
3. Mr. Ferlazzo is an old teacher.
4. Walter is tall.
5. Luther Burbank is a big school.
6. Johanna has a blue pencil.
7. There are twenty-six desks in the classroom.
8. Ms. Smith has short hair.
9. Chue has a young sister.
10. Today is a sunny day.
11. The boy is wearing white shoes.
12. Tomorrow will be a rainy day.
13. The rice is very hot.
14. The ice cream is freezing.
15. Ms. Vue has a little baby.
16. There are twenty-four hours in a day.
17. There are three computers in our classroom.
18. Yesterday was a windy day.
19. Mr. Ferlazzo drives a gray car.
20. The students in our class are young.
21. The water is cold.
22. The ant is tiny.

Critical Pedagogy

Critical pedagogy is the term often used to describe a teaching approach whose most well-known practitioner was Brazilian educator Paulo Freire. Freire was critical of the "banking" approach towards education, where the teacher "deposits" information into her students. Instead, he wanted to help students learn by questioning and looking at real-world problems that they, their families, and their communities faced. Through this kind of dialogue, he felt that both students and the teacher could learn together.[7] Freire was careful to call his learning approach a "problem-posing" one, not a "problem-solving" exercise. He wanted to put the emphasis on teachers raising questions through this process and not giving solutions.[8]

There are many ways to use this strategy in the ESL classroom. One way is to first show a very short video clip, photo, cartoon, newspaper article, song, or comic strip or, if the English level of the class is advanced enough, students can act out a dialogue that represents a common problem faced by students (a teacher can also perform the dialogue on his own). Ideally, it should be connected to the thematic unit that is being studied at that time, and should reflect an actual problem students or their families have faced or are facing. However, there is no need to be strictly limited to the thematic unit, and issues may arise in students' lives at any time that can provide learning opportunities. The problems can be identified by the teacher first modeling an example and then by eliciting ideas of problems from students. Students can also draw their own representations of the problems.

For example, if the thematic unit is school, a short video clip from the movie *My Bodyguard* can be shown to illustrate the problem of bullying. Students can then work in pairs and small groups in a five-step process responding to the following questions,[9] with a class discussion after each one (certain words may need to be simplified and/or defined, especially when done for the first time):

1. Describe what you see: Who is doing what? What do they look like? What objects do you see in the video? Summarize what they are saying.

2. What is the problem in the video?

3. Have you, your family, or friends ever experienced the problem? Describe what happened.

4. What do you think might be the causes of the problem?

5. What solutions could a person do on their own? What solutions could people do together? Would one be better than the other? Why or why not? (The teacher might have to caution students that the solution(s) they choose must also be realistic).

Students can create simple posters and make presentations (including role-plays) illustrating the problem, sharing their personal connection to it, listing potential solutions, and choosing which one they think is best and why. As students become more advanced, they can develop this outline into a problem-solution essay using the same outline (see Chapter Six for more ideas on how to support students writing a problem-solution essay). Students can also take real-world actions to confront the problem, as one of our classes did by organizing a fair bringing ten different job training agencies to our school so they and their families could learn what services were available (see Chapter Six for more information on action projects).

This five-step outline can be used to approach multiple problems on a weekly or biweekly schedule for different thematic units—perhaps discussing the problem of unemployment when learning about jobs, not having health insurance when discussing a medical unit, or landlord issues during a week on home. Each time the problem can be demonstrated in a different form, and each time students can be challenged to present their answers in an increasingly more sophisticated way.

As ELLs increase their language proficiency, an extra step can be inserted into the five-point outline to incorporate another level of inductive learning: it can be numbered 2.5 or later in the process. Students can be asked to make a list of questions they would need answered about the problem in order to solve it (during the first time using this strategy, teacher modeling might be necessary). For example, questions about the bullying video could include:

- How old are they?
- Are they in the same class?
- What is the school policy on bullying?
- Does the teacher know what is going on?
- How might the bully respond?
- Do their parents know each other?
- Was there a specific incident that started it?
- Are other students being bullied too?
- Are there other students the bully seems to listen to?

Students can then be asked to categorize the questions into the broad areas needed to solve most problems—researching information, identifying allies, and preparing for a reaction. They can then use similar questions and categories to develop their own specific action plan to solve the more personal problems they identify and present those plans with their solutions. Finally, students can perform short role-plays or draw a comic strip portraying how they would solve the problems.

Using the critical pedagogy correlates with California ELD domains 1, 2, 3, 5 and 6.

Supporting Research. Using the kind of problem-based learning exemplified in these kind of critical pedagogy lessons has brought many benefits to the ESL classroom. These include the more authentic issues represented in the process promoting enhanced language acquisition, compared to prepackaged dialogues and worksheets or role-plays. In addition, it has been found to increase the likelihood of learners applying the classroom content to their outside lives.[10]

Tech Tool
Digital Storytelling

Students can portray the problems, and their potential solutions, online through the use of video, animations, or slideshows. Smartphones make the creation of these digital stories even easier, and they can be created by even the least tech-savvy students and teachers. Multiple digital storytelling tools for smartphones and computer use can be found in "The Best Digital Storytelling Resources" at http://larryferlazzo.edublogs.org.

Free Voluntary Reading and Reading Strategies

Free Voluntary Reading, also called Extensive Reading, Silent Sustained Reading, and recreational reading, is the instructional strategy of letting students choose books or other reading material they want to read with minimal or no academic work connected to it. Its purpose is to promote the enjoyment of reading. It's expected that since students are choosing the books they will read, they will also feel more motivated to want to learn the new vocabulary that appears in them. Students are also encouraged to change books if they find the one they are reading to be uninteresting.

Though students are typically not assessed on what they are reading, students can be encouraged to interact with the text through the use of reading strategies. Without this kind of encouragement, students can more easily fall into the trap of learning to "decode" words without truly understanding their meaning. Teachers can model what good readers do through short and simple "think-alouds" (see Exhibit 3.4). Teacher comments are noted in the exhibit. (Read-alouds, where short passages are read to students without modeling reading strategies, are also an effective instructional method. See Chapters Five and Six for further information.)

A teacher can identify short, accessible passages and over a period of a few weeks use this sequence with students:

1. Teacher models a think-aloud (showing it on a document camera or overhead projector), focusing on one of several reading strategies—asking questions, making a connection, predicting what happens next, evaluating, visualizing, monitoring and repairing, and summarizing.

2. Small whiteboards with markers and erasers (or white sheets of paper) are distributed to students.

3. Teacher shows and reads another short passage and asks students to apply the previously modeled reading strategy. Students hold up their boards when they are ready for teacher feedback so all students can see many examples.

EXHIBIT 3.4. Think-Aloud

Note: The names used here should be changed to reflect you and your own students. Teacher think-aloud comments appear in italics.

The students were working very hard in class one day (*I wonder what they were doing?*). In the middle of a lesson, Jose screamed, "Look, there's a mouse!" (*This makes me see a picture of a little tiny mouse in my mind.*) All the students started yelling, and some jumped on their desks. Tou threw his pencil at it, and Chou threw his pen. The teacher was very afraid, too. Pang wasn't worried. (*I wonder why she wasn't afraid?*) She took two books and used them to push the mouse out the door. The mouse was free, and Pang was a hero. (*This makes me see a picture in my mind of the teacher and students cheering Pang.*)

Students can be given a simple form (see Exhibit 3.5) that asks them to show a few reading strategies each week. It is less important that students are using all the reading strategies correctly. It is more critical for them to recognize that genuinely understanding any text requires readers to be proactive and not passive.

Students can begin each class with fifteen minutes of silent reading (part of that time can also be spent with partners reading the same book together if they choose). An important consideration is what the teacher is doing during this period of time. Though some suggest that the teacher should also be a model and read during the same time, we feel strongly that it is more important to be walking around, asking students questions, having them read aloud short passages, and so forth. Not only does this kind of interaction serve as a good formative assessment, but at least one important study has also found it to be a good instructional strategy. In an article in the *Journal of Educational Psychology*, researchers found that teachers providing individual feedback to students during this kind of reading time was by far one of the most effective ways to help improve students' reading ability. It primarily looked at students using their silent reading time to read class text (though not exclusively), but it seems close enough to the basic ideas of Free Voluntary Reading that we should carefully consider what they found.[11] Reading at home for twenty minutes each night could also be homework.

In addition, students can be encouraged to talk with their classmates using simple Book Talks, which are explained more in Chapter Five and in Exhibit 5.4.

EXHIBIT 3.5. Reading Log

Name _____

Period _____

Date _____

Reading Log

Summarize: This book or story is about... ☐→☐

Predict: I predict that... ⟶

Ask questions: Will... ? Why... ?

Evaluate: I agree (or disagree) with... I like (or do not like)... ☺ or ☹

Visualize: Reading this book or story makes me see a picture of... ☺✿

Connect: This makes me remember...

Movie · Book · Personal Experience

Date	Book or Story Title	Reading Strategy Used

Using Free Voluntary Reading and reading strategies correlates with California ELD domains 1, 2, 3, 4, 5 and 6.

Supporting Research. Numerous studies have shown the benefits of Free Voluntary Reading, particularly with English language learners.[12] A review of twenty-three studies showed that in all cases ELLs using Free Voluntary Reading had a higher gain in reading comprehension than those in classes not using the strategy. In addition, other research has demonstrated that ELLs using Free Voluntary Reading have greater gains in writing, grammar usage, and spelling.[13]

Research by Professor Jim Cummins also supports explicit teaching and learning of reading comprehension strategies.[14]

Tech Tool
Online Books

Thousands of free online books are available and accessible to English language learners and provide audio and visual support for the text. These are particularly useful for older ELLs because they help students read higher-level texts, as opposed to simpler ones designed for young children. In addition, many free and easily printable short books are available online. Lists of these online resources can be found in "A Collection of 'The Best . . .' Lists for Online Books Accessible to ELLs" at http://larryferlazzo.edublogs.org.

Communicative Dictation Activities

These three dictation exercises combine reading and writing skills with developing listening and speaking skills.

Interactive Dictation. In interactive dictation, students are assigned a simple passage or a book the class has been using, so students are familiar with it. They are then divided into pairs or triads, and each student is given a small whiteboard, marker, and eraser (or blank sheets of paper). One student reads a few words while the other(s) write them down. The writers can look at their copy of the text as a kind of cheat sheet, but should be encouraged to work toward not using it. The reader can give feedback on the accuracy and errors of the writer.

Dictogloss. Dictogloss can be done a number of different ways but here is one variation. First, students divide their papers in half. Then the teacher reads a short text, often one students are familiar with. After the first time of just listening, the teacher reads it again and students write down notes on one-half of the paper about what they have heard. Next the teacher reads it a third time and again the students write down additional notes in the same space. Students then compare their notes with a partner and they work together to develop a reconstruction of the text—one that is not the exact wording, but that demonstrates its meaning accurately. Finally, the teacher reads the selection again and students judge how well they did.

Picture Dictation. In picture dictation, the teacher can draw or find a simple image and, without showing it to the class, describe it while students draw. It can also be a partner activity where half of the class is given one picture and the other half a different one. Students with different pictures are made partners and stand up a book or folder between them. One student describes her picture while the other draws. When it's complete and the student is given feedback, the roles can be reversed. Students can also be asked to write sentences describing the picture.

Picture dictation is one of many exercises (and our favorite one) that fall under the broad category of "information gap" activities. They are generally designed as partner exercises where one student has to get information from the other—speaking the target language—in order to complete the assignment.

Using Communicative Dictation Activities correlates with California ELD domains 1 and 6.

Supporting Research. Numerous studies have shown that communicative dictation activities can increase student engagement,[15] enhance English listening comprehension,[16] and improve grammar skills.[17] These communicative activities are different from the often deadly teacher-centered uses (passages repeated multiple times in a "drill-and-kill" fashion until students get it "right"), which can be particularly frustrating for beginning-level learners.

Tech Tool
Online Dictation Exercises

Many free online dictation exercises—using audio only or audio and video together—are available, providing automatic and immediate assessments. Some of the best ones are

Listen and Write: http://www.listen-and-write.com/audio

Dictations for Learning English: http://www.teacherjoe.us/Dicts.html

English Club Dictations: http://www.englishclub.com/listening/dictation.htm

English Online Dictations: http://eolf.univ-fcomte.fr/index.php?page=english
    -dictation-exercises

Concept Attainment

Concept attainment, originally developed by Jerome Bruner and his colleagues,[18] is a form of inductive learning where the teacher identifies both "good" and "bad" examples (ideally, taken from student work—with the names removed, of course) of the intended learning objective. After developing a sheet like the one in Exhibit 3.6, which is designed to practice conjugating the verb "to be" correctly, the teacher would place it on a document camera or overhead projector. At first, everything would be covered except for the "Yes" and "No" titles, and the teacher would explain that he is going to give various examples and he wants students to identify why certain ones are under "Yes" and others are under "No."

EXHIBIT 3.6. Concept Attainment Example

Yes	No
Hmong food is good.	
	Many people is big and heavy.
The food is spicy.	
	Hmong foods is good.
It is a sort of soup that Hmong people eat.	
	Ginger and galangal is good
The foods are spicy.	
	Hmong food are natural.
American foods are not spicy.	
	Papaya salad are good and spicy.

After the first "Yes" and "No" examples are shown, students are asked to think about them and share with a partner why they think one is a "Yes" and one is a "No." After the teacher calls on people, if no one can identify the reason, he continues uncovering one example at a time and continues the think-pair-share process with students until they identify the reasons. Then students are asked to correct the "No" examples and write their own "Yes" ones. Last, students can be asked to generate their own "Yes" examples and share them with a partner or the class. This inductive learning strategy can be used effectively to teach countless lessons, including ones on grammar, spelling, composition, and even speaking (using recorded audio).

We have even used this strategy to teach essay organization by taping parts of essays on the classroom wall under "Yes" and "No"—with names removed and after getting permission to do so from the student authors. This kind of exercise is much easier to do when there are positive relationships throughout the classroom.

Using concept attainment correlates with California ELD domains 1, 5 and 6.

Supporting Research. Concept attainment is another instructional strategy that builds on the brain's natural desire to seek out patterns. Judy Willis, neurologist, teacher, and author, writes: "Education is about increasing the patterns that students can use, recognize, and communicate. As the ability to see and work with patterns expands, the executive functions are enhanced. Whenever new material is presented in such a way that students see relationships, they generate greater brain cell activity (forming new neural connections) and achieve more successful long-term memory storage and retrieval."[19]

Numerous studies have shown that concept attainment has a positive effect on student achievement, including with second-language learners.[20]

Concept attainment, like the other forms of inductive teaching and learning discussed in this chapter (Picture Word Inductive Model and Text Data Sets) can also be described as an example of "enhanced discovery learning." In a recent meta-analysis of hundreds of studies, researchers found that "enhanced discovery learning" was a more effective form of teaching than either "direct instruction" or "unassisted discovery learning."[21]

Tech Tool

Online Writing Practice

Many free online sites, including blogs, provide interactive and engaging opportunities for English language learners to practice writing skills, including grammar, spelling, and sentence construction. You can find an extensive list of them in "The Best Places Where Students Can Write Online" at http://larryferlazzo.edublogs.org.

Language Experience Approach

The Language Experience Approach involves the entire class doing an activity and then discussing and writing about it. The activity could be

- Watching a short video clip
- Taking a walk around the school
- Doing a science experiment
- Playing a game
- Just about anything else you can think of!

Immediately following the activity, students are given a short time to write down notes about what they did (very early beginners can draw). Then the teacher calls on students to share what the class did—usually, though not always, in chronological order. The teacher then writes down what is said on a document camera, overhead projector, or easel paper. It is sometimes debated whether the teacher should write down exactly what a student says if there are grammar or word errors or should say it back to the student and write it correctly—without saying the student was wrong. We use the second strategy and feel that as long as students are not being corrected explicitly ("That's not the correct way to say it, Eva, this is"), it is better to model accurate grammar and word usage. Students can then copy down the class-developed description. Since the text comes out of their own experience, it is much more accessible because they already know its meaning.

The text can subsequently be used for different follow-up activities, including as a cloze (removing certain words and leaving a blank which students have to complete); a sentence scramble (taking individual sentences and mixing-up the words for learners to sequence correctly); or mixing-up all the sentences in the text and having students put them back in order.

Using the Language Experience Approach correlates with California ELD domains 1, 2, 5 and 6.

Supporting Research. Respected ESL researchers Suzanne Peregoy and Owen Boyle have found that "the language-experience approach is one of the most frequently recommended approaches for beginning second-language readers. The beauty of the approach is that the student provides the text, through the dictation, that serves as the basis for reading instruction. As a result, language-experience reading is tailored to the learner's own interests, social, and cultural strengths and interest the student brings to school."[22]

Tech Tool
Online Audio Recording

There are numerous free sites that, as long as the user has a microphone, let students easily make an audio recording. Some of these tools also allow you to either upload your own photo or grab others off the Web to illustrate the recording. Students can record a text developed through the Language Experience Approach (LEA) and then record it again weeks or months later so they can actually see and hear the progress they are making. A teacher with a smartphone can also assign

LEA sentences to individual students or pairs that they can practice, record in the classroom, and, with a tap on the phone's screen, immediately upload to a site so that it can be replayed to the class. Some of the best free online tools we've used include

Audioboo. Audioboo lets you easily create what is basically a voice blog. After signing up (which is quite easy), you can make recordings of up to five minutes in length. (http://audioboo.fm)

Fotobabble. Fotobabble is a supereasy application that lets you upload a photo (or grab one from the Web) and provide a one-minute audio recording to go along with it; then it provides a link and an embed code that can be used for sharing. It's a simple tool students can use to practice their speaking skills. (http://www.fotobabble.com)

Voki. A Voki is a talking avatar that students can design and use to record a message. (http://www.voki.com)

Vocaroo. Vocaroo lets you record a lengthy message with no need for registration. It then provides a URL address or an embed code so you can post it to a student-teacher blog or web site or e-mail it. (http://vocaroo.com)

Sock Puppets. Sock Puppets is a simple iPhone app that lets you easily record a student and upload it to YouTube. It can be used to briefly record a student speaking or reading in class or even to have two or three students record a simple play. One major advantage of using this for speaking practice is that it's the sock puppet that's actually speaking on the display, not the student. (http://itunes.apple.com/us/app/sock-puppets)

Writing Collaborative Stories

Collaborative story writing can be done in a number of ways and bears some similarities to the Language Experience Approach.

One example is to start by dividing the class into groups of three. Within the small groups, each person is numbered either one, two, or three. Each group is given one sheet of paper, and at the top of each paper the group writes "Once Upon a Time . . ." (at times, it might make sense to provide some parameters for the story so it is connected to the thematic unit the class is studying—such as food or school—but, as we discussed earlier, it's okay not to have all activities directly connected to the theme at all times).

Next the teacher puts a piece of paper under the document camera and projects it on the screen and writes:

1. Who?

This means that the number ones in each group have to write one sentence describing who was going to be in the story. Students can be encouraged to have fun with it and pushed to write adjectives ("the ugly monster" and the "handsome boy"). Students are given no more than two minutes to write it, and their group members can help.

The teacher then writes:

2. Where?

All the number twos have to take the paper and write where the story was taking place. Students generally began to get engaged in the exercise at this point.

The process continues until the paper on the overhead looks like this:

3. When?

1. What is the problem?

2. Who said what? (indicating that someone in the story had to say something, which is a great time to reinforce quotation marks)

3. Who said what back to that person?

1. Something bad happens

2. Something good happens

3. Something funny happens

The entire small group then determines how the story ends.

Students can then be given a big piece of easel paper to convert their sentences into a story with illustrations. Next, in a round-robin fashion, each group can tell and show their story to the other groups.

Follow-up activities with the texts can be similar to the ones suggested in the Language Experience Approach section. In addition, students can even convert their story into a short skit they perform for the class.

Writing collaborative stories correlates with California ELD domains 1, 5 and 6.

Supporting Research. Working in small groups has consistently been found to develop second-language learner self-confidence and increase opportunities for language interaction. Specifically, it results in more student speaking practice and reduces future student errors because of those increased practice opportunities, along with students feeling more motivated and engaged in learning.[23]

Tech Tool
Online Collaborative Storytelling

Numerous free online sites and tools enable students to easily create collaborative stories. Some of our favorites that allow teachers and students to create stories whose contributors can be limited by invitation include:

Thumbscribes: http://www.thumbscribes.com

StoryTimed: http://www.storytimed.com

Folding Story: http://foldingstory.com

Protagonize: http://www.protagonize.com/groups. We especially like Protagonize because it easily allows students and teachers to create the added fun twist of turning their stories into choose-your-own-adventure tales with multiple options.

Phonics

Countless debates have taken place about the amount of time that should be spent on teaching phonics and which instructional method should be used to teach them. Extensive research supports the idea of spending limited time teaching what Stephen Krashen calls "basic phonics," the very basic consonant and vowel rules needed for students to comprehend text.[24] We believe that using an inductive process is the most effective and engaging way to teach these basic phonics.

The easiest tool to use in this process is the book *Sounds Easy* by Sharron Bassano.[25] A sample page from the book can be found in Exhibit 3.7. It is designed for use with beginning ELLs from grade five through adult education. The inductive method we recommend builds upon and adds to the instructional strategy suggested in the book.

First, copies of a page from the book are distributed to students. In the case of Exhibit 3.7, it is a page with a series of pictures that can be described by words with the long *a* sound. Each picture has one or more of the letters in the describing word missing. The teacher has the same sheet on the overhead or document camera. The teacher says the number of the picture, gives students a few seconds to complete the blanks with what they believe goes there, and then the teacher writes the correct letters (students correct their papers if they have made any mistakes).

EXHIBIT 3.7. Sounds Easy! Phonics, Spelling, and Pronunciation Practice

Sounds Easy! _____

a

1. _____	2. _____	3. _____	4. _____
5. _____	6. _____	7. _____	8. _____
9. _____	10. _____	11. _____	12. _____
13. _____	14. _____	15. _____	16. _____

Source: S. Bassano, _Sounds Easy! Phonics, Spelling, and Pronunciation Practice_ (Provo, UT: Alta Book Center, 2002). Copyright © 2002 Alta Book Center Publishers. Reproduced by permission.

After the sheet is complete it is reviewed again. The teacher can point rapidly to the different pictures and ask for a choral response, doing it faster and faster to make it a more fun activity. Then students work with partners to practice pronouncing the words. Next they work together to put the words into two or three categories. They could be "words that have *ai*," "words that have an *a* with a silent *e* at the end," or categories that reflect how they are used—such as food, for example.

Pairs then become groups of four to compare and explain the reasoning behind their categories. The groups then choose which categories they think are best and add words to them using what they learned from the Picture Word Inductive Model activity, dictionaries, or other resources. They can create posters of the categories and share them with the class, along with one, two, or three phonics rules they might have learned.

More often than not, students themselves will identify the key phonics "rules" that apply—in this case, that the letter *a* would be pronounced with a "long" sound if it was the third letter from the end of a word that ended with an *e* or if it was the second from the last letter if the last letter was a *y*. In addition, the letter *a* would likely be pronounced with a "long" sound if it appeared as an *ai*.

In reading activities later that day or shortly thereafter, the teacher and students can highlight instances where this rule applies.

Of course, it is not necessary to use this *entire* inductive process for every letter sound. Teachers should use their judgment about which sounds they think are the most important, how it fits into the other units they are teaching at the time, and the energy level displayed by their students on any given day.[26]

Teaching phonics inductively correlates with California ELD domains 1 and 2.

Supporting Research. Extensive research demonstrates that an intensive emphasis on explicit phonics instruction can lead students to focus on decoding instead of comprehension. Along with the previously cited studies by Krashen,[27] he has done further review of the confirming research (for a list of Krashen's publications see http://sdkrashen.com), as has Professor Brian Cambourne.[28]

Tech Tool
Phonics Practice

There are numerous free online sites where phonics can be reinforced in engaging ways through games and practice. Our favorites are

Reading Bear: http://www.readingbear.org
ABC Fast Phonics: http://www.abcfastphonics.com

The previously mentioned online Free Voluntary Reading sites are the best uses of technology, though, to move students from decoding to comprehension.

In addition to the support previously cited for inductive teaching and learning, studies have shown students in inductive learning classrooms scoring as much as 30 percent higher in assessments than those using deductive models.[29] In addition, ESL researcher H. D. Brown writes that "most of the evidence in communicative second language teaching points to the superiority of an inductive approach to rules and generalizations."[30]

LISTENING AND SPEAKING

Total Physical Response

The purpose of Total Physical Response (TPR) is to have students physically act out the words and phrases being taught by the teacher. One way to implement TPR is by first asking all students to stand, and they can move to the front or stay where they are. Two students are brought to the front. The teacher models a verb or two—for example, "sit" and "stand." She then asks the two students in front to "sit," "stand," "sit," and "stand." The two students are asked to return to their regular places, and the teacher then tells the class to "sit" and "stand" several times. Students can then divide into partners or in small groups and take turns giving each other commands.

TPR can be an engaging activity by spending ten minutes a day doing it and focusing on a few words each time. Once key verbs are learned, the commands can be made more complicated and even silly. More complicated play-acting scenes can eventually be used ("open the peanut butter jar, put some on your knife, and lick it"). One nice change of pace can be having a student give the commands to the class and creating opportunities where students can give commands to the teacher!

Using Total Physical Response correlates with California ELD domains 1 and 6.

Supporting Research. TPR was originally developed by Dr. James J. Asher and modeled from his analysis of how a child learns—by doing more listening than speaking and by often responding to commands from his parents.[31]

Tech Tool
Online TPR

Henny Jellema has developed one of the most creative sites on the Web for English language learners—the only way to describe it is as virtual TPR (http://www.digischool.nl/oefenen/hennyjellema/engels/tpr/voorbladtpr.htm). Images are shown of various gestures, and users must choose the correct written and/or verbal description of the activity. It does not substitute for the actual TPR activity. Instead, it should reinforce what is done in the classroom. As he states on the site, "For a student the exercises should not be a surprise of something new, but a surprise of recognition!"

Numerous studies have documented its effectiveness,[32] and TPR is used in ESL and EFL classes around the world.

Music

Songs can be an all-purpose tool in the ESL classroom. Many students who are reluctant to speak feel more comfortable singing with a group. Music is a universal language that most people enjoy. In addition to speaking practice, songs provide multiple opportunities for listening, reading, and even writing practice. Using pop songs can be much more engaging for older students. However, simple songs geared specifically to teaching children or ELL vocabulary can often be useful—and enjoyed by everybody!

Here are just a few ways to use songs in the classroom:

- Give students copies of lyrics to a song connected to the thematic unit you're studying and first review them together. Then practice singing the chorus, followed by playing the music and singing at the same time. Next do the same with verses, though for some songs you might just want to teach the chorus or the chorus and one or two verses. Different halves or thirds of the class can sing different portions and then switch, creating a friendly competition to see which groups sing the "best."

- Provide copies of the lyrics with some of the words blanked out (clozes). Students fill in the blanks as the song is played. The missing words can either be listed out of order at the bottom of the sheet or not listed anywhere so that students must come up with the words and correct spelling on their own.

- Provide the lyrics cut into separate lines (or cut every two lines). Another option is to copy and paste the scrambled lines in an electronic document, print it out, and have students cut them out. As the song is playing, students have to put the lines in the correct sequence. This may require periodically replaying portions (depending on the levels of student outrage!). Students can work together in pairs.

- Students develop comprehension questions about the song, which they use to quiz other students.

- Students can be challenged to write their own lyrics for certain lines of a song and perform them in small groups. For example, if students are learning the Beatles song "Hello, Goodbye," they can be asked to replace "hello" and "goodbye" in the line "You say hello, and I say goodbye" with any other pair of opposites they have been learning (for example, "You say short, and I say tall").

Using music correlates with California ELD domains 1, 2 and 6.

Supporting Research. Extensive research has shown that using songs is an effective language-development strategy with English language learners.[33] They are often accessible because popular songs use the vocabulary of an eleven-year-old, the rhythm and beat help students speak in phrases or sentences instead of words, and the word repetition assists retention.[34] Neuroscience has also found that music can increase dopamine release in the brain and generates positive emotions. This kind of emotional learning reinforces long-term memory.[35]

Tech Tool
Music Sites for ELLs

Many free online sites offer teacher resources for using songs in the classroom and online exercises similar to the classroom activities recommended in this section, such as clozes and sequencing. Karaoke is another activity that can be used either in the classroom or individually online. There are even sites designed to show music videos and have students complete clozes in the subtitles—individually or projected on a screen so the whole class can participate. In addition, plenty of free sites provide online audio access to just about any song you might want to use in class. You can find links to all of these tools in "The Best Music Websites for Learning English" at http://larryferlazzo.edublogs.org.

Chants

Carolyn Graham is well known for developing the concept of Jazz Chants to teach English. These are short, rhythmic chants that reinforce vocabulary and/or grammar lessons in a fun way.

She encourages teachers to create their own chants.[36] One of her recommendations is to start with three words—the first one having two syllables, the second three, and the third having one. For example, if your thematic unit is school, a vocabulary chant could be

> whiteboard, eraser, pen
>
> whiteboard, eraser, pen
>
> whiteboard, eraser, pen

Having students clap and chant in unison for a minute or two, with the teacher or a student pointing to each item, could be a fun reinforcing activity.

Or, as Graham suggests, the same words could be turned into a grammar chant:

> He uses the whiteboard
> She uses the eraser
> They use pens
> They use pens

These can be chanted together or in rounds.

Of course, just about anything can be turned into a chant, and chants don't always have to meet these criteria. For example, a chant can be structured in a question-and-response format with students on different sides of the room saying one or the other. Advanced students can also create their own chants and teach them to the class.

Using chants correlates with California ELD domains 1, 2 and 6.

Supporting Research. These kinds of chants have the same advantages cited by research supporting songs in the classroom[37] and are particularly helpful for teaching stress and intonation.[38] A big benefit to chants is that it is far easier and quicker to compose a chant than a song!

Dialogues

Short dialogues, ideally related to the thematic unit that is being studied and that has practical use outside the classroom, can be a useful tool for oral language practice. After teacher modeling, students—in pairs, threes, or fours—can practice and perform in front of the class or for another small group. It's often helpful to inject some humor into the dialogue.

There are several ways to vary this activity:

- The dialogue can have different options for students to choose from (see Exhibit 3.8).

- Dialogue performers can develop a few questions to ask their listeners about what was said.

- Students can develop their own dialogues after being given certain parameters (should be related to a certain topic and a certain length). They can use teacher-prepared dialogues as models and possibly be asked to create just one line and build from there as they develop more confidence.

- Students can be given the dialogue with sentences mixed up and asked to put them in the correct sequence.

Using dialogues correlates with California ELD domains 1, 2 and 6.

EXHIBIT 3.8. Dialogue Example

First Week of School Dialogue

Student One:
a. I am so happy to be in Mr. Ferlazzo's class!
b. I feel so sad that I'm in Mr. Ferlazzo's class.
c. I hate being in Mr. Ferlazzo's class. I feel sick when I'm there!

Student Two:
a. Me, too. I feel like my dream has come true.
b. I don't agree with you. Mr. Ferlazzo is a wonderful teacher!
c. Yes, I agree.

Student Three:
a. Let's go buy Mr. Ferlazzo a big present to show him how much we like him as a teacher.
b. Let's give him a chance. Let's tell him we don't understand something, and we can see if he's a good teacher and helps us or if he just gets angry.
c. Let's go talk to the principal to see if we can get transferred to a different class.

(Choose one of the following options and act it out.)

Next:
a. Go to store to buy a present.
b. Pretend not to understand something.
c. Ask the principal to change classes.

(Choose one of the following options and act it out.)

Last:
a. Give a present to a student pretending to be Mr. Ferlazzo.
b. A student pretending to be Mr. Ferlazzo responds to students not understanding something.
c. What does a student pretending to be the principal say?

Supporting Research. Dialogues have been found to be effective forms for language practice and confidence building. Students who have practiced within the relatively nonthreatening environment of the classroom will be more likely to actually use the language outside of school.[39]

Tech Tool
Online Dialogues

Videotaping students acting out a dialogue, uploading it to the Web, and then showing it to them in class is an excellent way for students to frequently assess their English skills and is always a fun activity. Students can also use the previously mentioned audio tools for recording their dialogues. In addition, there are numerous free sites that allow users to listen to dialogues, practice them, and be quizzed. Two of the best are

English Listening Lesson Library Online: http://www.elllo.org

J@M from the British Council: http://go4english.co.uk

3–2–1

This is a modification of an exercise developed by Paul Nation called the 4-3-2 Fluency Activity.[40] In his original activity plan, students line up (standing or sitting) facing each other. Each one must be prepared to speak on something that they are already quite familiar with. First, they speak to their partner for four minutes about the topic. Then they move down the line and say the same thing for three minutes to a new partner. Next they move again and speak for two minutes. Then the students on the other side do the same thing.

We developed a modification of this activity that could be called 3-2-1 or, for beginners, even 2-1.5-1. In it, students are told to pick any topic they know a lot about, and they will be asked to talk about it to a partner for three minutes (or two minutes, depending on the English level of the students), and then for two minutes and then for one. But first, they should write down notes about what they might want to say.

Next, if possible, students are taken to a computer lab where they practice speaking by recording all or part of what they want to say. Afterward, students are told they have two minutes to review their notes before they have to be put away. Next the teacher models questions that students who are listening can ask the speaker if they appear to be stuck. It is also useful to model characteristics of being a good listener (such as maintaining eye contact and not talking to other students). Then students begin the speaking and switching process described earlier. Later, if feasible, students can go back to the computer lab and record their speaking again so they can compare and identify improvement.

Using the 3–2–1 activity correlates with California ELD domains 1, 2 and 6.

Supporting Research. Regular use of the 4–3–2 exercise has been shown to improve learners' fluency, producing natural and faster-flowing speech.[41]

Video

We've already described one way of using videos with the Language Experience Approach. Another technique called Back to the Screen is adapted from *Zero Prep: Ready-to-Go Activities for the Language Classroom* by Laurel Pollard, Natalie Hess, and Jan Herron.[42] The teacher picks a short clip from a movie (the famous highway chase scene from one of the *Matrix* movies, for example) and then divides the class into pairs, with one group facing the TV and the other with their backs to it. Then, after turning off the sound, the teacher begins playing the movie. The person who can see the screen tells the other person what is happening. Then, after a few minutes, the students reverse places. Afterward, the pairs write a chronological sequence of what happened, which is shared with another group and discussed in class. Finally, everyone watches the clip, with sound, together.

Another way to use videos is to have students watch short clips and create questions about what they saw and heard. The questions can then be exchanged with a classmate to answer. An example of this strategy can be found in Chapter Five and in Exhibit 5.10.

It's important to show subtitles when using videos in an ESL class. Showing English subtitles during English videos improves listening and reading comprehension among English language learners.[43]

Using video in the described ways correlates with California ELD domains 1, 5 and 6.

Supporting Research. Substantial evidence suggests that the visual clues offered by video have a positive effect on student listening comprehension.[44] In addition, video use has been shown to have a positive impact on student motivation to learn.[45]

Improvisation

Improvisation is an activity done without student preparation. Here is one way to incorporate it into the classroom.

Tech Tool
Online Videos

A number of free video support sites for English language learners are available. You can find recommendations and links to video clips and associated lesson plans in "A Collection of 'The Best...' Lists for Online ELL Video Sites" at http://larryferlazzo.edublogs.org.

Even though English Central is included in many of the lists mentioned in this chapter, it deserves to be especially highlighted (http://www.englishcentral.com). The site shows engaging video clips and their subtitles and then assesses the accuracy of the user's pronunciation while repeating the lines—it even takes into account students' accents!

Each student can be given a small whiteboard—these are versatile and inexpensive, and if you don't want to buy them you can make them easily, too—along with a marker and cloth eraser. The teacher can explain (the first time—after that, students will understand what to do) that he will start off a conversation and that students will write on their board what they might say in response and hold it up so everyone can see it. The teacher then chooses one of the responses they wrote, and, in turn, responds to it, and so on.

Here is what happened in one of our classrooms when we first tried this activity:

> I began by saying that I was holding onto a cliff with my fingers and ready to fall. I then yelled "Help!" and told students to write a response on their whiteboards. Students immediately got the idea and the fun began. Responses included "No" "Why should I?" "What do you need?" and "Goodbye." Some students just held up their boards and I asked others to share their responses aloud. I chose "Why should I?" to respond to and said "I'm going to die if you don't help, please!" The next responses, with much laughter, included "I will step on your fingers to help you fall!" "What will you pay me?" and "Have a good trip." In print, it may sound like I have a class of crazed students, but it was all done in fun, and everybody participated. I would also point at various people for them to say what they wrote, too.
>
> I next asked them to imagine that I was a pretty girl or a handsome boy, and said, "Will you go on a date with me?" A similar process then began, including at one point my asking, "What restaurant will you take me to?" followed by "I don't want to go there." Many students

came back with responses like "Too bad," but one wrote "Where do you want to go?" I pointed out that the student who came up with that response was likely to get far more dates than the rest of them.

Lastly, I said "You are getting an F in this class and will have to repeat it again next year." Needless to say, an energetic conversation followed.[46]

Very simple scenarios can be chosen that relate to the thematic unit being studied, and students can begin taking turns up front, developing a scenario, choosing which responses they want to pick, and responding to them.

Using improvisation correlates with California ELD domains 1 and 6.

Supporting Research. Improvisation in music has been shown to deactivate parts of the brain that provide "conscious control, enabling freer, more spontaneous thoughts and actions," according to scientists.[47] These same researchers have discovered connections between music and language, suggesting that improvisation can lead to greater fluency in language, as well as music.

Additional resources, including further information on ELL instructional strategies like dictogloss and information gap activities, as well as additional ways to use photos in class, can be found on our book's web site at www.josseybass.com/go/eslsurvivalguide.

CHAPTER FOUR

Daily Instruction for Beginning ELLs

Nobody thought Juan was very capable. People didn't take him seriously when he said he wanted some land to farm. Finally, he was given a small plot, but everyone laughed because they believed it was poor soil and Juan wouldn't be successful. Juan, though, was a hard worker, and he had the knowledge that his friends the Zanate birds shared with him. Following their advice, he planted what are known as the "three sisters": corn, beans, and squash. The birds—and the indigenous people of Mexico—know that these three plants complement one another during the growing season. The townspeople were shocked to see the success of Juan's harvest. From that day forward he was known as Juan Zanate.[1]

In this Mexican folktale, people had a low opinion of Juan's ability. However, through his determination and his use of inner gifts—which most people didn't see he had—Juan succeeded beyond his neighbors' imagination.

The suggestions in this chapter for daily instructional activities, as well as the ideas found in every chapter in this book, are designed to help the gifts and assets carried by our ELL students shine as bright as those that were inside of Juan Zanate. Chapter Three provided an overview of different elements to include in a beginning ESL classroom. This chapter will describe what the application of these elements might look like on a day-to-day basis.

Reflection

Robert Marzano calls reflection "the final step in a comprehensive approach to actively processing information."[2] As such, it can also function as a useful formative assessment (see Chapter Thirteen).

We recommend having a short—five to seven minutes or so—reflection activity, usually a "think-write-pair-share," two or three times each week at the end of class. It could be useful to both student and teacher to collect these for monthly, bimonthly, or quarterly review, so keeping them in a separate folder or notebook is an option. We suggest that these activities fall into five different categories and that the reflection activity vary between them (and any other ideas you might want to try). Depending on the English level of the class, sentence starters to help students with their responses might be helpful in addition to asking the questions themselves.

SUMMARIZE

There is a wealth of research documenting the effectiveness of having students summarize what they have been studying.[3] Students can respond to prompts like:

What are two things you learned today?

What is the most interesting thing you learned today?

What do you know now that you didn't know before today?

What will you tell your parents tonight if they ask what you learned?

Draw something that represents the most important thing you learned today or that summarizes the day. Please write a short description.

SELF-ASSESS

Robert Marzano recommends students share how well they think they did in class and what they believe they could have done better.[4] Using the metacognitive strategy of reviewing what they did that helped them learn, along with what they did that was not particularly effective, can assist students in developing a greater sense of self-efficacy.[5] Here are a few more questions students can answer:

What did you do that helped you the most today to learn English?

What did you do to help yourself understand something when you were not clear?

What, if anything, do you think you need more help in understanding?

What, if anything, are you having difficulty doing?

After students complete the lesson on the Qualities of a Successful Language Learner in Chapter Twelve, they can periodically be asked to reflect on what they did to meet their goals or what they could have done differently to meet them.

ASSESS THE CLASS AND TEACHER

Asking students to share their perspectives on class activities and the teacher's style can help on a number of levels. This is best done anonymously to ensure candid responses. Questions can include

> What was your favorite class activity today, and why did you like it?
>
> What was your least favorite class activity today, and why was it your least favorite?
>
> Was the pace of this class too slow, too fast, or just right?

These one-day quick check-ins should not be confused with the more extensive class evaluation suggestions in Chapter Two and in Exhibit 2.2.

RELEVANCE

Some studies have shown that having students write a few sentences explaining how they can *specifically* apply what they learned to their lives resulted in higher achievement.[6] ESL teachers can apply this same concept in their classes. Students might write, "I will be able to ask someone for directions" or "I can fill out a job application" and, in addition to refreshing their memory, they might feel more encouraged to actually do these things.

HIGHER-ORDER THINKING

A Taxonomy of Student Reflection was developed by educator Peter Pappas.[7] In it, he applies the Revised Bloom's Taxonomy (see Chapter Six for more details on Bloom's Taxonomy) to critical reflection. He recommends looking at student self-reflection through this lens:

> *Top*
>
> > Creating: what should I do next?
> >
> > Evaluating: how well did I do?
> >
> > Analyzing: do I see any patterns in what I did?
> >
> > Understanding: what was important about it?
>
> *Bottom*
>
> > Remembering: what did I do?

Some of these questions obviously also connect to the previous reflection ideas. After students become more experienced in self-reflection, and as their English levels advance, the teacher might want to start framing the reflection questions in the context of this taxonomy. In this way, not only may students become more aware of the strategy behind self-reflection, but they will also be introduced to the Revised Bloom's Taxonomy, which they will surely encounter during their academic career.

Homework

This section presents the homework that we give our beginning and early intermediate English language learners. It covers all four domains: reading, writing, listening, speaking. All homework is shared and turned in on Fridays, and twenty minutes of class time is sometimes provided to students during the week to work on it.

- Read a book in English at home for at least twenty minutes each night and demonstrate the use of at least three reading strategies (see the Reading Log in Exhibit 3.5). In addition, students must complete a Weekly Reading Sheet (see Exhibit 6.1 in Chapter Six).

- Write a journal sharing two or three good events that occurred that week and one event that was not necessarily positive. In the last instance, share if there was something that the student could have done differently to improve the outcome. If the student is an early beginner, he or she can draw or paste pictures representing the same events. In class, students share what they wrote with a partner, and the partner should ask at least one question.

- Complete a Four Words sheet with new words they learned that week—in or out of class—that they think are important (see Exhibit 4.1 in this section). In class, students share the words they chose with a partner.

- Spend at least ten minutes each day "talking to themselves" (while riding a bicycle or walking to school, for example) or to someone else in English (this could sometimes happen during reading time at the beginning of class), and complete the Conversation Log in Exhibit 4.2. Note that the log is set up to also include a ten-minute conversation each day with an in-class tutor or another classmate, and uses a conversation cheat sheet (Exhibit 4.3). Teachers may or may not be working in schools that can provide other students who can act as peer tutors.

- Watch a movie or television program in English for at least fifteen minutes each night.

- Depending on whether students have computers and Internet access at home, online practice can substitute for the last two assignments (see the Tech Tool box later in this section).

Supporting Research. Cathy Vatterott, the author of *Rethinking Homework: Best Practices That Support Diverse Needs*, recommends these guidelines for homework:

EXHIBIT 4.1. Four Words Sheet

Name _____ **Period** _____ **Date** _____

Word and Definition in English
Definition in Primary Language
Picture
Sentence

Word and Definition in English
Definition in Primary Language
Picture
Sentence

Word and Definition in English
Definition in Primary Language
Picture
Sentence

Word and Definition in English
Definition in Primary Language
Picture
Sentence

EXHIBIT 4.2. Conversation Log

Date	I talked to my tutor about...	I talked to myself about...	Tutor Signature and Student Signature
Oct. 17, 2010	1. What is your favorite fruit? 13. What is your name? 19. What did you eat for lunch yesterday?	What I saw on the street My lunch	

EXHIBIT 4.3. Conversation "Cheat Sheet"

1. Q: What is your favorite fruit?
   A: My favorite fruit is (a banana, an apple, a peach, a melon, a nectarine).

2. Q: How are you?
   A: I am fine.

3. Q: How do you feel?
   A: I feel (happy, sad, tired, angry, hungry, sick).

4. Q: Did you have a good weekend?
   A: Yes, I did. (No, I did not.)

5. Q: What did you do over the weekend?
   A: I (read, slept, played soccer, went to the park, watched TV, went to Fresno, played with my baby).

6. Q: Can I use the telephone please?
   A: Yes, you can. (No, you cannot.)

7. Q: How old are you?
   A: I am _____ years old.

8. Q: What grade are you in?
   A: I am in _____ grade.

9. Q: I'm cold. Can you turn the air conditioner off?
   A: Yes, I can. (No, I cannot.)

10. Q: I don't understand. Can you repeat that?
    A: Yes, I can. (No, I cannot.)

11. Q: What are you going to do this weekend?
    A: I am going to (read, sleep, do homework, go to the park, watch TV, play with my baby).

12. Q: What is your address?
    A: My address is _____.
    Q: Is it close or far away?
    A: It is _____ _____.

13. Q: What is your name?
    A: My name is _____ _____.

14. Q: What is the word for this in English?
    A: The word in English is _____ _____.

15. Q: What do you buy at the store?

A: I buy (food, clothes, vegetables, fruit, bananas, rice).

16. Q: Where do you buy food?

A: I buy food at (Main Street Grocery).

17. Q: What is your telephone number?

A: My telephone number is _____ _____.

18. Q: What did you eat for lunch yesterday?

A: I ate (rice, a burrito, a hamburger, a sandwich).

19. Q: What did you eat for breakfast today?

A: I ate (rice, cereal, bananas, toast).

20. Q: Who is your favorite teacher?

A: My favorite teacher is _____ _____.

21. Q: What is your favorite story on Mr. Ferlazzo's web site?

A: My favorite story is about ____ _____.

22. Q: What is your favorite meal?

A: My favorite meal is _____ _____.

23. Q: What was your favorite field trip?

A: My favorite field trip was when we went to _____.

24. Q: How do you get to school?

A: I (drive, walk, ride my bike, run).

25. Q: Do you have any brothers or sisters?

A: Yes, I have _____ brothers and _____ sisters. (No, I don't have any brothers or sisters.)

26. Q: When is your birthday?

A: My birthday is on _____.

27. Q: What is today's date?

A: Today's date is _____.

28. Q: Are you feeling okay?

A: I'm fine. (No, I'm feeling sick.)

29. Q: Excuse me, I can't see. Can you move please?

A: Sure, I can.

30. Q: What time is it?

A: It is _____.

31. Q: Was the (homework, test) easy or hard?

A: It was _____.

32. Q: How long until we get to (San Francisco, Thailand, New York, St. Paul)?

A: We will get there in _____ (minutes, hours, days, weeks).

33. Q: How far is (downtown, the restaurant, San Francisco, New York, St. Paul)?

A: It is _____ (blocks, miles) away.

34. Q: How do you get to (San Francisco, Burbank, the grocery store, downtown)?

A: You drive to the (first, second, third) stoplight, then make a (left, right) turn, then go to _____ (street, road) and make a (left, right) turn. It will be on your (left, right).

35. Q: What size is this (jacket, shirt, pair of pants)?

A: It is (small, medium, large, extra large).

36. Q: How much does this (shirt, TV, jacket) cost?

A: It costs _____ (cents, dollars).

37. Q: First Person: I (love, like, hate) you.

A: Second Person: I (love, like, hate) you, too.

38. Q: What time does the movie start?

A: The movie starts at (1:00, 7:30).

39. Q: What are you going to do this weekend?

A: I am going to (read, play soccer, sleep).

40. Q: What are you going to do tonight?

A: I am going to (study, read, eat).

41. Q: What are you going to eat for dinner tonight?

A: I am going to eat (rice, papaya salad).

42. Q: What do you usually eat for breakfast?

A: I usually eat (cereal, rice, toast) for breakfast.

43. Q: What time do you usually go to sleep?

A: I usually go to sleep at (9:30, 10:00).

44. Q: What time do you usually get up?

A: I usually get up at (7:00, 7:30).

45. Q: Can I use the restroom (bathroom)?

A: Yes, you can. (No, you cannot right now; please wait five minutes.)

46. Q: Can I borrow that book?

A: Yes, you can. (No, you cannot.)

47. Q: How is your (father, mother, baby, brother)?

A: (He, She) is (okay, sick, fine, tired).

48. Q: Would you like to go to dinner (tonight, this weekend, next Friday)?

A: Yes, that would be nice.

49. Q: What kind of work would you like to do when you graduate from high school (college)?

A: I would like to be a (doctor, teacher, cook).

50. Q: I would like to go home now. Is that okay?

A: Sure it is. I'll take you home.

51. Q: I have a headache. Do you have an aspirin?

A: Yes, here's one. I hope you feel better.

52. Q: I have a stomachache. Can I call home?

A: Sure, you can. (No, you cannot.)

53. Q: Can I put a CD on?

A: Sure, you can. (No, you cannot.)

54. Q: Can you give me a ride home?

A: Sure, I can. (No, I cannot.)

55. Q: What is that?

A: That is a _____.

56. Q: What is this?

A: This is a _____.

57. Q: I'm hungry. What time is (breakfast, lunch, dinner)?

A: We'll eat at (7:30, 12:00).

58. Q: Where does it hurt?

A: My (nose, arm, leg) hurts here.

59. Q: Can you call the police?

A: Sure, I can. (No, I cannot.)

60. Q: I'm sorry, I don't understand. Can you repeat that and speak slowly?

A: Yes, I can. (No, I cannot.)

61. Q: Can I keep this book?

A: Yes, you can. (No, you cannot.)

62. Q: Can you get a teacher to help?

A: Sure, I can. (No I cannot.)

63. Q: First person: I'm tired. I'm going to bed.

A: Second person: Me, too.

"The best homework tasks exhibit five characteristics. First, the task has a clear academic purpose, such as practice, checking for understanding, or applying knowledge or skills. Second, the task efficiently demonstrates student learning. Third, the task promotes ownership by offering choices and being personally relevant. Fourth, the task instills a sense of competence—the student can successfully complete it without help. Last, the task is aesthetically pleasing—it appears enjoyable and interesting."[8]

We feel confident that the homework we assign meets these guidelines.

In addition, research supports the particulars of these assignments. For example, in addition to the journals facilitating writing practice, the sharing of positive events can develop trust,[9] which is an important quality to cultivate in an ESL classroom.

Tech Tool
Online Homework

A number of free or low-cost engaging sites—many of which are very accessible to English language learners—let teachers register entire classes so that students can sign in to the site and the teacher can see the work of individual students. These sites can be used as homework or during school time. Our favorites include:

USA Learns. USA Learns offers an exceptional multimedia online course for ELL beginners and intermediates. (http://www.usalearns.org)

Raz-Kids. Raz-Kids provides a large number of "talking books" at multiple levels that speak the text at the same time the words are highlighted. There's a wide range of fiction and expository text that is suitable for beginning and intermediate readers. (http://www.raz-kids.com)

My Testbook. My Testbook lets students study math, science, and English. (http://www.mytestbook.com)

Zondle. Zondle has tons of content in different subjects and, if you can't find what you need, it's easy to just add your own. The ingenious part is that once you pick the topic you study, you have the option of studying the info in *forty* different games! (http://www.zondle.com)

Study Ladder. Study Ladder has impressive literacy, science, and math interactives. (http://www.studyladder.com)

English Central. We have mentioned English Central before, and we'll mention it again. In addition to all its exceptional activities, it also lets students create virtual classrooms. (http://www.englishcentral.com)

Field Trips

Simple field trips, including lessons to prepare for them and classroom follow-up activities, can be excellent learning opportunities, especially when they are connected to thematic units being studied.

Scavenger hunts can be engaging and reinforcing. For example, when studying clothes in the classroom, a class can visit the mall or a thrift store and students can be given a list of different kinds of clothes (such as a blue skirt or a large boot) and asked to take photos of each item with either their cell phone or digital camera. Students can later create slide shows or posters with them. Similar hunts can be done in food stores, around a school, looking for signs, or the like. When visiting some of these places, though, it's courteous to let staff know ahead of time and schedule the visit during times when the business is not crowded.

Other field trips can include ordering a soda at a fast food restaurant, asking a local bank for a tour, or just playing a sports game. The list is really endless! They also make great fodder for using the Language Experience Approach.

Logistically, we recommend that students be organized ahead of time in groups of two or three (with a student leader) to take advantage of the learning benefits inherent in small groups, to help ensure student safety, and to help maintain teacher sanity.

Supporting Research. ESL researcher Heide Spruck Wrigley, in a study for the U.S. Department of Education, emphasized the importance of field trips with English language learners and called it "bringing in the outside."[10] She particularly recommends trips and minitrips that relate to language and situations students have to regularly deal with in their lives.

Tech Tool
Uploading Field Trip Photos

Several sites let multiple people upload photos to the same account by simply using a URL address. These are great for having a class upload field trip pictures. Students can then use these photos to create slide shows, or the photos can be used in the Picture Word Inductive Model. Our favorites include

Troovi: http://troovi.com

Yogile: http://www.yogile.com

Packmule: http://usepackmule.com

Photocollect: http://photocollect.net

Tech Tool
Virtual Field Trips

Though they do not offer anywhere near the kind of personal interaction and direct experience of a real, physical field trip, virtual field trips can offer a change of pace and an opportunity to see places that cannot realistically be seen in person. Some of our favorite sources for virtual field trips include

Google Earth Virtual Field Trips: http://www.ctap10.org/gfeportal

Google Maps Historic Sites: http://maps.google.com

Utah Education Network Virtual Field Trips: http://www.uen.org/tours

Internet4Classrooms Virtual Trips: http://www.internet4classrooms.com/vft.htm

Assessment

Chapter Thirteen will cover assessment—formative and summative—in depth. Since the "typical week" section in this chapter will refer to one formative assessment in particular, however, we wanted to explain it a little further here.

Each Friday, at the end of a Picture Word Inductive unit, a teacher might want to give a quiz. For a very early beginners' class, the picture can remain on the wall, but in most cases you will want to remove it.

The first twenty questions could be a basic spelling test with the teacher saying the word, using it in a sentence, and then saying the word again. The next ten questions could be a combination of other exercises reflecting the texts and vocabulary studied during the week (see Exhibit 4.4). They include sentences that do not have the words separated and that require students to write them correctly; short cloze sentences where students need to write the correct word (any word that makes sense would be correct); sentence scrambles, where students have to put the words and punctuation in the correct order; a question that students have to answer; and a sentence that has a mistake in it that students have to correct.

An easy way to assess the test is to have students give it to the person behind them, who will put a check mark next to the correct responses, while having two students take the lead in front writing the correct answers on the board or overhead and pointing to the picture (with the teacher monitoring, of course, to ensure the answers are indeed correct). Students can score the test by writing a fraction—the number of correct answers above the total number of test questions. Students return the papers, and any scoring disputes can be discussed among students and the teacher.

EXHIBIT 4.4. Sample Friday Test

1. Thewheelrollsthroughthebarn.

2. Pigeonsliveincities.

3. Juanhadarottenday.

4. Squirrels _____ nests in trees.

5. Juan _____ a giant hug.

6. The wheel _____ toward the river.

7. in live cities . dogs

8. had . day Rosie horrible a

9. What are you going to do this weekend?

10. Bee and Jose hits the teacher.

Picture Word Inductive Model Unit Plan

Chapter Three discussed the major instructional strategies that we recommend using in a beginning ESL class (and in fact they can be used effectively in many other classes as well).

The Picture Word Inductive Model Unit Plan discusses one of those strategies in more detail because we believe it can be the centerpiece of the beginning ELL curriculum. The unit plan is followed by a sample week schedule, which is in turn followed by a list of specific ways to implement our recommended strategies in many units throughout the entire school year.

INSTRUCTIONAL OBJECTIVES

Students will:

1. Learn at least twenty new theme-related vocabulary words.
2. Develop categorization skills.
3. Write an essay.

DURATION

Five approximately twenty- to thirty-minute lessons over a five-day period.

ENGLISH LANGUAGE DEVELOPMENT STANDARDS: CALIFORNIA ENGLISH LANGUAGE DEVELOPMENT (ELD) DOMAINS

1. Students use English for everyday communication in socially and culturally appropriate ways and apply listening and speaking skills and strategies in the classroom.
2. Students apply word analysis skills and knowledge of vocabulary to read fluently.
3. Students will write well-organized, clear, and coherent text in a variety of academic genres.
4. Students will apply the conventions of standard English usage orally and in writing.

MATERIALS

1. Enlarged laminated photo representative of a thematic unit (such as food, sports, or school) mounted on poster board with border space around the

image. The photo should reflect a real-life incident, and should show a variety of objects. See Figure 3.1 for a sample photo.

2. A photocopy of the photo for each student.

3. A data set composed of a list of sentences about the picture with blanks in them (see Exhibit 3.2). Potential answers should appear below each sentence. Provide enough copies for each student.

PROCEDURE

First Day

1. Teacher asks all students to come to the front of the room and stand in front of the laminated picture. He asks if students can say some of the things that they see in English. As students say a word and point to it in the picture, the teacher writes each letter and asks students to repeat it, and then says the word, again asking students to repeat. He then draws an arrow from the word to the object. This process should continue until there are approximately twenty words on the photo, including new words that the teacher has added.

2. Students then return to their seats and copy the words in the same way on their individual photos.

3. Teacher reviews the words again.

4. After class, the teacher develops a data set of cloze sentences about the picture using all the words that were labeled.

Second Day

1. Teacher reviews the words on the image, asking students to repeat.

2. Students are asked to put the words into three or four categories on a sheet of paper, leaving space for additions. Then they can work individually or in pairs. The teacher might want to encourage students to look at particular word qualities during their categorization, including word endings or plural versus singular forms.

3. After a few minutes, the teacher asks students to share a few of the category names they have identified and writes them on the board (words that start with *p*, people-related words, things that are red). This is to help students who are having a difficult time categorizing. A few minutes later, the teacher asks one or two students he has identified to share one list of words they have categorized—without saying the name of the category. He will then ask students to think for a moment—without saying anything—about which category might work for those words. He next asks students to share their answer with a partner and then calls on students to share their guesses. After

each time a student says what they think it is, the teacher will ask the student who originally gave the words if it is correct or not.

4. Next the teacher will ask students to use their dictionaries and prior knowledge to add three or four new words to their categories.

5. Students share their completed work—orally and in writing—with a partner.

Third Day

1. Teacher reviews the words on the image, asking students to repeat.

2. Teacher distributes a data set composed of a list of sentences with blanks in them. Potential answers appear below each sentence.

3. Students fill in the blanks and then share—both orally and in writing—their answers with a partner.

4. Teacher reviews the answers with the class.

5. Teacher asks the students to put the sentences into at least three categories (either by cutting and pasting each sentence under the name of a category or by writing the name of a category and underneath writing the numbers of the sentences that belong there). The teacher can provide the categories or ask students to develop their own. Students then categorize and are asked to share (similar to step 3 from the previous day). Students must also underline the clue words they used to place each sentence in a particular category.

6. Students then write three additional sentences about the picture under each category, either in class or as homework.

Fourth Day

1. Teacher reviews the words on the image, asking students to repeat.

2. Teacher asks students to rewrite their categories as paragraphs and explains some structures of an essay (such as indents for paragraphs and a single line separating them).

Fifth Day

1. Teacher reviews the words on the image.

2. Teacher asks students to develop a title for their essay. Students share their titles, which are recorded by the teacher or students on easel paper next to the laminated photo (this can also be done on the fourth day, if desired).

3. Essays are turned in, and student writing is used for lessons using concept attainment (discussed in Chapter Three) in the following days.

ASSESSMENT

1. Teacher gives a test that includes all twenty words. Teacher says the word, uses it in a sentence, then says the word again. The test also includes completing sentences with blanks, sentence scrambles (mixing up the words in a sentence and having students reorder them correctly), and other items covered during the week.

2. Students exchange papers with each other for checking as the teacher says the correct answer or asks students to contribute them. Students are told to put check marks next to the answers that are correct. Papers are returned to students and then given to teacher for review.

POSSIBLE EXTENSIONS AND MODIFICATIONS

1. After the second day, the teacher can have students lead the class in reviewing the words at the beginning of the lesson.

2. Depending on the class level, more sophisticated writing elements (such as topic sentences and thesis statements) can be taught and used.

3. Depending on the class level, students can label the laminated photo with sentences they generate the first day, which can also be used in the data set.

Source: L. Ferlazzo, *English Language Learners: Teaching Strategies That Work* (Columbus, OH: Linworth, 2009). Copyright ©2010 by ABC-CLIO, LLC. Reproduced with permission of ABC-CLIO, LLC.

A Sample Week in a Two-Period Beginning ESL Class

This sample schedule is not designed to be scripted curriculum—it's a sample, that's all. It's designed to provide a general snapshot of an effective ESL classroom, one that balances reading, writing, listening, and speaking; one that provides a flexible routine and time for reflection; one that incorporates music and movement; and one that includes fun and higher-order thinking skills.

It does not use all the strategies discussed in Chapter Three—it's only one week, after all. If you want to include more writing one week, you can replace Total Physical Response lessons with one on critical pedagogy. One week you might use improvisation instead of a dialogue. If you have three periods with your students instead of two, then you can incorporate more of the key elements more often.

If your students are a little more advanced, you can begin to include some of the activities discussed in Chapters Five and Six. If you have a mixed-level class, you can incorporate activities from Chapters Three though Six (see the section on multilevel classes in Chapter Twelve for more ideas). If you have to, or want to, integrate a standard textbook into this routine, please see the section on that topic in Chapter Twelve.

Again, this is not a scripted curriculum. It is a compass, not a road map.

MONDAY

1. Reading and writing. Students enter the classroom and immediately begin copying down a short and simple plan for the day that is written on the board. Bridging words will vary, such as "*First,* we are going to . . . " and *then* and *next* and the like. When the bell rings, the teacher asks students to stop writing and she reads what is on the board while pointing to the words. Students then finish writing and begin reading a book of their choice alone or quietly with another person. (fifteen minutes)

2. Listening and speaking. A short round-robin dialogue takes place. For example, the teacher first models "What did you do on the weekend?" and then lists potential responses on the board with student brainstorming assistance. The teacher asks the question of the first student who then answers, and that first student quickly asks the next one, and so on. Many other questions can be used, including "What did you learn yesterday?" and "What do you remember from yesterday?" (five minutes)

3. Reading and writing. A picture on the theme of school is introduced. Students are asked to come close to the wall where the picture is hung, and the first stage of the Picture Word Inductive Model process begins (labeling the picture). (twenty minutes)

4. Reading and writing. Individual whiteboards are distributed to each student, along with markers and an eraser. Each student also gets a copy of a common book the class is reading (ideally, though not necessarily, connected to the thematic unit the class is studying). The teacher might have a class set of a bound book or have student copies of a book printed from the Web. The teacher reads short phrases to the class, with students repeating them chorally. The teacher stops periodically to help the class understand words that are new to them (a nice thing about Internet books is that students can write down notes on them). Occasionally, the teacher models a reading strategy and asks students to demonstrate it on their whiteboards (such as writing a question or visualizing). Students are then divided into pairs and read those same pages to each other. (twenty minutes)

5. Listening and speaking. A Total Physical Response lesson is done. (fifteen minutes)

6. Listening and speaking. The song of the week is introduced. The song is played with the lyrics shown on the overhead or document projector. Students then practice the chorus (led by the teacher) and are given copies of the lyrics. As the song is played, the teacher points out the lines on the overhead and encourages students to sing the chorus. Next, each half of the room is assigned certain lines of the chorus in a friendly competition. (twenty minutes)

7. Reading and writing or listening and speaking. Game (see Chapter Eleven). (fifteen minutes)

8. Reading and writing. Reflection activity. (five minutes)

TUESDAY

1. **Reading and writing**. Students enter the classroom and immediately begin copying down a short and simple plan for the day that is written on the board. Bridging words will vary, such as "*First,* we are going to . . ." and *then* and *next* and so on. When the bell rings, the teacher asks students to stop writing and she reads what is on the board while pointing to the words. Students then finish writing and begin reading a book of their choice alone or quietly with another person. (fifteen minutes)

2. **Listening and speaking.** A short round-robin dialogue begins. For example, the teacher first models "What did you eat for breakfast today?" and then, with student brainstorming help, lists potential responses on the board. The teacher asks the question of the first student, who then answers, and that first student then quickly asks the next one, and so on. (five minutes)

3. **Reading and writing.** Students do the second stage of the Picture Word Inductive Model process (categorizing words). (fifteen minutes; students can complete as homework if not done)

4. **Listening and speaking.** Students sing the song of the week again, working on additional verses. Students complete a cloze of the song. (fifteen minutes)

5. **Listening and speaking.** A Total Physical Response lesson is done. (ten minutes)

6. **Reading and writing.** An inductive phonics lesson is done. (twenty minutes)

7. **Reading and writing.** Individual whiteboards are distributed to each student, along with markers and an eraser. Each student also gets a copy of a common book the class is reading (ideally, though not necessarily, connected to the thematic unit the class is studying). The teacher might have a class set of a bound book or have student copies of a book printed from the Web. The teacher reads short phrases to the class, with students repeating them chorally, though probably adding only one or two new pages. Afterward, students are divided into pairs or threes to do interactive dictation with the whiteboards. (twenty minutes)

8. **Listening and speaking.** A short video lesson or other Language Experience Approach lesson is done. (twenty minutes)

WEDNESDAY

1. **Reading and writing**. Students enter the classroom and immediately begin copying down a short and simple plan for the day that is written on the board. Bridging words will vary, such as "*First,* we are going to . . ." and *then* and *next* and the like. When the bell rings, the teacher asks students to stop writing and he reads

what is on the board while pointing to the words. Students then finish writing and begin reading a book of their choice alone or quietly with another person. (fifteen minutes)

2. Listening and speaking. A short round-robin dialogue begins. For example, the teacher first models "What did you learn in math class yesterday?" and then, with student brainstorming help, lists potential responses on the board. The teacher asks the question of the first student, who then answers, and that first student then quickly asks the next one, and so on. (five minutes)

3. Reading and writing. Students do the third stage of the Picture Word Inductive Model process (completing cloze sentences about the picture, categorizing them, and adding additional sentences). (twenty minutes)

4. Listening and speaking. Students practice and perform a short dialogue. (twenty minutes)

5. Listening and speaking or reading and writing. Students spend an hour in the computer lab reading or doing an activity. (fifty-five minutes)

6. Reading and writing. Reflection activity. (five minutes)

THURSDAY

1. Reading and writing. Students enter the classroom and immediately begin copying down a short and simple plan for the day that is written on the board. Bridging words will vary, such as "*First,* we are going to . . . " and *then* and *next* and the like. When the bell rings, the teacher asks students to stop writing and he reads what is on the board while pointing to the words. Students then finish writing and begin reading a book of their choice alone or quietly with another person. (fifteen minutes)

2. Listening and speaking. A short round-robin dialogue begins. For example, the teacher might first model "What are you going to eat for lunch today?" and then, with student brainstorming help, list potential responses on the board. The teacher asks the question of the first student, who then answers, and that first student then quickly asks the next one, and so on. (five minutes)

3. Reading and writing. Students do the fourth stage of the Picture Word Inductive Model process (putting categorized sentences into paragraphs and writing titles; twenty minutes).

4. Listening and speaking. Students sing the song of the week again, working on additional verses. Students have to complete a sequencing activity with the lines of the song cut out. (fifteen minutes)

5. Listening and speaking. A Total Physical Response lesson is done. (ten minutes)

6. Reading and writing. An inductive phonics lesson is done. (twenty minutes)

7. Reading and writing. Individual whiteboards are distributed to each student, along with markers and an eraser. Each student also gets a copy of a common book the class is reading (ideally, though not necessarily, connected to the thematic unit the class is studying). The teacher might have a class set of a bound book or student copies of a book printed from the Web. The teacher reads short phrases to the class, with students repeating them chorally, though probably adds only one or two new pages. The teacher stops periodically to help the class understand words that are new to them (a nice thing about Internet books is that students can write down notes on them). Occasionally, the teacher models a reading strategy and asks students to demonstrate it on their whiteboards (such as writing a question or visualizing). (fifteen minutes)

8. Listening and speaking or reading and writing. Game. (twenty minutes)

FRIDAY

1. Reading and writing. Students enter the classroom and immediately begin copying down a short and simple plan for the day that is written on the board. Bridging words will vary, such as "First, we are going to . . ." and *then* and *next* and so on. When the bell rings, the teacher asks students to stop writing and she reads what is on the board while pointing to the words. Students then finish writing and begin reading a book of their choice alone or quietly with another person. (fifteen minutes)

2. Listening and speaking. Students share their vocabulary homework and part of their weekly journal with a partner, and then homework is collected. (ten minutes)

3. Reading and writing. Concept attainment grammar lesson. (twenty minutes)

4. Reading and writing. Weekly test. (twenty minutes)

5. Listening and speaking or reading and writing. Students spend an hour in the computer lab reading or doing an activity. (fifty minutes)

6. Reading and writing. Reflection activity. (five minutes)

Year-Long Schedule

Teaching English language learners through the use of thematic units is a long-used, research-based, and effective instructional practice. As Suzanne Peregoy and Owen Boyle write in *Reading, Writing, and Learning in ESL,* "thematic instruction creates a meaningful conceptual framework within which students are invited to use both oral and written language for learning content. The meaningful context established by the theme supports the comprehensibility of instruction, thereby increasing both content learning and second language acquisition. In addition, theme-based collaborative projects create student interest, motivation, involvement and purpose."[11]

This section contains some suggested thematic units for a beginning or early intermediate ESL class. These themes are also covered in many beginning ESL textbooks, which facilitate integrating them into these activities. Though this chronology works well for us, it also offers a great deal of flexibility. Beginning with the theme of "school" is generally going to work well, which is why the activities listed under it also include a number of introductory and early phonetic exercises, as well as simple and inspiring songs. However, as the year goes on, intrinsic motivation will tend to be generated if students can have a voice in deciding when specific themes are studied. People are more confident and motivated if they feel they have control over their environment.[12] This is especially important for students who have had little choice in being moved to a different country and culture where a different language is spoken.

The ideas listed in each unit are not meant to be an exhaustive list. It's assumed that each thematic unit will include the Picture Word Inductive Model, so that strategy is not listed here. There are also many options for incorporating technology in all these units in addition to those mentioned in this section. Ideas on how students can easily create online content are discussed throughout this book. This section is designed to provide a few helpful ideas in addition to the ones already shared in this chapter, and it is likely that a creative teacher can develop countless more ideas that are as good or better than the ones here.

We will highlight only a few Tech Tools in this section, and you can find links to multiple reinforcing online activities at our book's web site.

1. School
   - Topics covered: school vocabulary, building relationships, and self-confidence
   - Introductory activities (see Chapter Two)
   - Introduce the alphabet and make an ABC book
   - Teach computer vocabulary, perhaps through Total Physical Response
   - If there are other subjects that beginners might not be able to take right now because they have to spend extra time in English, arrange short sample lessons by the relevant teachers (art, physical education, music, science, and so forth)
   - School scavenger hunt
   - Make two collages: one of words illustrated by pictures that they know and the other of ten words they do not know that they can learn through

dictionaries and other sources; then they need to teach them to the rest of the class

- School objects jazz chant
- Various songs, including:

"You Can Get It If You Really Want"

"Hello, Good-bye"

"Tutti Frutti," "Doo Wah Diddy," and "A Ram Sam Sam" are excellent songs for students to work on letter sounds; in addition to singing the lyrics as written, they can change them (Butti Lutti)

"The Vowel Song" (sung to the tune of "Bingo Was His Name," it goes "AEIOU, AEIOU, AEIOU, I won't forget my vowels, will you? These vowels are short, These vowels are long, I won't forget my vowels, will you?")

"Happy Birthday" song: a student's birthday is always a good opportunity for practice

"Twist and Shout" is a great song to get students feeling more comfortable singing, and it's like Total Physical Response for verbs

- Mr. Bean clips are very accessible to ELLs, and his "Back to School" episode works well for this theme; you can purchase a DVD inexpensively or find most of the episodes online
- Education data set (see Exhibit 4.5)
- Read the book *Teacher from the Black Lagoon* by Mike Thaler (Cartwheel Books, 2008)
- Critical pedagogy lesson on school bullying (see Chapter Three for the steps in a critical pedagogy lesson plan)

EXHIBIT 4.5. Education Data Set

Categories: Schools; Classes; Times

1. Most students go to high school for four years.
2. Students learn about the world in geography class.
3. First period starts at 8:15 in the morning.
4. Students can go to high school for free until they are eighteen years old.
5. Some students can go to high school for free after they are eighteen years old.

6. Students paint pictures in art class.
7. Most students go to elementary school for six years.
8. Most students go to middle school for two years.
9. Students use numbers in math class.
10. Sixth period ends at 3:15 in the afternoon.
11. Students play sports in physical education (PE) class.
12. Seventh period starts at 3:30 in the afternoon and ends at 4:30 in the afternoon.

Tech Tool
Vocabulary Reinforcement

There are plenty of free online sites where ELLs can reinforce new vocabulary, including words related to school and every other theme in this curriculum. These include

Kindersay: http://kindersay.com

Language Guide: http://www.languageguide.org/english

Learning Chocolate: http://www.learningchocolate.com

---

2. Describing people and things

- Topics covered: parts of body, clothes, colors, numbers, weather (including temperature), other adjectives (such as size, age, and attractiveness)

- Numbers

- Clothing store scavenger hunt (provide a list of twenty to thirty items, like "blue skirt" and "red shoes")

- Various songs, including:

   "What a Wonderful World"

   "You Are So Beautiful"

   "Heads, Shoulders, Knees, and Toes"

- "Hair by Mr. Bean of London" video

- Cut out pictures from magazines and describe them on a poster

- "The Tongue" read-aloud ("The tongue is the only part of the body that does not get tired"; Konrad Adenauer, former chancellor of West Germany)

- Describing things data set (see Exhibit 3.3); the categories are age, color, size, temperature, weather, and numbers. Sometimes students can be given the categories, and sometimes they can develop them on their own

- Crime Suspect Game: display pictures of different people on the walls of the classroom and tell students they are the police and you are a witness to a crime; you will describe the suspect, and they have to identify who you are describing (small whiteboards can be used) (see Chapter Eleven)

- Critical pedagogy lesson: someone doesn't understand something or is lost

- Spectrum exercise (explained in the Other Activities section of this chapter): "ugly, looks okay, attractive, handsome, beautiful" and "roasting, hot, warm, just right, cool, cold, freezing"

3. Data (or information)

- Topics covered: telling time, filling out forms, calendars and seasons, days of the week

- Getting around school or classroom (giving directions); blind man's bluff game (tie a blindfold around a student, and a partner has to give him or her directions around obstacles)

- Library field trip: getting a library card

- Various songs:

    "You've Got a Friend"

    "Happy Days"

    "Rock Around the Clock"

- Simple science experiments where students complete a simple lab report (see Chapter Nine)

- Time data set (see Exhibit 4.6; morning, afternoon, evening, or nighttime)

- Calendar data set (see Exhibit 4.7)

- Reading strategies data set (see Exhibit 5.3 in Chapter Five)

EXHIBIT 4.6. Time Data Set

1. First period starts at 8:15 A.M.
2. Students eat lunch at 12:25 P.M.
3. School ends at 3:15 P.M.
4. Seventh period starts at 3:30 P.M.
5. Mr. Ferlazzo goes to sleep at 10:00 P.M.
6. Zero period begins at 7:15 A.M.
7. Mr. Ferlazzo plays basketball at 7:00 P.M.
8. Second period ends at 10:15 A.M..
9. School starts at 9:30 A.M. on Wednesdays.
10. Families eat dinner after 5:00 P.M.

EXHIBIT 4.7. Calendar Data Set

Categories: Summer, Fall, Winter, Spring

1. School starts in September.
2. It is cold in December.
3. We plant our garden in late April.
4. It is hot in July.
5. Christmas is on December 25th.
6. School ends in June.
7. It rains a lot in January.
8. Students get a one-week vacation in early April.
9. The weather begins to get cooler in late September.
10. Thanksgiving is a holiday in November.
11. It begins to snow in the mountains in late October.
12. There are 31 days in March.
13. There are 31 days in May.
14. Mr. Ferlazzo's birthday is in December.
15. The new year begins in January.

4. Family
   - Topics covered: family members
   - Make a family tree including the work that each member does or did and project what they would like to see their future family tree look like
   - Various songs:

     "We Are Family"

     "Are You Sleeping?" lullaby (good to sing in a round)
   - Mr. Bean "Christmas Dinner" video
   - *Funniest Home Videos* has plenty of good family scenes
   - Scene in *My Big Fat Greek Wedding* film where everyone is going crazy getting ready for the wedding
   - Mr. Ferlazzo's Family cloze example (see Exhibit 4.8)
   - Critical pedagogy lesson: "A Family Is Poor" (use the beginning few minutes of the movie *Les Miserables*)

5. Friends and fun activities
   - Topics covered: sports, hobbies, nature, and anything students consider fun!
   - Students make a collage on what they do for fun and describe them with sentences
   - Various songs:

     "The Bowling Song" by Raffi

     "Take Me Out to the Ballgame"

     "Under the Boardwalk"
   - Field trips to a local park, shopping mall, bowling alley, museum, local amusement park, school playground, and so on
   - There are many Mr. Bean episodes that would fit this unit
   - Sports blooper videos
   - Great Moments in Sports videos
   - John Turturro's scene in the movie *The Big Lebowski* where he licks a bowling ball is always a big hit with students
   - Critical pedagogy lesson on trash or pollution in the park

6. Holidays
   - Topics covered: many different holidays
   - New Year's resolutions

EXHIBIT 4.8. Mr. Ferlazzo's Family Cloze

Mr. Ferlazzo has an interesting family. His father is from Italy. _____ mother is from Trinidad. They met in New York City.

Mr. Ferlazzo's aunts and uncles live in New York and in Florida. He has many cousins. His _____ live in many different places in the United States.

He is married. His wife is a nurse. She also teaches other nurses. _____ came to our classroom on Mr. Ferlazzo's birthday.

Mr. Ferlazzo has three children. One of his _____ is married. Two of his _____ go to high school. _____ also has two grandchildren.

Mr. Ferlazzo also has a dog and a cat that are part of his family. His dog is named Bella. His _____ is named Josie.

His wife has two _____. They are Mr. Ferlazzo's brothers-in-law. One lives in West Sacramento. His other brother-in-law _____ near Los Angeles.

His wife's parents live in Davis. Her father, Charles, is Mr. Ferlazzo's father-in-law. Her mother, Marilyn, is Mr. Ferlazzo's _____-in-law.

Mr. Ferlazzo loves his family. They love him, too.

- Various songs:

    "Jingle Bells"

    "We Wish You a Merry Christmas"

    "White Christmas"

    "The Marvelous Toy"

    "Rudolph the Red-Nosed Reindeer"

    "Monster Mash"

    "Feliz Navidad"

- Students can go around caroling to different classrooms
- Holiday data set (Exhibit 4.9)
- Halloween data set (Exhibit 4.10)
- Mr. Bean Christmas video
- *National Lampoon's Christmas Vacation* has a great scene of Chevy Chase setting up Christmas lights
- Clips from *Dracula, Frankenstein,* or other monster movies are great for teaching about Halloween
- Video clips with movies having love stories are good to relate to Valentine's Day
- Students create a Venn diagram and a short compare-and-contrast essay using the different holidays (see the Other Activities section in this chapter for more on this activity)
- Santa Claus dialogue (see Exhibit 4.11)
- Halloween dialogue (see Exhibit 4.12)
- Students can make a Big Book about all the holidays using large poster board: each student, or each pair, can make a page about one holiday
- Students make posters sharing holiday traditions from their native countries

EXHIBIT 4.9. Holiday Data Set

1. Christmas is on December 25th.
2. People often give candy or roses as gifts on Valentine's Day.
3. Thanksgiving is on the fourth Thursday in November.
4. Martin Luther King Jr. fought for African Americans to have equal rights.

5. Presidents' Day is on the third Monday in February.

6. Children wear costumes on Halloween.

7. Presidents' Day celebrates George Washington and Abraham Lincoln. They were both presidents of the United States.

8. Many people eat turkey on Thanksgiving.

9. Many people celebrate the birth of Jesus Christ on Christmas. People who believe that Jesus Christ is the son of God are called Christians.

10. Thanksgiving recognizes a meal that the first white settlers had in the United States with people who already lived here. Those people are called Native Americans or Indians.

11. Martin Luther King Jr. Day is on the third Monday in January.

12. People eat a lot of candy on Halloween.

13. Valentine's Day is on February 14th.

14. People celebrate love on Valentine's Day.

15. People celebrate the fight for equality on Martin Luther King Jr. Day.

16. A heart is a symbol for Valentine's Day.

17. People often decorate a Christmas tree in their house.

18. Jewish people celebrate Hanukkah at around the same time Christians celebrate Christmas.

EXHIBIT 4.10. Halloween Data Set

Categories: Pumpkins, Imaginary Monsters, Children

1. A ghost is a person who died but is still here.

2. Children say "trick or treat!" when they go to homes on Halloween.

3. When children say "trick or treat!" they mean "Give me a treat or I will play a trick on you."

4. A vampire is a monster who drinks blood at night.

5. Children are given candy on Halloween.

6. Frankenstein is a monster made from parts of different dead people.

7. Carved pumpkins are called *jack-o'-lanterns*.
8. Pumpkins are vegetables.
9. Children wear costumes and visit homes on October 31st.
10. People can make pies using the inside of pumpkins.
11. Monsters can be scary.
12. A mummy is a dead person wrapped with cloth. A mummy is a monster when it is alive.

EXHIBIT 4.11. Santa Claus Dialogue

Santa Claus: Ho, ho, ho! Merry Christmas! Have you been a good (boy or girl)?

Boy or Girl: Yes, Santa, I have been a good (boy or girl).

Santa Claus: Great! What would you like for Christmas?

Boy or Girl: I would like a _____, a _____, and a _____.

Santa Claus: I will see what I can do for you. Is this your (mother or father)?

Boy or Girl: Yes.

Santa Claus: What would you like for Christmas?

Mother or Father: I would like a _____ and a _____.

Santa Claus: Okay. Merry Christmas and Happy New Year!

EXHIBIT 4.12. Halloween Dialogue

Student One and Student Two: Trick or treat!

Adult: You scared me! What do you want?

Student One: We want a treat!

Adult: I only have one piece of candy left, and there are two of you. Will you share?

Student Two: No, I want it!

Student One: No, I want it!

Student Two: *I want it!*

Student One: *I want it!*

Adult: Since you can't share, I'll eat it.

Student One and Student Two: We don't like you!

Tech Tool
Learning About Holidays Online

There are many free sites where ELL students can deepen their understanding of different holidays. Here are four of our favorites:

ESL Holiday Lessons: http://www.eslholidaylessons.com

ESL Courses, Festivals, and Celebrations: http://www.esolcourses.com/topics/world-festivals.html

Michelle Henry Holidays: http://www.michellehenry.fr

EL Civics: http://www.elcivics.com/holiday-lessons-usa.html

7. Home
   - Topics covered: types of homes, rooms, items found in them
   - A scavenger hunt in a large store for items used or found in a home
   - *Pink Panther* movies with Peter Sellers have many funny scenes with Sellers and his valet fighting in his apartment and wreaking havoc in the process; these scenes are excellent to use with the Language Experience Approach to identify items in the house—usually getting destroyed!
   - Several Buster Keaton and Charlie Chaplin movies have funny home scenes in them; many refugee students will be familiar with Chaplin, since his movies appear to be shown often in refugee camps
   - *The Money Pit* movie also has a number of good scenes for this unit
   - Sound Effects Game (see Chapter Eleven)
   - Draw and write about their childhood home

- Students do a Door Poster Project that opens to their room, or their ideal room: they label the items and on the inside flap describe what's inside and why it's their ideal room
- Students draw and write about their future home
- "Homeward Bound" song
- Critical pedagogy lesson on living in poor conditions

8. Community

- Topics covered: this unit could begin with the solar system and planets, then move to the Earth and continents, next to the state you live, followed by your town or city, and ending with your neighborhood; this unit also includes signs and transportation
- In this unit, in addition to using the Picture Word Inductive Model with a photo of an authentic community or activity, you might want to have a picture of the different planets in the solar system as well as world, state, and city maps
- Students can draw and/or create papier-mâché representations of the planets; they can also make a Big Book on the solar system by working in pairs to make a page on a planet from poster board
- A field trip with a scavenger hunt to identify different signs: students and teacher take photos to create a photo data set; then students place the images in categories (such as warnings or informational)
- Transportation (auto museum field trip or auto show if available)
- Various songs:

  "This Land Is Your Land"

  "Leaving on a Jet Plane"

  "It's a Small World"

  "I've Been Working on the Railroad"

  "What a Wonderful World"

  Songs about your local area or state
- Students make a poster about places they would like to visit
- Critical pedagogy lesson on neighborhoods with problems

9. Food

- Topics covered: food, menus, nutrition
- Scavenger hunt at a local food store (provide a grocery list of twenty to thirty items like "gallon of nonfat milk," "tomato," and so on)

- Various songs:

  "On Top of Spaghetti"

  "Crazy over Vegetables"

  "The Corner Grocery Store"

  "Lollipop" by the Chordettes

- Students write a recipe
- There are many easy food-related science experiments that can be done
- The movie *Cheaper by the Dozen* has a great scene where chaos reigns during breakfast
- Food-related Mr. Bean video clips
- Venn diagram and short compare-and-contrast essay comparing typical American food with food from another culture
- Food pyramid data set (see Exhibit 4.13; the federal government recently switched from the food pyramid to an image called My Plate, but we think the food pyramid is more accessible to English language learners)
- Critical pedagogy lesson: a person or family is hungry (similar to the lesson in the unit on family earlier in this chapter)

Tech Tool
Learning About Money Online

There are many free sites that allow students to deepen their understanding of money. Three of our favorites are

Everyday Life. Everyday Life has excellent interactive exercises on many money-related issues. (http://www.gcflearnfree.org/everydaylife)

Banking on Our Future. You have to register for Banking on Our Future, but it's free, quick, and easy. It's a very complete and accessible financial literacy site. (http://www.bankingonourfuture.org)

Savings Quest. Savings Quest walks you through an engaging step-by-step process that shows how to budget money. It would be ideal if the audio reflected the text, but it doesn't always match up. (http://www.mysavingsquest.com)

EXHIBIT 4.13. Food Pyramid Data Set

1. The food pyramid shows grains, vegetables, fruits, milk, meat and beans, and oils.
2. It is good to eat 2-1/2 cups of vegetables every day.
3. The United States government made the pyramid to show people how to be healthy.
4. It is good to eat three cups of milk products every day.
5. It is good to eat six ounces of grains every day.
6. It is good to eat oils every day. You can get your oils from eating fish, nuts, and cooking oil.
7. It is good to exercise thirty minutes each day.
8. It is good to eat 1-1/2 cups of fruit every day.
9. It is not good to eat a lot of candy and sugar.
10. You can drink fruit juice if you do not want to eat fruit.
11. You should eat more of the foods with the bigger stripes on the food pyramid.
12. Apples, bananas, and grapes are fruits.
13. Milk, yogurt, and cheese are milk products.
14. It is good to eat five ounces of meat and beans every day.
15. Bread, rice, and cereal are grains.
16. Turkey and chicken are meats.
17. Eating too much candy, sugar, and oil is bad for your heart.
18. Dancing, walking, working in a garden, and playing soccer are all good ways to exercise.
19. Carrots, broccoli, and spinach are vegetables.

EXHIBIT 4.14. Money Cloze and Data Set

1. One is equal to one hundred pennies. (dollar)

2. You can save your money a bank. (in)

3. One quarter equal to two dimes and one nickel. (is)

4. Can pay for things with cash, a credit card, a debit card, or a check. (you)

5. A will pay you interest on money you save in it. (bank)

6. A cashier give you change if you pay them more than the price of the item. (will)

7. You can take money out of a bank with an ATM card. An ATM card also called a debit card. (is)

8. A bank open an account for you if you save money there. (will)

9. One dollar is to four quarters. (equal)

10. Fifty is equal to .50 or 50. (cents)

11. A bank almost the same as a credit union. (is)

12. Many people borrow from a bank to pay for a house or a car. (money)

13. Two quarters is to five dimes. (equal)

10. Money
    - Topics covered: money and financial transactions
    - In this unit, in addition to using the Picture Word Inductive Model with a photo of an authentic activity related to money, teachers might want to display a picture showing the different kinds of coins and currency used in the United States
    - Field trip to a bank, ideally with a tour
    - Students imagine that they have $500, and they make a poster of how they would spend it and why
    - "Money, Money, Money" song
    - Money cloze and data set. (See Exhibit 4.14. Note that this is both a cloze and a data set. The cloze is a little different—there is no blank, and the missing word is after the sentence in parentheses. Students have to determine where the word correctly belongs without the clue of a blank space.)
    - Critical pedagogy lesson: someone earns a very low salary at their job and can't support their family

11. Jobs and careers
    - Topics covered: occupations, job training, college
    - In this unit, in addition to using the Picture Word Inductive Model with a photo of an activity related to work, teachers might want to display a picture showing images of many different kinds of occupations
    - Students can go on a field trip and take a tour of a local college and job training agency
    - The class can have various guest speakers talk about their jobs (and it's especially helpful when guests are of the same ethnicities as students)
    - Students can create a photo collage showing different occupations they are interested in and why
    - Students can make a poster describing their family's work history
    - Critical pedagogy lesson: someone telling you you're not smart enough to go to college

12. Animals
    - Topic covered: animals
    - Various songs:
      "Going to the Zoo"
      "The Lion Sleeps Tonight"
      "Old McDonald Had a Farm"

Tech Tool
Learning About Jobs and Careers Online

There are many free sites where students can learn more about jobs and careers. We think some of the best are

The Learning Edge. The Learning Edge is a Canadian newsletter for English language learners that offers animations about careers with audio support for the text. (http://www.thewclc.ca/edge)

Career One Stop. Career One Stop has closed-captioned short videos on just about every career imaginable. (http://www.careerinfonet.org)

Hot Shot Business. Hot Shot Business is a great interactive site from Disney that allows students to start virtual businesses. (http://disney.go.com/hotshot/hsb2)

- Field trip to zoo
- Many Funniest Animals or Funniest Pets videos are available
- *The Bear* movie is very accessible to ELLs
- The *Free Willy* movies are accessible to ELLs and, combined with a trip to the zoo, can lead to a discussion on the ethics of animal captivity
- Sound effects game with animal sounds (see Chapter Eleven for details)
- Students can use a graphic organizer to write about an animal (see Figure 4.1 and Exhibit 4.15)

13. Feelings
    - Topics covered: feelings and emotions
    - In this unit, in addition to using the Picture Word Inductive Model with a photo of an activity related to feelings, the teacher might want to display a picture showing many different kinds of facial expressions communicating different feelings, such as the well-known "How Are You Feeling Today?" print
    - Students create posters depicting experiences when they felt different emotions
    - Students cut out pictures from magazines of people and make posters describing how they feel and why

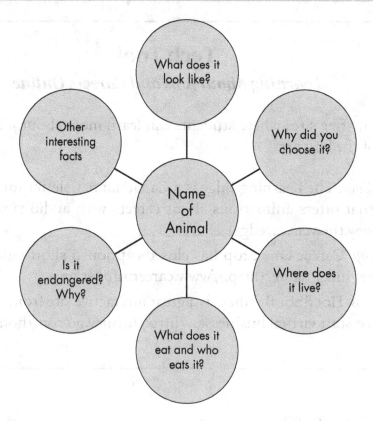

Figure 4.1. Graphic Organizer

EXHIBIT 4.15. Animal Report Example: Parrots

Parrots are beautiful birds and live in rain forests around the world. Most live in the jungles of South America. They are many different colors, though many are green.

They can be between four and forty inches long. They are very smart. They can talk and have been kept as pets for two thousand years. Parrots can live to be seventy-five years old.

Parrots eat seeds, berries, nuts, and fruit. They hang upside down when they search for food.

Parrots are popular pets. They are endangered because they don't give birth to many baby parrots, and so many people want them as pets. Bigger birds, like hawks, also attack and eat them.

I chose to write about parrots because I saw a movie about a group of them living in San Francisco.

Tech Tool

Learning About Animals Online

There are many free sites where students can learn more about animals. A few of the best sites are

All About Animals: http://ngfl.northumberland.gov.uk

National Geographic Creature Features: http://kids.nationalgeographic.com/kids /animals/creaturefeature

San Diego Zoo Animal Bytes: http://www.sandiegozoo.org/animalbytes

BBC Roar. Roar is a great game from the BBC. Players have to create their own zoo, including picking habitats, the animals, their food, and their feeding routines. There is audio support for some text, and the English is simple. It's a fun way to learn about animals and practice language skills. (http://www.bbc .co.uk/cbbc/roar)

- Various songs:
  "Feelings"
  "I Feel Good"
  "I Just Called to Say I Love You"
  "Don't Worry, Be Happy"
  "Happy and You Know It"
  "Stand by Me"
  "Happy Together"
  "Sing" by the Carpenters
- Critical pedagogy lesson: you're angry because someone broke into your home
- Critical pedagogy lesson: someone calls you an ethnic slur

14. Art and music
  - Topics covered: art and music
  - Students can make simple musical instruments (see Tech Tool next for further information)
  - Ask the school's art teacher to give the class a lesson, or arrange to go to his classroom and ask his students to teach the ESL students

- Ask the school's music teacher to give the class a lesson, or arrange to go to her classroom and ask her students to teach music to the ESL students

- Do some of the many easy classroom science experiments related to sound

- Field trip to a local museum

- Students can write, design, and create a puppet show to perform at a local elementary school (see the Other Activities section later in this chapter for further information)

- "I'm Your Puppet" song

- Any of the STOMP videos

- Watch the Mr. Bean video about him and a saxophone

Tech Tool
Learning Music and Art Online

Earlier in this chapter we listed web tools that could be used for musical activities. In addition, there are many others that can be used in an art unit. Students can create artwork and describe what it is in writing and/or verbally, do the same with online comic strips, or make animations that include audio. Links to all these sites can be found in "A Collection of 'The Best . . .' Lists for Sites Where ELLs Can Create Art" at http://larryferlazzo.edublogs.org.

15. Health

- Topic covered: health

- Have guest speakers such as nurses, nurse practitioners, or physicians come to class

- Take a field trip to a local clinic

- "Moonshadow" song

- Watch the video of Mr. Bean going to the dentist

- Students make a collage of healthy habits

- Critical pedagogy lesson: an ill or injured person cannot be treated because they do not have insurance

Tech Tool
Learning About Health Online

There are many free sites where students can learn more about health issues. They include

Healthy Roads Media. Healthy Roads has many multilingual health-related resources. (http://www.healthyroadsmedia.org)

Medline Plus. Produced by the National Institutes of Health, Medline Plus offers a large number of multimedia presentations on health issues. (http://www.nlm.nih.gov/medlineplus)

REEPWorld Health English. REEPWorld offers many very accessible interactive exercises for English language learners. (http://www.reepworld.org/englishpractice/health)

The Center for Applied Linguistics (CAL). CAL has an excellent series of Picture Stories for Adult ESL Literacy, several of which can be easily modified for younger students. (http://www.cal.org/caela/esl_resources/Health)

Other Potential Units

- End the year with small groups of students making units on topics of their own choice using the common teaching strategies (such as the Picture Word Inductive Model, text data sets, songs, clozes, and video clips; groups can teach portions of their units to other small groups
- A unit on heroes, including examination of the qualities of good leaders, studying leaders from student native cultures and from the United States, and doing compare-and-contrast work on them
- A unit on preparing for the United States Citizenship exam
- A unit on continuous verbs and opposites
- A unit on tools, which could include a scavenger hunt at a hardware store

Other Activities

There are hundreds, if not thousands, of lesson ideas that have been used in ESL classes over the years. We believe the ones we have discussed so far are the ones that can regularly offer superior opportunities for language learning. However, there are a few others that we have also found useful as lessons to use periodically throughout the year.

TONGUE TWISTERS

Tongue twisters are short phrases that use alliteration, like "Sally sells sea shells by the sea shore." They are easy to create at various levels of difficulty using vocabulary being taught in the classroom. It is also fun to have students try saying them—chorally or in pairs. Teaching one to students, and then having them say it three times quickly can help develop accurate pronunciation skills and bring some levity into the classroom—especially when the teacher makes a mistake! Students can create their own tongue twisters, make a poster illustrating them, and then perform and teach them to the entire class.

IDIOMS

Countless idioms are used in the English language. Teaching some of them when they are at least peripherally connected to a thematic unit ("It's raining cats and dogs" with the animal theme, for example) might be a good strategy to help students remember them. However, they are good to teach at any time. Having students write them, practice them, and draw a representational picture can be a quick and useful activity.

Tech Tool
Online Idiom Practice

There are many free sites designed to help English language learners become familiar with idioms. These three in particular offer audio, text, and animated explanations of their meanings:

Idioms 4 You: http://www.idioms4you.com/index.html

In 2 English: http://www.in2english.com.cn

On the Tip of My Tongue: http://www.ccdmd.qc.ca/ri/expressions

DIALOGUE JOURNALS

Dialogue journals have often been used in ESL classes. Typically, students write a journal entry and then a teacher writes a response—not pointing out errors in grammar or spelling, but instead correctly reflecting back what the student wrote.

For example, the student might write "I go to the piknik yesterday and have fun" and the teacher might respond, "That's great that you went to the picnic yesterday and had fun." ESL teachers can choose to let their students know in advance about these "recasts" or let them figure it out on their own.

Realistically, however, we feel it's not very practical for teachers to write these responses—there is just not enough time in the day for teachers with multiple classes to take on this responsibility. However, it can still be done—and we believe it can be done more effectively—by developing a sister class relationship with proficient speakers, either in the same school or another school. Students generally will feel more engaged with their peers than with their teacher, and other English teachers may welcome the opportunity to have their students become grammar and spelling tutors. Of course, such a relationship does not have to be limited to a journal—we have had sister classes come in and teach lessons in small groups to our English language learners (and our ELLs have taught a lesson about their culture to them), as well as having joint celebrations. This kind of social engagement has been found to be critical to language learning.[13]

Supporting Research. Numerous studies have documented the positive effect that dialogue journals have had on improving writing and how that improvement transfers to better essay writing, increased fluency, and enhanced learner motivation by providing a low-stress opportunity to write for an authentic audience.[14]

Tech Tool
Online Sister Classes

There are many free sites that help classes from around the world make connections with others. They include:

iEarn: http://www.iearn.org
Global School Net: http://www.globalschoolnet.org
ePals: http://www.epals.com
People to People: http://www.ptpi.org/community
eLanguages: http://www.elanguages.org
Rafi.ki: http://www.rafi.ki/site

PUPPETS

Puppets are often used in ESL classes with students of all ages. They often remove inhibitions to speaking a new language and can provide an opportunity to develop writing skills, especially if a full-fledged story will be performed. Sometimes the show can be performed not only in the classroom but also at a nearby elementary school. Puppets can be made out of paper bags, regular paper, or papier-mâché.

Supporting Research. Studies have shown that using puppets is an effective tool for helping English language learners enhance reading, writing, speaking, listening, and especially oral skills.[15]

READERS THEATER

Readers Theater typically entails having a group of students dramatically perform a short story only using their voices and directly reading from a script. There are hundreds of Readers Theater scripts available online that are accessible to English language learners. We prefer, after sufficient teacher modeling, to have students write their own scripts and then perform them.

Supporting Research. ESL researchers have found that performing Readers Theater improves fluency and comprehension. It also enhances learner motivation.[16]

SPECTRUM

Teaching words within a spectrum—such as "always, usually, sometimes, seldom, never" or "depressed, sad, okay, feeling good, happy" or "I can't do it, it's hard; I can do it, it's easy"—can be an engaging learning activity. The teacher can write the words across the whiteboard and ask students questions that can be answered by one of the words. Students can then stand underneath the word they chose. If it's done in a fun way ("Can you jump thirty feet in the air?" or "How would you feel if you got an F in this class?"), students can enjoy and learn from this type of exercise.

PAST, PRESENT, AND FUTURE CHART

As students learn new vocabulary, having a three-column Past, Present, and Future chart on the wall can function as a helpful reminder. Teachers can display one chart for regular verbs and one for irregular ones. When teaching the tenses, don't forget to have students use gestures—have them stand, point, and look backward when using the past tense, point down when using the present tense, and point and take a step forward when using the future tense. Connecting words to physical action enhances student learning.[17] Even more research supporting physical movement and gestures in learning can be found in Chapter Five.

VENN DIAGRAMS

A Venn diagram is a useful graphic organizer with two or more circles that partially overlap. It is a very accessible scaffolding tool for students to compare one or two events, people, planets, holidays, or ethnic foods, for example, and can be a first step toward writing a simple compare-and-contrast essay. (See Chapters Six through Ten for information on many other useful graphic organizers.)

Tech Tool
Online Compare-and-Contrast Tools

Many free interactive tools are available online to help students understand and use Venn diagrams and write a compare-and-contrast essay. A scaffolded example using these tools can be found in "Unit Project on Reformers" at http://unitedstateshistory.edublogs.org.

K-W-L CHARTS

A K-W-L chart—a three-column sheet that stands for What do you know? What do you want to know? and What have you learned?—can sometimes be a good tool for activating students' prior knowledge on a topic at the beginning of a unit. In addition, it can help them track new information they have learned and look for patterns. Finally, it can be used to support reflective activities.

It is important to note that there are many ways to activate student prior knowledge. The Picture Word Inductive Model, for example, always begins by asking students to identify words that they know and describe items they see. K-W-L charts are just one more tool to occasionally use. K-W-L charts are discussed more in Chapter Six.

Supporting Research. Advance organizers like the K-W-L chart and other questioning strategies have long been found to be effective in increasing student achievement.[18]

"WORDS YOU WANT TO KNOW"

Periodically giving students time to identify ten words they want to learn can be a nice change of pace (especially if they are going to have a substitute that day). They can identify a picture or concept that they want to know the word for by drawing a representation or cutting out a picture from a newspaper or magazine. With teacher and/or tutor assistance, students can learn the words, make an illustrated poster of all ten, and teach them to other classmates in pairs or in slightly larger groups.

ACADEMIC VOCABULARY

Chapters Five and Six discuss developing academic vocabulary with intermediate ELLs, but that doesn't mean it can't start with beginners! Using simple sentence starters is one good strategy for developing academic language. We have also found that regularly showing a short engaging video and combining it with questions, sentence starters, and partner and classroom discussion can work effectively. For example, show the very brief video titled "What Are Your Reasons for Learning English?" (at http://www.englishcentral.com) and then give students a sheet that says:

How do you think learning English can benefit you?

It can assist me to:

1.

2.

3.

You can find a list of academic vocabulary words categorized by content area and grade level at the Jefferson County Schools' site (http://jc-schools .net/tutorials/vocab/index.html).

GIVING INSTRUCTIONS, WAIT TIME, USING GESTURES, AND CHECKING FOR UNDERSTANDING

All these important points were described in Chapter One, but they can't be repeated too many times!

- Give verbal *and* written instructions.
- After asking a question, wait a few seconds before calling on someone to respond.
- Don't speak fast, do use gestures to help reinforce what you are saying, and if a student says he didn't understand what you said, never, ever, repeat the same thing in a louder voice!

- Regularly check for understanding through the use of thumbs-up or thumbs-down, sticky notes, and whiteboards.

Links to free online student exercises for all the thematic units described in this chapter can be found on our book's web site at www.josseybass.com/go/eslsurvivalguide.

PART THREE

Teaching Intermediate English Language Learners

CHAPTER FIVE

Key Elements of a Curriculum for Intermediate ELLs

One day a poor man visited his wealthy friend. The friends ate and talked well into the night. When the poor man went to bed, he fell into a deep sleep. In the middle of the night, the rich man was summoned by a messenger to travel to a distant land. Before he left, he wanted to do something for his poor friend to show how much he cared for him. Because he didn't want to disturb his sleeping friend, the rich man sewed a beautiful colored gem inside the hem of his poor friend's robe. This jewel had the power to satisfy all of one's desires.

The poor man awoke to find himself all alone in his wealthy friend's house. He left and wandered from place to place, looking for work. All the while, he was completely unaware that he possessed a priceless jewel in the hem of his robe.

A long time passed until one day, the wealthy friend came upon the poor man in the street. Seeing the man's impoverished condition, the wealthy friend asked him: "Why have you allowed yourself to become so poor? You could have used the jewel that I gave you to live your life in comfort. You must still have it, yet you are living so miserably. Why don't you use the gem to get what you need? You can have anything you want!"

Confused, the poor man fumbled through the inside of his robe and, with the help of his friend, found the gem. Ashamed of his ignorance yet overcome with joy, he realized for the first time the depth of his friend's compassion. From then on, the poor man was able to live comfortably and happily.[1]

In this Buddhist parable, a poor man is completely unaware of the amazing jewel he is carrying around inside of his robe. He suffers many hardships until he encounters his wealthy friend, who helps him discover the priceless gem within his robe.

As educators, it is easy to feel overwhelmed by what our students "don't know." However, every student comes to the classroom with a wealth of experiences and knowledge. It is the teacher's job to remind students of the treasures they already possess, the "gems within their robes," and to use them as a foundation upon which to build new knowledge and skills.

English language learners sometimes view themselves and are viewed by others as "deficient" or "lacking" because they are not proficient in English. This "deficit" attitude hinders learning and can have long-term negative effects on students. Teachers must recognize the assets their students bring to the classroom in order to promote a healthy and effective learning experience. The activities in our book reflect this philosophy.

At the beginning level, students need to learn key "survival" language to begin interacting in a new school, community, and country. Many of our students arrive without a formal education in their native language. As they progress to the intermediate level, students need continued language development. They also need to learn the academic language necessary for the reading, writing, and speaking they will do in their secondary classes, in college, and in the workplace. A sense of urgency exists when working with English learners at the secondary level because they face the challenge of developing their proficiency in English while also striving toward the looming deadline of graduation and navigating their way through adolescence.

As adolescents, they deserve a curriculum that directly connects to their lives and is intellectually challenging. For this reason, when teaching intermediates, it is important to focus on developing students' analytical and academic writing skills. This chapter will present several research-based and highly effective instructional strategies for use with intermediate English learners. You will notice a shift from themes more relevant to beginners (such as school, family, or feelings) to thematic teaching based on academic topics and writing genres. The sample unit plan in this chapter models how to integrate these reading, writing, and oral language activities in order to connect to students' lives, build new background knowledge, and strengthen their academic English skills.

This chapter also indicates where each instructional strategy or lesson fits into the six standards domains the state of California mandates for its English language development (ELD, also known as ESL) classes. Similar standards exist in most other states. To make these standards more easily understandable, a one-sentence description developed for each domain by the Sacramento City Unified School District will be used, and its appropriate numbers will be cited throughout this chapter. The full one-sentence summary of each domain can be found in Exhibit 3.1.

Key Elements of a Curriculum

This section presents key learning and teaching activities that we regularly use in a beginning ESL classroom. Though they are divided into two sections for organization purposes—"Reading and Writing" and "Speaking and Listening"—you will find that many of them incorporate all four of these domains.

READING AND WRITING

Free Voluntary Reading and Reading Strategies

As previously described, Free Voluntary Reading, also called Extensive Reading, Silent Sustained Reading, and recreational reading, is an effective way to elevate the level of student interest in reading while increasing literacy skills at the same time. Students are allowed to choose whatever reading material they are interested in and are given time to read each day (fifteen to twenty minutes has worked well with our students). At the beginning of each semester, students can set reading goals for themselves that they can periodically reflect on and revise throughout the school year (see Exhibit 5.1). Setting goals increases intrinsic motivation and gives students ownership of their learning. By setting goals for their reading, students also learn what readers can do to improve their skills.

EXHIBIT 5.1. Reading Goals

1. What do you want to learn about through reading? What topics are you interested in? What genres (types of books) would you like to try?

2. What is your reading time goal for this quarter? How many minutes? How many days? Where will you do your reading?

3. Which reading strategies do you want to practice more this quarter?

4. How will you help yourself accomplish these goals? List three things you need to do in order to accomplish your goals.

Helping students realize the importance of practice can be a great way to keep them engaged. In our classroom, we emphasize that reading is like a sport or anything else—if you want to improve, you have to practice. However, it is much easier to practice something you enjoy, hence our classroom rule, "You must be reading a book you like!" See Chapter Twelve for ideas on helping students select interesting and challenging books. Also, sharing research with students on the benefits of reading (see the Supporting Research section on Free Voluntary Reading in Chapter Three) can help students develop intrinsic motivation for reading.

Visiting the school library and developing a relationship with the school librarian is an important strategy for promoting literacy in the classroom. Taking students to the library on a regular basis helps keep engagement levels high. Having students fill out a Library Goal Sheet each time they go to the library can promote a positive and productive experience (see Exhibit 5.2).

EXHIBIT 5.2. Library Goal Sheet

Name _____

Date _____

My goal(s) for the library today: _____

_____

I _____ did (or did not) accomplish my goal today because

_____

_____

My behavior today in the library was (excellent, good, okay, poor) because

_____

_____

As discussed in the previous chapter, Free Voluntary Reading serves to generate student motivation for reading and is typically not formally assessed. However, the teacher may use free reading time to learn about students' reading strengths and challenges in English. Spending one-on-one time with students—listening to them read, talking about new words, and discussing their books—is critical to their progress.

During this daily twenty-minute Free Reading Time, students begin to apply the strategies they see modeled and practiced in class to their personal reading. One way to review these strategies at the beginning of the year is to have students do a Text Data Set on reading strategies to identify the characteristics of each strategy (see Exhibit 5.3). Text Data Sets were explained in Chapter Three and will be described in more detail later in this one.

The teacher can assess how well students are using these reading strategies in their personal reading by asking students periodically to respond in Reading Logs (see Exhibit 3.5 in Chapter Three). Intermediate students should be moving toward using higher-order thinking in their reading log responses. One way to practice this is by teaching students about the Revised Bloom's Taxonomy and having them practice higher-level questions—focusing more on analysis and evaluation as opposed to recall and comprehension (see the Other Activities section at the end of Chapter Six for more on Bloom's Taxonomy). Concept attainment is a great way for students to see the difference between lower- and higher-level questions (see Chapter Three for more explanation of concept attainment).

Warning: Reading Logs can become a tedious task if they are assigned too often (one or two times a week works well for our students), so students should be invited to respond to their reading in other ways as well.

Book Talks are a great way for students to interact with their reading and gain valuable speaking practice. Students answer questions about the book they are currently reading and turn these answers into a Book Talk where they discuss their book with a partner, in a small group, or with the whole class. This allows students to hear about other interesting books their classmates are reading (see Exhibit 5.4).

Using Free Voluntary Reading correlates with California ELD domains 1, 2, 3, 4, 5 and 6.

Supporting Research. As stated in Chapter Three, numerous studies show the effectiveness of Free Voluntary reading with English learners.

There are also many studies showing the benefits of goal setting for students, especially when students set "learning goals" (to read more challenging books, to take more leadership in small groups, to be more organized, for example) as opposed to "academic performance goals" (higher test scores or a higher GPA, for example). Research shows that when students focus on learning goals they actually raise their GPA more than students who had emphasized performance goals related to improving their grades.[2]

EXHIBIT 5.3. Reading Strategies Data Set

Predict, Ask Questions, Make Connections, Visualize, Summarize, Evaluate

1. This book reminds me of another book I read titled *A Child Called It*. Both authors experienced horrific child abuse and survived to tell about it. They both wrote books in order to help others in similar situations.

2. Why did the girl lie to her mother about where she was? Was she scared she would get in trouble?

3. As I read the last chapter of the book, I visualized the look of fear on Victor's face and felt his thumping heart as he was being chased by the dogs. I could imagine what it looked like as he tried to climb the chain-link fence and kept turning his head to see if the dogs were getting closer.

4. I predict that Justin will break up with Karina because she has been lying to him. He will probably find out about her lies when he reads her texts on her phone.

5. This chapter was about DeShawn's decision not to join the basketball team. He decided that he didn't want to give up his part-time job, which he needed to help his family. He felt sad about the decision and wished things could be different.

6. The problem in this book is similar to a problem I have been experiencing with my best friend who would rather spend time with her boyfriend than with her friends. I also feel frustrated and hurt by my friend.

7. While reading this section of my book I can picture how beautiful the mountains looked covered with sparkling snow. I can picture how the sunrise gave them a pink and orange glow.

8. I predict that Sundara's family will not be happy about her relationship with Jonathan because they don't want her to date anyone outside of her own culture. They want her to date a Cambodian young man.

9. I think that the friends will go inside the haunted house because they are curious and want to see if ghosts are real or not. Maybe they will run out if they get too scared.

10. The main character, Billie, decided to run away from home. She left during the middle of the night and went to her best friend's house. Billie's mom was worried and kept calling her phone, but Billie wouldn't answer it because she was so mad.

11. I think the ending of this book was too short. I want to know more about what happened to Johnny and Susan after high school. I don't like that it ended on their graduation day because I want to know if they decided to attend different colleges and if they stayed together or not.

12. I predict the next chapter of this book will describe what happened to Cesar Chavez as a teenager because the previous chapter was about his childhood.

13. What does the word "arrogant" mean? Is it similar to bragging?

14. As I read this sentence, I see many students bumping into each other in a crowded hallway, making lots of noise. I can see Johnny and Maureen holding hands, looking at each other, and ignoring everybody else around them.

15. I wonder why many teenagers don't like to talk about their problems with their parents. I also wonder why many parents feel uncomfortable talking to teenagers about important issues such as drug abuse or sexual activity.

16. I don't agree with Billie's decision to run away. I think she needed to take some time and calm down before making any decisions.

17. I can relate to Maria because she feels so sad and powerless because her parents are getting a divorce and that is how I felt when my parents got a divorce. I felt like I had no choice about what was happening to our family.

18. Why did the author of this book decide to write about the problem of bullying in schools? Did he ever experience being bullied by someone?

19. This character reminds me of my aunt because she is also very determined to reach her goals, no matter what obstacles get in her way.

20. The first chapter of the book focused on Cesar Chavez's childhood. His parents were migrant farm workers who moved a lot to find work. Cesar attended many different schools, but had to drop out after eighth grade in order to go to work to help his family.

21. If I were the author, I would have added more of DeShawn's thoughts so the reader could know more about his feelings. I also would have added more description of what his school was like so I could really visualize what it looked like.

EXHIBIT 5.4. Book Talk

1. Say the title of your book and show it to the other person.

2. Say the name of the book's author.

3. Explain why you picked the book.

4. Explain what the book is about.

5. Share what you like about the book. (You shouldn't be reading it if you don't like it!)

6. Share a quote from the book and why you picked it.

Tech Tool
Online Book Trailers

Book Trailers are a fun way to engage students and encourage speaking practice. Students write a script in which they review a favorite book (see Exhibit 5.5). They then practice aloud several times before being recorded using a video recorder or smartphone. These trailers can easily be posted on YouTube or on a class blog. They can also simply be presented in front of the class or in small groups.

There are many ways to have students share their Book Trailers online. Fotobabble is a great site that allows students to record themselves for one minute (http://www.fotobabble.com). They can easily publish their recording online, along with a picture either from the Internet or from uploaded photographs. The teacher can also record a video of students presenting their Book Trailers, then upload it to YouTube, and even embed it in a class blog. This can be done very easily with a smartphone.

EXHIBIT 5.5. Book Review Trailer

You will prepare a short "trailer" about your favorite book that you read this year. It will be recorded and posted on YouTube and will be used next year to help students find good books.

Your book review trailer must include:

- Book title and author
- A brief summary of the book (you want to make someone interested in the book without giving away the good parts!)
- Give two specific reasons why you liked this book and explain why someone else should read it

Remember—a trailer is like a commercial—you are trying to "sell" this book to someone. Be convincing and support your opinions with specific reasons. You will need to show the book while you are talking about it. Be creative and *practice, practice, practice!*

Academic Vocabulary Instruction: Word Charts and Word Walls

Word charts are critical tools used to front-load and reinforce vocabulary that students will encounter in academic reading, writing, listening, and speaking. Before starting a unit, the teacher can identify words students will need to know in order to understand the reading and writing assignments. These words may be related to a writing genre (such as persuasive or problem-solution) or to minithemes being used to help teach that genre (such as immigration or goal-setting). We will go into more detail on genre units and minithemes later in Chapter Six.

Teachers and students can create various formats of word charts. Exhibit 5.6 shows an example of a word chart from a persuasive writing unit. It contains key words students will need to know in order to understand the features of a persuasive essay. Students first make connections and guesses for the words they've heard. Students may translate the words into their native language. After students have time to share in partners and as a class, the teacher builds upon this knowledge and guides students toward an accurate definition of each word, which they write in the Meaning column of the word chart. Students can then list any related words or synonyms in the Related Words column (they can also write the word in their native language in this space). Students next draw a sketch or image to represent each word. Finally, a body movement or gesture is taught to go with each word. First the teacher models the movement, and then students repeat it. For example, with the word *fact* the teacher could point to the ground, stomping her foot, and with the word *opinion* the teacher could point to her mind. The teacher should look for opportunities to repeat the gesture and reinforce student understanding throughout the unit. Students enjoy collaborating to come up with the best movement for each word.

EXHIBIT 5.6. Persuasive Word Chart

Word	Meaning	Related Words	Picture
fact			
opinion			
persuade			
reason			
argument			
convince			
opposing opinion			
counterargument			
audience			

Students can keep individual word charts in their binders or folders and can staple their word charts to the front of their folders for easy reference. It is important to post the words on the classroom wall as well. The key to making word charts and word walls effective tools is to use them! In other words, they are living documents that should be added to, revised, and referred to on a daily basis.

Using word charts and word walls correlates with California ELD domains 1, 2, 3, 5 and 6.

Supporting Research. Many researchers have focused on the benefits of using drawing and movement to increase vocabulary development.[3] In the book *Building Background Knowledge for Academic Achievement: Research on What Works in Schools,* Robert Marzano states that academic vocabulary development involves students being able to express their knowledge of the words through both "linguistic and nonlinguistic representations."[4] He describes nonlinguistic representations as "drawings, pictures, graphic organizers, acting the word out, etc."[5] Also, studies of adolescent learners indicate that nearly 75 percent of those studied were better learners when movement was incorporated into their classroom environment.[6]

It is important to clarify that word charts can be an effective way to preteach and reinforce vocabulary, but only if they contain a limited amount of key words. We are not suggesting that teachers have students create an endless chart or glossary of a zillion new words. In fact, researchers have suggested that providing students with lengthy vocabulary lists or glossaries to use while reading can create a "cognitive load that splits the learner's attention" as he goes back and forth between text and glossary, and that it is more effective to have students write down a word's meaning right next to the difficult word on the text itself.[7]

Tech Tool
Academic Vocabulary Online Resources

There are many online reinforcement activities for academic vocabulary, as well as teaching resources. You can see a list of them in "The Best Websites for Developing Academic English Skills and Vocabulary" at http://larryferlazzo.edublogs.org. In particular, Vocabahead is a site with numerous free vocabulary resources for students at the intermediate and advanced levels (http://www.vocabahead.com).

Read-Alouds and Think-Alouds

A read-aloud is used to model fluent reading for students. The teacher selects a short piece of text related to the unit of study and reads it aloud with prosody (intonation, rhythm, and expression). The teacher does not stop during the reading to share his or her ideas. Sometimes it is necessary to supply easier synonyms for difficult vocabulary, but the teacher shouldn't spend a lot of time defining the words. In order to help students understand the concept of prosody, the teacher can read a passage twice—one time in a robotic tone and then again with feeling and intonation. Students can instantly hear the difference between the two styles. Students should have copies of the text in front of them or be able to see it on an overhead or document camera. Read-alouds can be followed by writing or speaking prompts ("What would you have done in this situation?" or "What does the author mean by _____?"). The teacher can quickly check for understanding by asking students to use whiteboards to share their responses.

A think-aloud also models fluent, prosodic reading for students, but additionally models interacting with text through the use of reading strategies. As mentioned in the previous chapter, the teacher can model his or her thinking while reading a short piece of text. Students can then replicate the think-aloud process on their own by writing their thoughts in the margins of a different piece of text. Next, students can share their think-alouds with a partner.

Doing this kind of guided and independent practice with the class gives students more exposure to the reading strategies they employ during free voluntary reading. As researchers Roger Farr and Jenny Conner explain: "We are encouraging them to think about why and when to use certain strategies, and providing them with the tools they need to successfully monitor their own comprehension. With enough modeling and coached practice, students will be on their way to becoming independent users of strategies. Eventually they will become their own coaches. Ultimately, using the strategies will become more automatic for them, so that activities they have practiced will be happening automatically in their heads."[8]

Reading in pairs in a positive learning environment and with familiar text is one way to help students build fluency. However, doing round-robin reading or popcorn reading, where individual students are called on to read aloud for the class without any prior practice, is an ineffective practice that can be harmful to students. We never recommend having students do these "cold reads" because, as studies have shown, it can lead to embarrassment and frustration for the student who is called on to read. It also does not provide an engaging or valuable learning experience for the other students in the class.[9]

Read-alouds and think-alouds are also great ways to build background knowledge and vocabulary within a unit, which can lead to better writing. For further explanation of both strategies and some great tips, see Instructional Strategies at http://pebblecreeklabs.com.

Exhibit 5.7 shows a think-aloud used in our intermediate class as part of a persuasive writing unit.

See the Tech Tool on online audio recording in Chapter Three for easy ways students can practice reading with prosody, record themselves online, and listen to their recordings.

Using read-alouds and think-alouds correlates with California ELD domains 1, 2, 3 and 4.

EXHIBIT 5.7. Persuasive Think-Aloud

Note: Teacher think-aloud comments appear in italics.

Many middle schools and high schools have adopted school uniform policies in recent years. (*I wonder if our school has ever considered uniforms?*) Some proponents claim uniforms can increase school unity and promote a focus on academics rather than fashion. (*Yes, I've heard this argument before when I worked at a middle school.*) However, opponents of school uniform policies argue that uniforms inhibit individuality and prevent students from expressing themselves at an age when self-expression is very important. (*Could students express themselves in other ways?*) They also argue that many families may not be able to afford uniforms, which can be costly. Some schools have tried to compromise by not requiring students to purchase a specific uniform, but instead requiring they wear certain colors of clothing such as blue or khaki on the bottom and white on top. (*This is an interesting compromise—I wonder what students think of this?*)

Supporting Research. Research indicates that prosodic reading may serve as an aid to comprehension. As well-known researcher Dr. Timothy V. Rasinski states: "When readers embed appropriate volume, tone, emphasis, phrasing, and other elements in oral expression, they are giving evidence of actively interpreting or constructing meaning from the passage. Just as fluent musicians interpret or construct meaning from a musical score through phrasing, emphasis, and variations in tone and volume, fluent readers use cognitive resources to construct meaning through expressive interpretation of the text."[10]

Reading aloud to students also promotes literacy development and generates interest in reading. In one recent study, children whose families were educated about the benefits of read-alouds and who were given free books showed consistent gains in vocabulary development.[11]

Clozes

Clozes (also known as fill-in-the-blank or gap-fill) are another activity students can do to practice reading strategies and build background knowledge for writing. As explained in Chapter Three, a cloze is a piece of text from which several words have been removed and replaced with blanks. Students must use higher-level thinking skills in order to choose words to fill in the blanks. Students can also respond to a cloze orally once they are familiar with the text.

Depending upon the cloze, students may be asked to demonstrate linguistic knowledge (for example, if the teacher replaces prepositions with blanks) or to demonstrate textual comprehension by using context clues to make guesses. Challenging texts can be made more accessible by offering a word bank of answers at the bottom of the cloze or by simplifying some of the language. When creating a cloze for students, it is important to carefully consider which words are removed and replaced with blanks. Students should be able to use contextual clues to make a guess and should circle those clues. In order to preserve meaning, blanks should not be put in the first or last sentence of the passage. Cloze passages should be relatively short (a few paragraphs) and generally should not contain more than fifteen blanks.

Many variations of clozes can be used, and Pebble Creek Labs offers some helpful guidelines for using the cloze strategy under Instructional Strategies (http://pebblecreeklabs.com).

Teachers of intermediate-level students can use clozes to teach reading strategies like predicting and using context clues, while also teaching students about metacognition (or "thinking about their thinking"). After students complete the cloze, the teacher can ask them to explain *why* they chose the answers they did. Students could use the following sentence frame to explain their thinking: "I chose the word _____ because _____." The teacher should first model this process of explaining the clues he or she used when choosing a word for a specific blank; in other words, making his or her thinking transparent for students. This strategy of challenging students to explain their thinking in writing helps them become more conscious of the reading strategies they are using and reinforces the idea that good readers employ these tools while reading. Another way for students to reinforce metacognitive skills is by creating their own clozes for classmates to complete. During the process of developing the clozes, students need to be very aware of ensuring that gap words have clues somewhere in the text. So that you can ensure accuracy, these clozes should use text from books or articles related to class lessons, not pieces of original student work.

Clozes can also be used to assess the reading progress students are making. They can be given to students several times throughout the year to measure growth in reading comprehension and vocabulary development.

Additionally, clozes can serve as models for the types of writing that students will be expected to produce. The teacher can have students do a cloze and then evaluate the features of the writing that he or she would like students to practice. Students can then do a mimic write and replicate the features on their own. Exhibit 5.8 is an example of a cloze designed to reinforce persuasive concepts along with a mimic writing scaffold. Figure 5.1 is the mimic write a student produced using that cloze as a model. Mimic writing will be explained in more detail later in this chapter.

The cloze strategy correlates with California ELD domains 1, 2, 3 and 6.

EXHIBIT 5.8. Persuading My Parents Cloze and Mimic Write

Sometimes I need to persuade my parents to let me do things that I want to do. Last week, when I wanted to _____ up late and watch a movie, I had to convince my parents that it was a good idea. First, I had to think of a convincing _____ and support this reason with facts. For example, I told them that the reason I _____ be able to watch a movie is because I already completed my homework and set my alarm clock. My parents disagreed with me and presented an _____ viewpoint. They argued that if I stayed up to watch a movie, then I would be too tired to _____ up on time and get ready for school in the morning. I reminded them that just last week I stayed up late finishing my homework and the next _____ when my alarm clock went off at 6:00 a.m., I got up and got ready for _____ on time. This was a great counterargument because they were convinced and they agreed to let me watch my movie!

Sometimes I need to persuade _____ to let me do things that I want to do. Last week, when I wanted to _____, I had to convince _____ that it was a good idea. First, I had to think of a convincing reason and support this reason with facts. For example, I told them that the reason I should be able to _____ is because _____
_____.
_____ disagreed with me and presented an opposing viewpoint.
_____ argued that if I _____, then
I _____. I presented a counterargument when I said _____
_____
_____
_____.

<u>Persuade My Parents</u>

One times I tried to persuade my parent to let me do things that I want to do. Last week, I wanted to wake up early to play basket in my brother school. I had to convince my parents that it was a good idea. One reason I used was it help me to get exercise and my body get stronger. Another reason was I already finished cleaning the house and I already did my homework.

Figure 5.1. Persuading My Parents Student Sample

Supporting Research. Numerous research studies have shown the cloze procedure to be effective with English learners in developing self-monitoring of their reading skills. It is a strategy that can be varied by teachers according to their instructional goals and the levels of proficiency of their students. Researchers have concluded, "Cloze technique is recommended as a useful strategy for English Language Learners who are developing or fine tuning their English language skills and developing and applying their reader comprehension strategies."[12]

The metacognitive aspect of cloze has many benefits for learners. Judy Willis, a neurologist and teacher, explains the importance of metacognition as "one of the distinct learning behaviors that enhances students' competence and confidence and helps them become optimal learners."[13]

Tech Tool
Creating Clozes Online

If teachers do a search on "interactive online clozes," they can find many versions that students can do online. However, many of the interactive clozes available online do not appear to have blanks inserted strategically. In other words, they may have been placed there randomly. For that reason, we suggest you first review online interactive clozes prior to recommending them to your students. The safest and best way to ensure that students are getting the most learning they can from online interactive clozes is for teachers to create them. Teachers and students can create clozes online by copying and pasting text of their choice using a site such as Learnclick (http://www.learnclick.com).

Text Data Sets

The Picture Word Inductive Model (PWIM) and Text Data Sets are key strategies to use with beginners. With these strategies students seek patterns and use them to identify their broader meanings and significance. Inductive learning can also be powerful at the intermediate level through the use of more sophisticated Text Data Sets.

As previously explained, Text Data Sets can be composed of short examples of text which can be organized into categories. Each example may be a sentence or a paragraph in length, and the level of text can be adjusted depending upon the proficiency level of the students.

Students use their reading strategies to decode and comprehend the text first and then employ a higher level of thinking to recognize patterns in the text. They organize the examples into categories either given to them by the teacher or generated by the students themselves. For example, a data set on a country might include the categories of history, climate, and economy.

Students can then add to each category using information presented in further reading (read-alouds, think-alouds, and clozes) and from videos or the Internet. Students can organize their information using a graphic organizer or by simply folding their paper so they have a box for each category. This is an opportunity for the teacher to emphasize the note-taking skills students are practicing that will help them as they advance into mainstream classes.

Organizing information into categories can also serve as a scaffold for writing an essay. Once students have enough information, they can use their notes to write sentences in their own words about each category. As with the PWIM, the teacher can model how to structure each paragraph with a topic sentence and supporting details. Once students have written about a certain number of categories, these paragraphs can serve as body paragraphs. The students can then work on adding introductory and concluding paragraphs and they have an essay!

Having students create their own Text Data Sets is another writing opportunity. Students can first select a topic and then identify categories within it. After researching the categories, they can write examples in their own words. Students can also create online Text Data Sets. Their categories can be presented in different online formats, including online books or on an online "wall" with pictures. Students can then read each other's data sets and work to categorize them. See the Tech Tool on online writing practice in Chapter Three for resources on web tools that allow students to easily write online.

This type of inductive teaching and learning pushes students to develop both their reading and critical thinking skills and saturates them with language and ideas to use in their writing. Further explanation of how to use inductive teaching with intermediate English language learners can be found in the Inductive Lesson Plan in Chapter Six. For more explanation of data sets and inductive teaching, see Instructional Strategies at http://pebblecreeklabs.com.

Using Text Data Sets correlates with California ELD domains 1, 2, 3, 4, 5 and 6.

Supporting Research. As stated in the previous chapter, using the inductive process builds on the brain's natural desire to make connections and seek patterns. This results in higher levels of literacy for English language learners.

Also see Supporting Research under Mimic Writing in the next section for additional research on inductive teaching.

Mimic Writing

Mimic writing can sometimes be confused with copying and therefore some teachers are hesitant to use it with English learners. However, it can be quite successful in improving student writing. It can be used to practice numerous features of writing related to organization, style, and grammar.

Students first evaluate a sample text, identifying the features they will be mimicking. For example, students may identify how an author uses imagery and figurative language to describe a person. It is important for students to participate in identifying both good and bad examples of the feature of writing they will be mimicking. Concept attainment is a good way to do this (see Chapter Three). Writing techniques can also be examined by having students use inductive teaching. For example, students can read a Text Data Set with multiple examples of figurative language and categorize them by type (such as simile or metaphor). See Exhibit 5.9 for a sample figurative language data set.

After viewing multiple examples, students mimic the features they have just studied. Students can then generate their own examples of figurative language. Or, if the model text contains a description of a person, students can then write a description of a different person or a place.

Using mimic writing correlates with California ELD domains 5 and 6.

Supporting Research. Bruce Joyce and Emily Calhoun describe the benefits of the mimic writing process used with fourth graders who used inductive learning to "explore the techniques used by published authors to accomplish tasks such as announcing the main idea clearly, introducing characters, establishing setting, and describing actions. The students … then experimented with those devices in their own writing … Their end-of-year scores for writing quality were higher than the end-of-year scores for eighth grade students the previous year!"[14]

EXHIBIT 5.9. Figurative Language Data Set

1. I was as quiet as a mouse so I wouldn't wake up my little sister.
2. My alarm clock screamed at me to wake up.
3. The girl's soft voice was music to his ears.
4. The fog wrapped us in a blanket of cool mist.
5. Our car was a hot, dry desert when the air conditioner broke.
6. The medicine my mom gave me for my stomachache was as pink as a flamingo.
7. The moon was playing hide-and-seek among the clouds in the night sky.
8. Juan's new shoes were as white as my grandma's hair.
9. Her eyes sparkled like diamonds when she looked at me.
10. Drew was a wall, deflecting every shot on goal made by the other team.
11. The tall trees shivered in the cold wind.
12. Sitting in my English class and listening to the teacher was as boring as watching paint dry.
13. My best friend was a potato chip about to be crushed by the group of boys approaching him.
14. The boys on the opposing basketball team were as tall as redwood trees!
15. The raindrops danced across the windowpane.
16. The frozen lake was a smooth glass mirror.
17. The warm sun greeted me as I stepped outside onto the front porch.
18. The trees were a huge, green umbrella shielding the road from the rain.

Note: The Answer Key is below. Teachers may or may not want to give it to students after they complete their own categories.

Categorized Similes

1. I was as quiet as a mouse so I wouldn't wake up my little sister.
6. The medicine my mom gave me for my stomachache was as pink as a flamingo.
8. Juan's new shoes were as white as my grandma's hair.
9. Her eyes sparkled like diamonds when she looked at me.
12. Sitting in my English class and listening to the teacher was as boring as watching paint dry.
14. The boys on the opposing basketball team were as tall as redwood trees!

Categorized Metaphors

3. The girl's soft voice was music to his ears.
5. Our car was a hot, dry desert when the air conditioner broke.
10. Drew was a wall, deflecting every shot on goal made by the other team.
13. My best friend was a potato chip about to be crushed by the group of boys approaching him.
16. The frozen lake was a smooth glass mirror.
18. The trees were a huge, green umbrella shielding the road from the rain.

Categorized Personification

2. My alarm clock screamed at me to wake up.
4. The fog wrapped us in a blanket of cool mist.
7. The moon was playing hide-and-seek among the clouds in the night sky.
11. The tall trees shivered in the cold wind.
15. The raindrops danced across the windowpane.
17. The warm sun greeted me as I stepped outside onto the front porch.

Sentence Frames

Similar to mimic writing, sentence frames (also called templates) help students become familiar with organizational patterns and syntactic and grammatical features of various genres. When students are given a frame (sentence starters, transitions) to help structure the academic language and organization of their writing, it often frees them up to focus on the ideas they want to communicate in their writing. As they use these frames they begin to internalize the structures and language, eventually becoming less dependent on that support over time. The Sample Unit in Chapter Six contains a more detailed explanation of using sentence frames and outlines.

Using sentence frames correlates with California ELD domains 5 and 6.

Supporting Research. In the book *They Say, I Say: The Moves That Matter in Academic Writing*, Gerald Graff and Cathy Birkenstein write, "One virtue of such templates, we found, is that they focus writers' attention not just on what is being said, but on the *forms* that structure what is being said. In other words, they help students focus on the rhetorical patterns that are key to academic success but often pass under the classroom radar."[15]

Using Images to Generate Writing

Using images is a key strategy in an ESL classroom. Pictures are immediately engaging and often less daunting for students than texts. Images can be used to push language development and thinking skills within a unit by asking students to look at an image posted on the wall, on a document camera, or overhead. The image may be related to a thematic unit or may reflect a problem (similar to the critical pedagogy example in Chapter Three).

First, students describe in writing what they observe, trying to record as many details as possible. Then the teacher asks students to write as many questions they can think of about the image and the details they have listed. Once students have shared their questions with a classmate, the teacher asks them to use the inductive process to organize these questions into categories. These questions could serve as writing entry points for students to develop a longer writing piece based on the image.

See the Tech Tool on photos on the web in Chapter Three for a collection of web sites and lessons related to using images in the ESL classroom.

Using images to generate writing correlates with California ELD domains 1, 5 and 6.

Supporting Research. Research has shown that these types of inquiry activities—where students are asked to analyze a piece of concrete data such as a picture or an object in order to generate ideas for writing—are an effective instructional practice for improving the writing of adolescent learners.[16]

LISTENING AND SPEAKING

Video Clips and Questions

Chapter Three explained how to use video with beginners in the Language Experience Approach and the Back to the Screen activity. Another technique that can be used with intermediate learners involves students watching a short video clip and generating questions. Students divide into pairs, exchange their papers, and answer their partner's questions. Students then exchange papers again and "grade" their partner's answers.

Using the concept attainment strategy, the teacher can show student samples that illustrate yes and no examples of answers to questions. The fact that students are writing questions for a real audience (a classmate) tends to lead to better questions. Students may also take more time answering the questions because they know a classmate will be "grading" them.

Our students have enjoyed watching the *Connect with English* video series by Annenberg Media. It is available for free online at http://www.learner.org. Exhibit 5.10 can be used with the *Connect with English* series or with any video.

See Supporting Research in the Video section and the Tech Tool on online videos in Chapter Three for research and resources related to using videos in the ESL classroom.

Using video clips and questions correlates with California ELD domains 1, 5 and 6.

Dialogues

Dialogues can be written by the teacher or by students on any topic and can be performed in numerous ways. They can be frequently used to reinforce the concepts and vocabulary within a unit. Students can be given a list of unit-related words and work together to produce a dialogue or skit using the words. Not only does this provide oral language practice, it also serves to assess student understanding of the vocabulary words.

Students can also generate a list of real-life "speaking situations" that they would like to practice (such as going to the doctor, asking a teacher for help, dealing with a landlord, or asking for directions). The teacher can then lead students in developing key words and phrases for these situations that can be turned into dialogues by the teacher or by students.

Students at the intermediate level need to practice saying, and listening to, the academic language they are learning. For example, students can discuss a topic of study using academic phrases such as "I understand your point; however, I disagree because _____", "I partially agree with your point

EXHIBIT 5.10. Practicing English Sheet

Name_____ My partner _____

Before watching:

The title of today's episode or film is _____.

Write two predictions about this episode or film based on the title:

1.

2.

While you watch the episode or film, write three questions about this film for a classmate to answer. After the episode or film, give your paper to a classmate so that he or she can write answers to your questions.

Question 1:
Answer:

Question 2:
Answer:

Question 3:
Answer:

After watching:

Were your predictions correct? Explain why or why not.

1.

2.

because _____," "Based on my experience, _____." These academic sentence frames can be posted on a classroom wall. Dialogues that incorporate academic language can be acted out in front of class, in a group, or even recorded online using a site such as Fotobabble (http://www.fotobabble.com).

Using dialogues correlates with California ELD domains 1, 2 and 6.

3–2–1

As mentioned in Chapter Three, we use a modified version of the fluency activity called 4–3–2 created by Paul Nation, where students choose a familiar topic and talk about it for three minutes, then two minutes, and then one minute.[17] Students can first write down notes about the topic to help generate ideas for speaking. After studying their notes, students put them away and form two rows facing each other. Students then talk about their topics for three minutes with a partner, and then one row moves to the right and students talk for two minutes with a new partner. The process is repeated one more time, with students talking to a new partner for one minute.

While beginners might do 2–1.5–1, intermediate-level students can do 3–2–1 or 4–3–2. See Chapter Three for a more detailed explanation of this activity.

Using the 3–2–1 activity correlates with California ELD domains 1, 2 and 6.

Presentations: "Speed Dating"

Similar to 3–2–1, Speed Dating is a quick way for students to gain speaking practice while presenting their work to classmates. Students divide into two rows and stand facing each other or remain seated and turn their desks to face each other. The teacher assigns one row to be the "movers" and then announces that each pair will have a certain amount of time to speak. When the teacher says "Switch," everyone in the movers row stands and moves to the right (or to the left). The idea is for students to share with several different partners. Students can share their work in numerous ways (by explaining or reading something they have written, for example). The teacher may also encourage students to ask their partners questions.

Using the Speed Dating activity correlates with California ELD domains 1, 2 and 6.

Additional resources, including ones on student book trailers and online activities where students can build vocabulary, can be found on our book's web site at www.josseybass.com/go/eslsurvivalguide.

CHAPTER SIX

Daily Instruction for Intermediate ELLs

One day a large buck went to drink at a spring. As he bent down, he noticed his own reflection in the clear water. He admired his great, strong horns, but as he looked at his legs and feet, he suddenly felt angry and thought "Why are they so thin and weak?" While the buck was immersed in his negative thoughts, a lion approached the spring, ready to hunt his prey. The buck immediately turned and shot off into the distance, his strong legs carrying him far across the plains to safety. "It was my legs, not my mighty horns, which saved me from death," the buck said to himself.[1]

In this story the buck wasn't able to see his most valuable strength until he was faced with a challenging situation. In the classroom, our students sometimes have a hard time seeing their valuable qualities. The strategies and lesson ideas presented in this chapter are designed to build upon students' strengths and experiences in order to promote greater learning and help students see the value both in their learning and in themselves.

Reflection

Reflective activities can be a rich experience for both students and teachers. We recommend that intermediate-level students end class with a reflective activity a few times a week. These activities can fall into the five categories—summarize, self-assess, assess the class and teacher, relevance, and higher-order thinking—explained in Chapter Four.

Homework

The homework we give our intermediate students covers the four domains of reading, writing, listening, and speaking and is similar to the homework we assign our beginners and early intermediates, with a few variations:

- Read a book in English at home for at least twenty minutes each night and have a parent or guardian sign a Weekly Reading Sheet (see Exhibit 6.1).

- Complete one Reading Log and demonstrate the use of at least three reading strategies (see Exhibit 3.5 in Chapter Three).

- Write a journal sharing two or three good events that occurred that week and one event that was not necessarily positive. In the last instance, share whether there was something that the student could have done differently to improve the outcome.

- In class, students share what they wrote with a partner, and the partner should ask at least one question.

- Complete a Four Words sheet with new words learned that week—in or out of class—that students think are important (see Exhibit 4.1 in Chapter Four). In class, students share the words they chose with a partner.

- Spend at least ten minutes each day talking to someone else in English (for example, with a teacher, another student, or a coworker) and complete the Conversation Log (see Exhibit 4.2 in Chapter Four).

- Extra credit: read a book aloud to a child and complete the Read a Children's Book sheet (see Exhibit 6.2).

Please see the Homework section in Chapter Four for the research support behind effective homework activities and for Tech Tools on homework.

Field Trips

As discussed in Chapter Four, field trips can be a great way to extend the classroom learning that students are doing within a thematic unit. For intermediate students, the activities students do in preparation for the trip and as a follow-up can involve more writing and higher-level analysis than for beginners.

For example, as part of a unit on persuasive writing, we have students research, visit, and critically evaluate two different neighborhoods according to various criteria such as public transportation access, housing costs, diversity, and overall livability. Afterward, students write a persuasive essay choosing the best neighborhood. For more explanation of this project and a lesson plan, see *Helping Students Motivate Themselves: Practical Answers to Classroom Challenges* by Larry Ferlazzo.[2]

EXHIBIT 6.1. Weekly Reading Sheet

Name_____

Date	Book Title	Minutes Read	Student Signature	Parent Signature

EXHIBIT 6.2. Read a Children's Book

Student name _____

1. What is the name of the child you read the book to?

2. What is this child's relationship to you?

3. What is the title of the book you read?

4. Why did you pick that book?

5. Did the child enjoy having you read the book to him or her? How could you tell?

6. How did you feel about reading the book to him or her? Why?

Assessment

Please see Chapter Thirteen for an in-depth explanation of the different types of assessments that can be used with intermediate-level students.

A Sample Unit: Problem-Solution

Thematic teaching can be an effective way to build vocabulary and provide students with many opportunities for rich reading and writing experiences. At the intermediate level, students are moving further toward proficiency in academic writing in English. It can be helpful to organize thematic units around an academic writing genre. In their book *Literacy Techniques for Building Successful Readers and Writers*, David Wallace Booth and Larry Swartz point out that a genre study is similar to a thematic unit—it "explores a type of writing, understanding the nature of the medium on the message."[3]

When you are selecting these genres, the following questions may be important to consider: Is this type of writing commonly used in secondary courses? Is this a genre students will need to know to be successful on district and state writing exams? Is this a genre students will frequently be required to use at the postsecondary level? Does this genre exist outside the academic world of school in real-world writing?

There are also several criteria to keep in mind when designing a thematic, genre-based unit. In order to promote "language development, critical thinking, independence, and interpersonal collaboration," Suzanne Peregoy and Owen Boyle describe these six criteria for organizing thematic instruction for English learners:[4]

- *Meaning and purpose:* connecting topics of study to students' lives and offering students choice in topics studied

- *Building on prior knowledge:* making connections to students' life experiences

- *Integrated opportunities to use oral and written language for learning purposes:* promoting a variety of oral language and literacy experiences that are aligned with student interests

- *Scaffolding for support:* using multiple scaffolds to support students who are at various levels of language proficiency

- *Collaboration:* providing opportunities for students to work together in pairs and small groups for learning tasks

- *Variety:* creating a dynamic learning environment that emphasizes variety and flexibility in all aspects of the classroom

These criteria have guided the development of the genre units we use with our intermediate level students throughout the year. If students are scheduled into a two-hour block, it is possible to teach several genres a year. Problem-solution, persuasive, and autobiographical are three genres that are commonly taught and assessed in high school, and also exist in college and in real-world writing. Of course, these are not the only genres that students need to be exposed to, but they each contain critical thinking and writing techniques that students will use both in and outside of school.

This section will explain the key components of a problem-solution genre unit for intermediate students. Problem-solution is a powerful genre for students to practice because it involves elements of both persuasive and narrative writing. There are many activities students can do in order to build their knowledge of both persuasive and narrative techniques used by writers. Students must be exposed to the features of this type of writing many times in order to replicate these features in their own writing.

The following sections describe ways to both develop student knowledge of the problem-solution genre *and* provide opportunities for valuable listening, speaking, reading, and writing practice. The learning process is one of guided discovery using inductive learning as a key component. While students demonstrate this learning by producing a problem-solution essay at the end of the unit, you will also see that students can practice other types of writing, including responses to on-demand writing prompts. This unit takes six to eight weeks, depending upon the level of the class and whether the students take the class for one or two periods.

STUDENT CONNECTIONS AND PRIOR KNOWLEDGE

When you are starting any unit of study, it is critical to make connections to students' lives and to help students make connections to what they already know about the topic.

Research has shown that activating prior knowledge is a crucial step in the learning process: "it is the proper entry point for instruction, which should build on what is already known, and a major factor in comprehension—that is, making sense of our learning experiences."[5]

There are many ways to activate prior knowledge: students may draw, write, or talk in response to a question or series of questions relating to the unit topic. The key is to validate what students know and what they have experienced so they are able to make new connections and new learnings, and so they can see the relevance of a unit of study to their own lives.

Exhibit 6.3 shows a quick-write called Problems All Around for use at the beginning of the problem-solution unit. Students are asked to think about a problem in their lives (at school, at home, or with friends) and a problem in the community or in the world. Then students are asked to sketch each problem, write a few sentences about each problem, and then share with a partner. This activity

EXHIBIT 6.3. Problems All Around Quick-Write

Think about a problem in your life (at home, at school, or with friends, for example). Quickly sketch the problem below:

Now write a few sentences describing this problem:

Think about a problem in your community or in the world. Quickly sketch the problem below:

Now write a few sentences describing this problem:

helps students see the connections between the problem-solution unit and their daily lives. This type of quick-write can be used at the beginning of any genre unit. For example, with a unit on persuasive writing, students can respond to a prompt like "Write about a time when you wanted something or wanted someone to do something. How did you convince that person to do what you wanted?"

The section on critical pedagogy in Chapter Three describes another powerful activity that challenges students to think critically about problems and make connections to their experiences and beliefs.

At the beginning of the year, students can quickly demonstrate what they've learned about writing essays by responding to the prompt "Write down anything you know about writing essays" or "What do you think of when you see or hear the word *essay*?" We are not looking for a formula. Instead, this can be an opportunity for you to validate what students have already learned and for both teacher and students to discover areas that need to be further explored.

BUILDING BACKGROUND KNOWLEDGE AND ACADEMIC LANGUAGE

Along with students making connections to their own lives, it is important for them to begin building the academic language related to the problem-solution genre. Students need to learn the key words associated with writing about problems and presenting solutions. Following are strategies that can be used to develop student knowledge of the topic, as well as the academic language necessary to talk and write about problems and solutions:

- *Reading the prompt.* Exhibit 6.4 shows the prompt we give our students for this unit. We teach our students how to carefully read and "attack" a prompt. The first step is to read it carefully and underline any key words or phrases, especially words that are telling them to do something. Then we have students number the specific tasks (what they must do first, second, third, and so on). We also have them draw a box for each number that they can use as a graphic organizer to list ideas and words. Sometimes, with more complicated prompts, we have students rewrite the key tasks in their own words. For more on this process, see the Using Text to Generate Analytical Writing Lesson Plan later in this chapter.

- *Word chart.* At the beginning of the unit, students are given a Problem-Solution Word Chart (see Exhibit 6.5; also see Exhibits 6.6 and 6.7 for word charts for other genres). Students can access this chart on a daily basis as a tool for writing and speaking. The word charts serve as a key way to reinforce the features of the problem-solution genre—describing a problem, stating the causes and effects of the problem, proposing realistic solutions to the problem, evaluating both the benefits and potential problems of each solution, formulating counterarguments to anticipate the arguments against a solution, and identifying the best solution and presenting reasons why it is the best.

- *Read-alouds and think-alouds.* Finding texts to make into read-alouds or think-alouds is fairly easy in a problem-solution unit. One can find numerous articles about current problems. Some articles may need to be simplified to fit the language proficiency level of students. There are also many stories about problems and solutions. The book *I Felt Like I Was from Another Planet: Writing from Personal Experience* by Norine Dresser contains fifteen multicultural student-written stories about issues of immigration, assimilation, and cultural differences.[6] Each one is accompanied by preteaching ideas and follow-up writing activities. A story from this anthology is used in the Using Text to Generate Analytical Writing Lesson Plan later in this chapter.

- *Clozes.* A text about a problem can be turned into a cloze and then be used as a read-aloud or think-aloud (see Exhibit 6.8).

- *Text data sets.* Text data sets can be used for different reasons within the unit. If the class is focusing on a particular problem (such as gangs, smoking, or obesity), students can learn new information about the problem while practicing their reading and thinking skills. Students can also practice identifying the different features of a problem-solution essay by doing a data set (see Exhibit 6.9). The Inductive Lesson Plan later in this chapter explains how to use this type of text data set.

EXHIBIT 6.4. Problem-Solution Writing Prompt

We all experience problems that make us feel frustrated. Sometimes we face problems at home, at school, or in our communities.

Choose a problem you see at home, at your school, or in your community and describe it. Think about and explain the causes of the problem. Describe the effects of this problem. Propose several solutions to this problem. Analyze the pros and cons of each solution. Choose the solution you feel is the best and explain why you feel it is the best.

EXHIBIT 6.5. Problem-Solution Word Chart

Word	Meaning	Related Words	Picture
problem			
solution			
fact			
opinion			
cause			
effect			
convince			
opposing argument			
counterargument			

EXHIBIT 6.6. Autobiographical Incident Word Chart

Word	Meaning	Related Words	Picture
autobiographical			
incident			
hook			
context			
dialogue			
sensory details			
interior monologue			
significance			
narrative			

EXHIBIT 6.7. Response-to-Literature Word Chart

Word	Meaning	Related Words	Picture
plot			
character			
setting			
imagery			
figurative language			
historical context			
theme			
symbol			
tone			

EXHIBIT 6.8. Problem-Solution Cloze

One of the biggest health problems in our country is obesity. Many adults, teenagers, and even _____ are overweight and experience many negative health effects as a result.

There are many causes of obesity. Some people are more likely to gain _____ than others because their bodies don't burn calories as quickly. This is sometimes called a "slow metabolism." Other people become overweight because they eat for emotional reasons. For example, some people turn to food as a comfort when they are _____ sad, mad, or anxious. Many people are overweight due to unhealthy food choices and a lack of exercise. Today people eat _____ fast food and other "junk" foods, which are high in fat and calories, and then they do not burn off these calories through exercise and an active lifestyle.

Obesity can lead to many health effects. Being overweight increases the risk of developing diabetes, heart disease, high blood pressure, and many other serious health conditions. Obesity can also affect a person's overall health and well-being. For example, it _____ affect energy levels, sleep, and self-esteem.

While obesity is a major problem in our society, there are steps we can all take in order to _____ it. Making an effort to get more exercise each day can help. Even simple things like taking the stairs or walking to school can have a positive effect. Cutting down on fast food and sugary drinks is _____ way to lead a healthier lifestyle. Learning about the causes and effects of obesity and sharing this information with others are big steps toward solving this problem.

Source: Adapted from Mary L. Gavin, "Review of 'When Being Overweight Is a Health Problem,'" 2010. Retrieved from http://kidshealth.org.

Completed Problem-Solution Cloze

Note: This portion of the exhibit should not be reproduced for student use.

One of the biggest health problems in our country is obesity. Many adults, teenagers, and even **children** are overweight and experience many negative health effects as a result.

There are many causes of obesity. Some people are more likely to gain **weight** than others because their bodies don't burn calories as quickly. This is sometimes called a "slow metabolism." Other people become overweight because they eat for emotional reasons. For example, some people turn to food as a comfort when they are **feeling** sad, mad, or anxious. Many people are overweight due to unhealthy food choices, larger portion sizes, and a lack of exercise. Today people eat **more** fast food and other "junk" foods, which are high in fat and calories, and they then do not burn off these calories through exercise and an active lifestyle.

Obesity can lead to many health effects. Being overweight increases the risk of developing diabetes, heart disease, high blood pressure, and many other serious health conditions. Obesity can also affect a person's overall health and well-being. For example, it **can** affect energy levels, sleep, and self-esteem.

While obesity is a major problem in our society, there are steps we can all take in order to **solve** it. Making an effort to get more exercise each day can help. Even simple things like taking the stairs or walking to school can have a positive effect. Cutting down on fast food and sugary drinks is **another** way to lead a healthier lifestyle. Learning about the causes and effects of obesity and sharing this information with others are big steps toward solving this problem.

Source: Adapted from "When Being Overweight Is a Health Problem," reviewed by Mary L. Gavin, 2010. Retrieved from http://kidshealth.org.

EXHIBIT 6.9. Problem-Solution Features Data Set

Categories: Hooks, Thesis, Causes, Effects, Solutions

1. Childhood obesity is a widespread problem that needs to be addressed immediately.

2. One of the main causes of childhood obesity is lack of healthy food choices.

3. When I've taken students on field trips, I've been amazed at all the junk food they eat. I once saw a student who ate three whole bags of potato chips in one hour.

4. A real solution to the growing problem of childhood obesity is to motivate students to exercise and to eat healthy by participating in contests at school.

5. Another cause of childhood obesity is that children don't spend enough time outdoors getting exercise.

6. Another solution to childhood obesity is to only allow fresh, healthy foods at school.

7. Imagine if schools only served fresh fruits and vegetables and other healthy foods to students. What would be the effect? Would the problem of childhood obesity be reduced?

8. In my opinion, childhood obesity is a growing problem that must be stopped.

9. My friend Juan eats fast food every day on his way to school, and when he goes home he drinks a soda and eats a bag of Cheetos. He is always complaining that he is tired and doesn't feel like doing anything. Do you know anyone like this?

10. Childhood obesity can affect how children perform in school. If they are eating unhealthy foods and are overweight, then they may have less energy for their schoolwork.

11. Have children stopped eating healthy foods? Does junk food really taste better than fresh fruit? Is it easier to buy junk food?

12. A big problem facing my community is childhood obesity, and something must be done.

13. Childhood obesity can result in devastating health effects like diabetes or heart disease.

14. I believe the biggest problem facing my community is childhood obesity.

15. Childhood obesity is also caused by parents who model unhealthy eating habits for their children.

16. In order to reduce childhood obesity rates, we must educate both children and parents about the dangerous effects of being obese.

17. One effect of being overweight as a child is low self-esteem.

Categorized Hooks, Thesis, Causes, Effects, Solutions

Note: This portion of the exhibit should not be reproduced for student use.

Hooks

3. When I've taken students on field trips, I've been amazed at all the junk food they eat. I once saw a student who ate three whole bags of potato chips in one hour.

7. Imagine if schools only served fresh fruits and vegetables and other healthy foods to students. What would be the effect? Would the problem of childhood obesity be reduced?

9. My friend Juan eats fast food every day on his way to school, and when he goes home he drinks a soda and eats a bag of Cheetos. He is always complaining that he is tired and doesn't feel like doing anything. Do you know someone like this?

11. Have children stopped eating healthy foods? Does junk food really taste better than fresh fruit? Is it easier to buy junk food?

Thesis

8. In my opinion, childhood obesity is a growing problem that must be stopped.

1. Childhood obesity is a widespread problem that needs to be addressed immediately.

12. A big problem facing my community is childhood obesity, and something must be done.

13. I believe the biggest problem facing my community is childhood obesity.

Causes

2. One of the main causes of childhood obesity is lack of healthy food choices.

5. Another cause of childhood obesity is that children don't spend enough time outdoors getting exercise.

15. Childhood obesity is also caused by parents who model unhealthy eating habits for their children.

Effects

13. Childhood obesity can result in devastating health effects like diabetes or heart disease.

17. One effect of being overweight as a child is low self-esteem.

10. Childhood obesity can affect how children perform in school. If they are eating unhealthy foods and are overweight, then they may have less energy for their schoolwork.

Solutions

16. In order to reduce childhood obesity rates, we must educate both children and parents about the dangerous effects of being obese.

6. Another solution to childhood obesity is to only allow fresh, healthy foods at school.

4. A real solution to the growing problem of childhood obesity is to motivate students to exercise and to eat healthy by participating in contests at school.

- *Mimic writing.* Students can examine multiple examples of certain writing features through strategies like concept attainment, text data sets, and teacher modeling. Then students can mimic these writing features by creating their own examples. For example, students can examine several Yes and No examples of topic sentences and identify the features of a good topic sentence. Then students can write their own topic sentences and evaluate them according to these features. See Exhibit 6.10 for a data set that can be used to teach effective openers or "hooks" through the mimic writing process.

- *Minithemes and practice essays.* Within a larger problem-solution unit, various minithemes based on problems chosen by the teacher, or preferably by students, can be explored using many of the strategies in this sample unit plan. For example, we have focused on problems like smoking, gangs, obesity, immigration laws, and many other current issues within the larger problem-solution unit. After students have been exposed to enough text and information on one of these minithemes, they can write a practice problem-solution essay on that theme. It can work well for the class to do one together first, with the teacher modeling some sentence frames. Students can do a few of these practice essays before doing their final problem-solution essay on a topic of their choice.

- *Dialogues.* Students need a lot of practice with the academic vocabulary required for a problem-solution essay. They need to see it, write it, and *say* it! Students can write dialogues depicting various problems and solutions (see Exhibit 6.11).

- *Research.* Students can choose a problem that they would like to write about for their final problem-solution essay. The topic can be a problem in their lives, at their school, or in the larger community or world. The teacher can lead students in a brainstorming process to select their topic using criteria such as "Is it interesting to you? Would it have an impact on others?" Part of their research can involve interviewing students, family, and teachers (see Exhibit 6.12). This activity allows students to practice their interviewing and speaking skills while also collecting more ideas for their writing.

- Students can also spend time in the computer lab researching their problem. They can use a simple graphic organizer divided into sections for notes on causes, effects and solutions to their problem. This tool helps them categorize the information, allows them to keep all their research in one spot, and provides a graphic organizer for their use while drafting the essay.

EXHIBIT 6.10. Types of Hooks Data Set

Categories: Critical Thinking Questions, Anecdotes and Observations, Interesting Facts and Statistics

1. Imagine if schools only served fresh fruits and vegetables and other healthy foods to students. What would be the effect? Would the problem of childhood obesity be reduced?

2. Last year, over twenty thousand high school students in California passed all required classes, but didn't receive a diploma because they didn't pass the High School Exit Exam.

3. There is a problem I see every day in my neighborhood. It affects the old, the young, and teenagers. When someone you live with smokes, then there is no way to escape the effects of second-hand smoke.

4. How would you feel if you worked for years to get something and then didn't get it because you couldn't pass a two-hour test?

5. My aunt was diagnosed with lung cancer in 2009. Did she smoke a pack a day? No. Did she smoke earlier in her life and then quit? No. Did she live with my uncle who has smoked for the last thirty years? Yes.

6. Almost 20 percent of children and adolescents in the United States are overweight, and 70 percent of diabetes risk in the United States can be attributed to excess weight.

7. My friend Chan never missed a day of school in all four years he was in high school. He received a 3.5 grade point average. He took zero- and seventh-period classes every day. However, because he didn't pass the English part of the High School Exit Exam, he didn't receive a high school diploma.

8. Have children stopped eating healthy foods? Does junk food really taste better than fresh fruit? Is it easier to buy junk food?

9. Second-hand smoke kills tens of thousands of people every year in the United States and causes life-threatening illnesses for thousands more.

10. My friend Juan eats fast food every day on his way to school, and when he goes home he drinks a soda and eats a bag of Cheetos. He is always complaining that he is tired and doesn't feel like doing anything.

11. Imagine being told you are dying of lung cancer when you've never even smoked a cigarette before. Is that even possible? How would you react? Unfortunately, this situation can happen to nonsmokers who have been exposed to second-hand smoke.

12. Childhood obesity has more than tripled in the past thirty years, and the percentage of obese adolescents aged twelve to nineteen years increased from 5 percent to 18 percent over the same period.

Critical Thinking Questions

Note: This portion of the exhibit should not be reproduced for student use.

1. Imagine if schools only served fresh fruits and vegetables and other healthy foods to students. What would be the effect? Would the problem of childhood obesity be reduced?

4. How would you feel if you worked for years to get something and then didn't get it because you couldn't pass a two-hour test?

8. Have children stopped eating healthy foods? Does junk food really taste better than fresh fruit? Is it easier to buy junk food?

11. Imagine being told you are dying of lung cancer when you've never even smoked a cigarette before. Is that even possible? How would you react? Unfortunately, this situation can happen to nonsmokers who have been exposed to second-hand smoke.

Anecdotes and Observations

3. There is a problem I see every day in my neighborhood. It affects the old, the young, and teenagers. When someone you live with smokes, then there is no way to escape the effects of second-hand smoke.

5. My aunt was diagnosed with lung cancer in 2009. Did she smoke a pack a day? No. Did she smoke earlier in her life and then quit? No. Did she live with my uncle who has smoked for the last thirty years? Yes.

7. My friend Chan never missed a day of school in all four years he was in high school. He received a 3.5 grade point average. He took zero- and seventh-period classes every day. However, because he didn't pass the English part of the High School Exit Exam, he didn't receive a high school diploma.

10. My friend Juan eats fast food every day on his way to school, and when he goes home he drinks a soda and eats a bag of Cheetos. He is always complaining that he is tired and doesn't feel like doing anything.

Interesting Facts and Statistics

2. Last year, over twenty thousand high school students in California passed all required classes, but didn't receive a diploma because they didn't pass the High School Exit Exam.

6. Almost 20 percent of children and adolescents in the United States are overweight, and 70 percent of diabetes risk in the United States can be attributed to excess weight.

9. Second-hand smoke kills tens of thousands of people every year in the United States and causes life-threatening illnesses to thousands more.

12. Childhood obesity has more than tripled in the past thirty years, and the percentage of obese adolescents aged twelve to nineteen years increased from 5 percent to 18 percent over the same period.

EXHIBIT 6.11. Problem Dialogue

Student 1: I hate going to the bathrooms at school. They are so dirty!

Student 2: I know—the floors are disgusting and the sinks look like they haven't been cleaned in a long time.

Student 1: The soap dispenser is empty, and there aren't any paper towels.

Student 2: How are we supposed to wash our hands and stop the spread of germs if we don't have any soap?

Student 1: What can we do about it? Should we tell our teacher?

Student 2: I think we should talk to our teacher and the principal. This is a big problem and we need help.

Student 1: You're right. We have to do something if we want to make a change.

Student 2: Come on—let's go talk to the teacher.

Student 1: Okay, maybe she can tell us how to meet with the principal.

Student 2: Good idea! Let's go!

EXHIBIT 6.12. Problem-Solution Interview

My name _____

Your assignment is to ask two students, one adult who works at Luther Burbank, and one family member, the following questions about the problem you have chosen as the topic of your problem-solution essay. You will write their answers in the space below the questions.

Name of student interviewed: _____

What do you think are the causes of _____?

_____

_____

What do you think are the consequences (effects) of _____?

_____

_____

What do you think are possible solutions to this problem?

_____

_____

_____

Name of student interviewed: _____

What do you think are the causes of _____?

_____

_____

_____

What do you think are the consequences (effects) of _____?

_____

_____

_____

What do you think are possible solutions to this problem?

_____

_____

_____

Name of staff member: _____

What do you think are the causes of _____?

_____

What do you think are the consequences (effects) of _____?

_____

_____

What do you think are possible solutions to this problem?

_____

_____

_____

Name of family member: _____

What do you think are the causes of _____?

_____

_____

What do you think are the consequences (effects) of _____?

_____

_____

What do you think are possible solutions to this problem?

_____

_____

_____

Tech Tool

Search Engines for English Language Learners

Doing research online can be especially challenging for ELL students as they try to navigate through all the clutter of search engine results. Following are a few search engines that we have found particularly accessible for English language learners:

Qwiki. Qwiki is a search engine that combines images and text in the search results. The text is not only very accessible, but audio support for it is also provided. (http://www.qwiki.com)

Quintura. Quintura is a search engine that provides search results in a visual "cloud." (http://www.quintura.com)

Carrot Search Engine. The Carrot search engine returns search results divided into themes. (http://search.carrot2.org/stable/search)

- *Sample essays.* It is important for students to see several models of problem-solution essays. These samples can be generated by the teacher or be student examples from previous years. If you don't have student samples, many examples can be found online (see the upcoming Tech Tool on online writing resources). Students can read the sample essays and identify features of problem-solution writing. This process is explained in the Inductive Lesson Plan later in this chapter.

SCAFFOLDING THE WRITING PROCESS

In the activities on building background knowledge, students did a variety of reading, thinking, speaking, and writing about problems and solutions. They also learned and practiced the academic language needed for a problem-solution essay. They are now ready to begin the process of drafting their essay.

- *Frames or outlines.* Before students begin the drafting process, the students can consult all of the activities in their problem-solution folder (including the problem-solution writing prompt) and use this prewriting to complete an outline of their essay. Depending upon the range of language levels within a class, the teacher can decide whether some students need the additional support of sentence frames to help structure their outlines. For example, the teacher and students can develop topic sentences together, or the teacher can give students several examples of transition words. The outline can lay out a paragraph structure for students to follow (see Exhibit 6.13). For higher-level classes, the teacher can remove some of the scaffolds within the outline.

EXHIBIT 6.13. Problem-Solution Outline

Use this outline to organize your thinking before writing your essay. You don't need to write complete sentences. Instead, write *key words* and *ideas* that will help you as you begin to draft your essay.

Introduction

Hook:

_____

_____

The problem/my thesis:

_____

_____

Causes of problem:

_____

_____

Effects of problem:

_____

_____

So what? (What are the consequences if the problem isn't solved?)

_____

_____

Body Paragraph 1

Solution:

_____

_____

How it will work:

_____

_____

Pros:

_____

_____

Cons:

_____

_____

Counterargument(s) to address cons:

_____

_____

Body Paragraph 2

Solution: _____

How it will work: _____

_____

_____

Pros: _____

_____

_____

Cons: _____

_____

_____

Counterargument(s) to address cons:

_____

_____

Conclusion

Restate problem and its consequences:

_____

Best solution: _____

_____

Reasons why it is best:

_____

_____

_____

- *Oral outlining.* Having students do an oral outline of their essay can also be an effective way to reinforce the essay structure. Students can explain aloud step-by-step how they will write their essay: "In my introduction, I will start with a hook, then I will introduce the problem, and then I will write my thesis statement." The teacher can provide students with a cloze to complete (see next example) or ask students to write out the steps on their own. Then students can practice reciting their oral outline aloud with a partner or can record it online using a site such as Fotobabble and then post it to a class blog.

- Here is an example of a cloze our students completed before writing their problem-solution drafts:

  Tomorrow, I will begin writing my problem-_____ essay. I will start my essay with a _____. Then I will describe the _____ of the problem and the effects of the _____. In each of my body paragraphs, I will present a _____ to the problem and will explain how it will work. Then I will describe the pros and _____ of each solution. In my conclusion, I will restate the _____ and explain which solution is the _____. I will give specific _____ to support why I believe it is the best solution.

- *Revising and editing.* Once students have produced a draft, it is important that they receive immediate feedback in order to make revisions. Research shows that the quality of student work increases when students are expecting to receive "rapid" feedback from the teacher—a teacher's verbal or written response shortly after the work or test is completed.[7] This can be done effectively by circulating around the room as students are drafting and offering verbal feedback. Conferencing one-on-one with students after they have finished a draft is also a good way to give both verbal and written feedback. To make the process go more smoothly, it is important for all students to be engaged in an activity while the teacher is conferencing with individual students. One activity could be having students exchange papers and complete a Problem-Solution Peer Checklist (see Exhibit 6.14). Having students identify one or two parts of the draft they want the teacher to help them with can make these conferences more effective.

- Error correction is best addressed through concept attainment and games—activities that teach students grammar in context and without a red pen! See Chapter Three for a description of using concept attainment for error correction. Chapter Eleven also shares examples of error correction exercises. Chapter Twelve describes other error correction strategies and the research behind them.

EXHIBIT 6.14. Problem-Solution Peer Checklist

My name: _____ **My partner's name:** _____

1. Is there a **hook** at the beginning of the essay?
Yes   No
What kind of **hook** is it?

2. Does the writer state the problem and his or her thesis?
Yes   No

3. Does the writer explain the **causes** of the problem?
Yes   No
Copy the **causes** here:

4. Does the writer explain the **effects** of the problem?
Yes   No
Copy the **effects** here:

5. Does the writer propose **two solutions** to the problem?
Yes   No
Copy each **solution** here:

    1.

    2.

Is there a separate **body paragraph** for each solution?
Yes   No
Does each paragraph have a **clear topic sentence**?
Yes   No
(Highlight each topic sentence.)
Does the writer explain how the **solution** will work?
Yes   No

6. Is there a **conclusion** where the problem is restated?
Yes   No
Does the writer explain which solution is **best** and give reasons **why**?
Yes   No

7. Did your partner read his or her essay **aloud** to you in order to catch errors?
Yes   No

- *Publishing or presenting.* As mentioned earlier in chapter five, "speed dating" is a way for students to share their work. When sharing an essay, students can read their whole essay or just choose specific parts. Another way to share their final products is to post them online. This can be done on an individual class blog or through creating a sister class relationship where students from different schools post their work on a shared blog and can read and comment on each other's writing. Students can also share their writing with peers the old-fashioned way by exchanging essays with another class and writing comments on sticky notes.

- Writing for an authentic audience of their peers is motivating for most students. As educator Anne Rodier powerfully states, "Students have to believe that what they have to say is important enough to bother writing. They have to experience writing for real audiences before they will know that writing can bring them power."[8]

Tech Tool
Online Writing Resources

A variety of activities available online reinforce the thinking and language required for problem-solution writing and many other genres of writing. Plenty of these activities allow students to write for an authentic audience, thus increasing student motivation. For a list of the best sites containing these online reinforcement activities and sites where students can write for an authentic audience, see "The Best Websites for K–12 Writing Instruction Reinforcement" at http://larryferlazzo .edublogs.org.

- *Assessment.* If they wish, teachers can create a rubric appropriate for their classroom situation. For a more detailed discussion of using rubrics and other forms of assessments with student writing, see Chapter Thirteen.

- *Action projects.* The problem-solution unit provides students with the opportunity to extend their writing into action projects. For example, one of our ESL classes was studying the issue of getting a good job and the problems involved with this pursuit. The class decided to take action by organizing a meeting focused on job training opportunities. They organized, planned, and led a multilingual meeting of area job training providers that was attended by 150 parents and students![9]

Tech Tool
Online Rubrics

There are many free online sites where teachers can find premade rubrics or create their own. A few we have found helpful are:

Kathy Shrock's Assessment Rubrics. This site contains hundreds of rubric resources that include sample rubrics in various subject areas, research, and tools for creating rubrics. (http://school.discoveryeducation.com/schrockguide/assess.html)

Rubistar. Rubistar is a site where teachers can find or create their own rubrics. (http://rubistar.4teachers.org)

R Campus. This site features a rubric gallery with thousands of free rubrics available. (http://www.rcampus.com)

- *On-demand writing practice.* The above activities are designed to support students as they move through the writing process over the course of several weeks. However, English language learners also need practice with on-demand writing assessments (writing to a prompt in a timed situation). See the lesson plan on Using Text to Generate Analytical Writing at the end of this chapter for ways to help students practice this type of writing and thinking. A list of these key elements of a writing genre unit appears in Exhibit 6.15.

EXHIBIT 6.15. Key Elements of a Writing Genre Unit

Student Connections and Prior Knowledge

Drawing
Talking
Writing

Building Background Knowledge and Academic Language

Word charts
Read-alouds and think-alouds

Clozes

Text data sets

Mimic writing

Minithemes or practice essays

Dialogues

Research

Sample essays or teacher models

Scaffolding the Writing Process

Frames or outlines

Oral outlines

Revising and editing

Publishing or presenting

Assessing

Extensions

Action projects

On-demand writing practice

A Sample Week in a Two-Period Intermediate ESL Class

This schedule is designed to provide a snapshot of a week in an effective intermediate level class where reading, writing, speaking, and listening are incorporated into challenging and engaging lessons. This schedule is not designed as a scripted curriculum and can be adapted in numerous ways.

MONDAY

1. **Reading and writing.** Students enter classroom and immediately begin reading a book of their choice quietly. (twenty minutes)

2. **Reading and writing and listening and speaking.** Students respond to their reading by completing a reading log. Students share what they wrote in their reading log with a partner. (five minutes)

3. **Shortened critical pedagogy lesson.** See Chapter Three for an example. (thirty minutes)

4. Reading and writing and listening and speaking. Teacher distributes a word chart for the problem-solution unit to students. Teacher reads each word aloud. Then students take a few minutes to write down the meanings of any words they might already know and share them with partners. Teacher begins a discussion of each word by asking students what they think it means and why: Where have they heard or seen this word before? Teacher guides students toward a correct definition of each word and writes on a copy of the word chart on the overhead or document camera. For each word, the teacher models a gesture or body movement, and students practice it. Students can participate in developing gestures by working in pairs to come up with ideas. After all the words are defined and have an accompanying gesture, students "quiz" each other and the teacher takes volunteers to demonstrate for the class. (forty minutes)

5. Reading and writing or listening and speaking. Game to review problem-solution words (see Chapter Eleven). (twenty minutes)

6. Reading and writing. Reflection activity. (five minutes)

TUESDAY

1. Reading and writing. Students enter classroom and immediately begin reading a book of their choice quietly. (fifteen minutes)

2. Reading and writing. Students work on Four Words homework sheet (see Exhibit 4.1). (five minutes)

3. Reading and writing. Teacher distributes a K-W-L chart and tells students they will be studying the problem of cigarette smoking in depth this week and then writing a practice problem-solution essay on the topic. Students fill in the K section, what they already know about smoking, and then the W section, listing questions of what they want to learn. Students share with each other and as a class. (twenty minutes)

4. Listening and speaking and reading and writing. Teacher conducts a read-aloud using a piece of text about smoking. Students have a copy of the text in front of them and follow along as the teacher reads with prosody. The teacher posts a question related to the read-aloud and students write their responses. Students share their responses with each other. Students add new learnings to the L section of their K-W-L chart. (thirty minutes)

5. Listening and speaking. Teacher passes out a dialogue (a conversation between two friends about smoking) and reads it aloud. Teacher quickly models reading in a monotone voice and then reads again, but this time with feeling. Teacher asks students which way is better and why. In pairs, students take turns performing the dialogue with prosody in preparation for recording themselves. (twenty minutes)

6. **Listening and speaking**. Students go to the computer lab and use Fotobabble to record their dialogues. (thirty minutes)

WEDNESDAY

1. **Reading and writing.** Students enter classroom and immediately begin reading a book of their choice quietly. (twenty minutes)

2. **Reading and writing and listening and speaking.** Students respond to their reading by completing a reading log. Students share what they wrote in their reading log with a partner. (five minutes)

3. **Listening and speaking**. Teacher uses speakers to play the Fotobabble recordings online and projects the web page onto the screen by using an LCD projector. Students listen to the dialogues they recorded the previous day. Teacher elicits student comments on good examples of reading with expression and clear pronunciation. (five minutes)

4. **Reading and writing.** Teacher distributes a cloze passage on smoking and reads it aloud to students. Then students work to complete the cloze on their own. Teacher asks students to share their guesses and clues for each blank and writes down all the possible answers on a copy of the cloze displayed on the overhead or document camera. Teacher and students go back through and discuss which word fits best in each blank and why (identifying the context clues). Students will have circled the clue words they used to make each guess. The teacher posts written directions for students to select one of their guesses and to explain their thinking behind that guess ("I chose the word _____ because _____."). (thirty minutes)

5. **Listening and speaking**. Students quickly practice saying the words and doing the gestures they learned on Monday for the problem-solution words. Students spend a few minutes "quizzing" each other (one student calls out a word and the other student says the meaning and does the gesture). (five minutes)

6. **Reading and writing.** Teacher distributes a text data set on cigarette smoking. The teacher reads the first three examples and models highlighting key words and using a reading strategy (asking a question, making a connection, or summarizing, for example). Students take turns reading the rest of the data set with a partner, stopping every three examples to compare their highlighting. Teacher specifies that students must demonstrate three reading strategies on each page. (forty minutes)

7. **Reading and writing or listening and speaking**. Game (see Chapter Eleven). (fifteen minutes)

8. **Reading and writing.** Reflection activity. (five minutes)

THURSDAY

   1. Reading and writing. Students enter classroom and immediately begin reading a book of their choice quietly. (fifteen minutes)

   2. Listening and speaking and reading and writing. Students respond to their reading by preparing a Book Talk (see Exhibit 5.4) to share with a classmate the following day. Students write down what they will say and then practice giving their Book Talk. (ten minutes)

   3. Reading and writing. Students take out the Smoking Data Set from the previous day and review their highlighting and annotations. Students begin to organize the data set into categories (such as health effects, quitting, cost) on a sheet of paper, writing the title of the category and the numbers that go in that category underneath. The teacher may give the categories to students, or students can be challenged to come up with them on their own. As students place each example in a category, they circle any clue words that make them believe it fits in that category. Students can work individually at first and then check their work with a partner. (thirty minutes)

   4. Reading and writing. Students take their category sheets to the computer lab and search for new information. Students add two to three new facts to each category. (thirty minutes)

   5. Listening and speaking. Students come back to class and share their new information with a partner. (five minutes)

   6. Reading and writing. Students add new information to their K-W-L charts. The teacher gives them a few minutes to review the category they find most interesting. Then students put away their notes and write a paragraph about that category with a topic sentence and supporting details. The teacher should model this process by first reviewing the information in one category. The teacher should then create a topic sentence for that category and select key facts to rewrite in his or her own words for supporting sentences. Teacher circulates and checks for understanding while students are writing their own paragraphs. (thirty minutes)

FRIDAY

   1. Reading and writing. Students enter classroom and immediately begin reading a book of their choice quietly. (twenty minutes)

   2. Listening and speaking. Students take out their Book Talk notes and share with a partner. The teacher takes a volunteer to do his or her Book Talk for the whole class. (fifteen minutes)

   3. Reading and writing and listening and speaking. Students have time to work on their weekly journal to reflect on the week, sharing two or three positive events that occurred that week and one event that was not necessarily positive and what they could have done differently to improve the outcome. Students share what they wrote with a partner, and the partner should ask at least one question. (twenty minutes)

4. Reading and writing or listening and speaking. Game to quiz students on problem-solution words and gestures (see Chapter Eleven). (twenty minutes)

5. Reading and writing or listening and speaking. Students go to the computer lab and visit interactive sites on problem-solution writing and vocabulary. (forty minutes)

6. Reading and writing. Reflection activity. (five minutes)

Inductive Lesson Plan

This lesson is used during a unit on problem-solution writing after students have done a number of activities to build knowledge and vocabulary related to this genre. See the sample problem-solution unit earlier in this chapter for the sequence of activities students would do before the lesson and afterwards.

INSTRUCTIONAL OBJECTIVES

Students will:

1. Read text and demonstrate use of reading strategies.
2. Identify different features of a problem-solution essay through categorization.
3. Apply knowledge of features of an essay by labeling them on a sample essay.

DURATION

Three 120-minute class sessions or six sixty-minute class sessions.

ENGLISH LANGUAGE DEVELOPMENT STANDARDS: CALIFORNIA ENGLISH LANGUAGE DEVELOPMENT DOMAINS

1. Students use English for everyday communication in socially and culturally appropriate ways and apply listening and speaking skills and strategies in the classroom.
2. Students apply word analysis skills and knowledge of vocabulary to read fluently.

3. Students will read and understand a range of challenging narrative and expository text materials.

5. Students will write well-organized, clear, and coherent text in a variety of academic genres.

MATERIALS

1. Copies of Obesity Read-Aloud (Exhibit 6.16) for students and teacher.

2. Copies of Problem-Solution Features Data Set (Exhibit 6.9) for students and teacher.

3. Copies of Problem-Solution Sample Essay (Exhibit 6.17) for students and teacher.

PROCEDURE

First Day

1. Teacher writes "Problem-Solution Essay" on the board and asks students to quickly brainstorm everything they have learned so far about problem-solution writing. Students list their ideas on a piece of paper and then share in pairs. Teacher facilitates a class discussion of what students have learned. The teacher then explains that students will be expanding upon this knowledge by reading a text data set that contains several important features of a problem-solution essay: hooks, thesis, causes, effects, and solutions. Students can use their Problem-Solution Word Charts (see Exhibit 6.5) to review the meanings of these words.

2. Teacher distributes a read-aloud on obesity (Exhibit 6.16). Teacher preteaches the word *obesity* in a sensitive way. Teacher conducts the read-aloud and posts the following prompt: "According to this article, what are the causes of obesity? What are the effects?" Students write their responses and then share with a partner.

3. Teacher explains that the data set is also on the topic of obesity, especially the problem of childhood obesity. Students will be doing this data set with two goals in mind: to learn new information about this topic, but more important, to identify the key features in a problem-solution essay. Teacher distributes the Problem-Solution Features Data Set (Exhibit 6.9) and models reading the first three examples, thinking aloud while highlighting key words (in this case, any problem or solution words) and writing questions and/or connections in the margin.

4. Teacher posts written directions for students to continue reading individually, to highlight any problem-solution words, and to write at least two more questions and make at least two more connections. Teacher circulates as students are working to check highlighting and to look for evidence of reading strategies. When finished, students share their highlighting and comments with a partner and add one new question from their partner's paper.

5. Teacher explains to students that next they will be putting the examples into categories. Students cut out all of the seventeen examples (being careful not to cut off the numbers) and spread the strips out on their desks. Depending on the class, the teacher may display the categories up front (Hooks, Thesis, Causes, Effects, and Solutions) or lead students in coming to some conclusions on their own by asking questions such as these: Are any of these examples similar? Why? Which examples would you group together? Why? What would you call that group? The teacher reads an example and models thinking aloud about why he or she thinks that example goes in a certain category and circles clue words.

6. Teacher posts written directions: "Put each example into a category and circle any clue words that make you think it belongs in that category." Students begin to group the examples into categories, working side-by-side with a partner. Teacher circulates and offers assistance and praises good thinking. The inductive process works best when *students* are doing the thinking, so it is important that the teacher remain neutral and not tell students where to put the examples. The teacher can respond to student questions with responses like, "Which category do *you* think it belongs in? What is your reasoning? Which category does that example *not* belong in? How can that help you figure this out?"

7. Once students have arranged the examples into categories on their desks, they compare their work with a partner. The teacher asks partners to share with the class which examples were difficult or placed in different categories. Teacher facilitates a class discussion about these examples and guides students to correct category placement by prompting them to do the thinking. Once all the examples are correctly placed, students make a category poster by writing the five category titles on a large piece of paper and then gluing or taping the examples underneath (see the student sample of a category poster in Figure 6.1).

Second Day

1. The teacher asks students to take out their category posters and review their categories from the previous day. Teacher explains that now that the data set

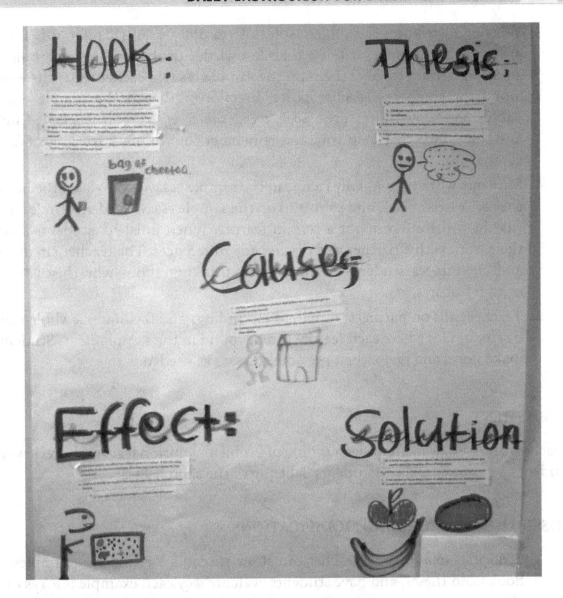

Figure 6.1. Student Sample of Category Poster for Data Set (Photo)

is categorized, students will examine the features, or characteristics, of each category. The teacher asks students questions like: "What do all the hooks have in common? How are all the causes similar?" Students work in pairs to make a list of common features underneath each category on their poster. Teacher explains that he or she will call on different pairs to share about one category.

2. Students take a few minutes to discuss their answers to the questions and then the teacher leads a whole-class conversation by calling on pairs to share what they talked about. Teacher records the features or characteristics of each category on the board, and students add any new ideas to their posters.

3. Teacher distributes a problem-solution sample essay (Exhibit 6.17) and explains that students will use their knowledge of the features of problem-solution writing to label them on the sample essay. Teacher reads the essay aloud for students. Teacher posts directions: "Reread the sample essay. Label the following features: *hook, thesis, causes, effects,* and *solutions*. Circle any clue words that help you, and remember the common features of each category."

4. Students work individually to reread the sample essay and to label the hook, thesis, causes, effects, and solutions on the sample essay. Students circle clues that help them figure out a certain feature. When finished, students share their work with a partner and discuss any differences. The teacher circulates and encourages students to share their thinking about why they labeled certain features.

5. Teacher calls on partners to share their findings and facilitates a whole-class discussion on where each feature can be found in the sample essay. Students make notes and revise their previous guesses as needed.

ASSESSMENT

Teacher can assess student understanding of problem-solution features by reviewing students' categories and the students' labeling of the sample essay.

POSSIBLE EXTENSIONS AND MODIFICATIONS

- *Concept attainment.* The teacher can show students Yes and No examples of hooks and theses, and have students evaluate *why* each example is a Yes or a No.

- *Mimic writing.* After examining the characteristics of each category, students can create their own examples for each category.

- *Jigsaw.* Students can be divided into groups and each group given a different sample problem-solution essay. Each group can label the features on their sample essay and then share with another group.

- *Synthesis.* Each group receives three different sample essays and creates a large chart, writing the five features—hook, thesis, causes, effects, and solutions—along the top and the three essay titles down the left-hand side. The group reads all three essays and identifies the different features by cutting them out and gluing them underneath the correct category on the large chart (see the student sample of synthesis in Figure 6.2).

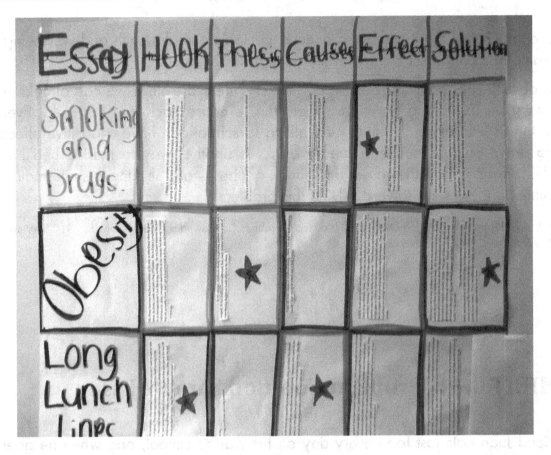

Figure 6.2. Student Sample of Synthesis Chart Poster (Photo)

EXHIBIT 6.16. Obesity Read-Aloud

One of the biggest health problems in our country is obesity. Many adults, teenagers, and even children are overweight and experience many negative health effects as a result.

There are many causes of obesity. Some people are more likely to gain weight than others because their bodies don't burn calories as quickly. This is sometimes called a "slow metabolism." Other people become overweight because they eat for emotional reasons. For example, some people turn to food as a comfort when they are feeling sad, mad, or anxious. Many people are overweight due to unhealthy food choices, larger portion sizes, and a lack of exercise. Today people eat more fast food and other "junk" foods, which are high in fat and calories, and then do not burn off these calories through exercise and an active lifestyle.

Obesity can lead to many health effects. Being overweight increases the risk of developing diabetes, heart disease, high blood pressure, and many other serious health conditions. Obesity can also affect a person's overall health and well-being. For example, it can affect energy levels, sleep, and self-esteem.

While obesity is a major problem in our society, there are steps we can all take in order to solve it. Making an effort to get more exercise each day can help. Even simple things like taking the stairs or walking to school can have a positive effect. Cutting down on fast food and sugary drinks is another way to lead a healthier lifestyle. Learning about the causes and effects of obesity and sharing this information with others are big steps toward solving this problem.

Source: Adapted from "When Being Overweight Is a Health Problem," reviewed by Mary L. Gavin, 2010. Retrieved from http://kidshealth.org.

EXHIBIT 6.17. Problem-Solution Sample Essay

My friend Juan eats fast food every day on his way to school, and when he goes home he drinks a soda and eats a bag of Cheetos. He is always complaining that he is tired and doesn't feel like doing anything. Do you know someone like this? Unfortunately, many teenagers and children in our country feel this way because they eat unhealthy food, don't get enough physical activity, and are becoming overweight. In my opinion, childhood obesity is a growing problem that must be stopped. If this problem is not addressed, then many children will be at risk of experiencing dangerous health effects in the future.

There are many causes of childhood obesity. Many kids don't have access to healthy food choices at school and in their homes. If their parents don't buy healthy foods and model unhealthy eating habits, then their children are more likely to eat unhealthy foods. Children also are less physically active because they spend time watching TV and playing video games. They don't burn as many calories when they are sitting on the couch. These factors can lead to unhealthy weight gain in children, which can have numerous health effects. Obese children are at a higher risk of developing diabetes and heart disease. They can also experience low energy levels, sleep problems, and emotional effects like low self-esteem.

While this is not an easy problem to fix, there are two solutions that can help address the problem of childhood obesity. My first solution involves education. Parents and children need to learn about the dangerous health effects of obesity and about how to maintain a healthy weight. This type of education should start in preschool and continue through high school. Schools could offer several workshops throughout the year for both parents and children in order to learn about healthy living choices. The main advantage of this solution is that it addresses the problem at its core and can have long-term effects if it is sustained over time. Some may argue that this solution would be too expensive for schools to implement. However, this initiative could be funded by government grants or even sponsored by health care agencies. This kind of education would even reduce health care costs in the future.

A second solution to the problem of childhood obesity is to ban junk foods from school campuses. If schools stopped selling unhealthy foods and drinks and provided fresh foods including fruits and vegetables, then many students would have access to a healthy breakfast and lunch five days a week. Over time this could really have an impact on the health of millions of children across the country. Children spend a lot of time at school and this would help them learn healthy eating habits for the future. Others may argue it is too difficult for schools to prepare and serve fresh foods. However, many schools already have gardens or land that could be turned into areas for growing fruits and vegetables. Students could participate in growing the food that is then served to them in the school cafeteria.

What is the best way to solve this growing problem of childhood obesity? I believe that educating parents and children is the best way to reduce the number of obese children and adults. This is the best solution because people can make better, healthier choices in their lives if they have access to information. Using schools to spread this information is the best way to reach millions of children and parents in our country. If we can address this problem with children now, we will see healthier, happier adults in our future.

Using Text to Generate Analytical Writing Lesson Plan

The following lesson plan uses the story "Monsy and Michelle" (see Exhibit 6.18) from the book *I Felt Like I Was from Another Planet: Writing from Personal Experience*, which contains a number of great stories for English learners. "Monsy and Michelle" engages students, spurs them to think more about problems and solutions, and challenges them to develop their analytical thinking and writing skills. While some of the activities described here are specifically tailored to this story, they can easily be adapted to work with other stories and be applied in multiple ways.

The style of the writing prompt in this lesson is based on the style of prompts used in the Analytical Writing Placement Examination (AWPE), the entry-level writing assessment that incoming University of California freshmen must take. Every AWPE assessment contains a piece of text and a multiple-step prompt that requires students to analyze the author's ideas and generate their own response supported by examples.

INSTRUCTIONAL OBJECTIVES

Students will:

1. Read a student-written story and demonstrate their understanding by completing a summarization chart.
2. Learn new vocabulary words.
3. Practice reading and dissecting an on-demand writing prompt.
4. Use the prompt to develop an outline and to write a draft.

DURATION

Two 120-minute class sessions or four sixty-minute class sessions.

ENGLISH LANGUAGE DEVELOPMENT STANDARDS: CALIFORNIA ENGLISH LANGUAGE DEVELOPMENT DOMAINS

2. Students apply word analysis skills and knowledge of vocabulary to read fluently.
3. Students will read and understand a range of challenging narrative and expository text materials.
5. Students will write well-organized, clear, and coherent text in a variety of academic genres.
6. Students will apply the conventions of standard English usage orally and in writing.

MATERIALS

1. Copies of the book *I Felt Like I Was from Another Planet: Writing from Personal Experience* by Norine Dresser (1994) or copies of the story "Monsy and Michelle" (Exhibit 6.18) for students and teacher.
2. Copies of prereading strategies (Exhibit 6.19) for students and teacher.
3. Copies of the summarization sheet (Exhibit 6.20) for students and teacher.
4. Copies of the writing prompt (Exhibit 6.21) for students and teacher.

EXHIBIT 6.18. Monsy and Michelle

I am Mexican American and my friends call me Monsy. In the seventh grade I met Michelle, an African American. From the beginning of that year, I had always felt scared of African Americans, so when I first saw Michelle in my history class I did not want to sit close to her. Many of the other students did not want to sit close to her either. The boys always made fun of her. They laughed at her because of the way she dressed, how she combed her hair, and because of her skin color. Although the teacher always told the class to be quiet when we laughed at jokes about Michelle, sometimes we got so carried away we made her cry.

At first I made fun of her too, but only because I didn't want other students to make fun of me. Since I have a brownish complexion, I thought they would probably make bad jokes about me, too. After two weeks I got tired and sad that some students still continued to make fun of her. The following week I began to sit next to her.

Michelle was surprised and smiled at me. Everyone in the class was shocked. They began making fun of me. They told me that I was dirty like her, that we were black because we didn't take showers. I felt very bad and I began to cry. I got so angry that one day I stood up in class and shouted at the other students. They all stood quiet. I told them that it wasn't fair to make fun of people because of their appearance and culture. In fact, Michelle was the smartest student in class. Michelle was so happy I stood up for her that we became very good friends.

Through this experience I learned that all people are the same no matter what they look like. I learned that because of the different cultures we have in this country we can learn many new things that help us have a more interesting life. By speaking out and proving to others what you are able to do, you can make a difference. Michelle and I found out that each human being is unique in appearance, but many feel the same inside. As a result of this experience I learned not to be scared of . . . those from different cultures.

Source: N. Dresser, *I Felt Like I Was from Another Planet: Writing from Personal Experience* (Boston: Addison Wesley, 1994). Pearson Education.

EXHIBIT 6.19. "Monsy and Michelle" Prereading Strategies

Talk with a partner and write anything you know about these words:

complexion:

appearance:

prejudice:

ethnicity:

Prereading Question

Have you or someone you know ever experienced prejudice because of your physical appearance, age, religion, or ethnicity? Explain what happened.

EXHIBIT 6.20. "Monsy and Michelle" Summarization Sheet

Work with a partner to complete this chart.

Problem:

Causes:

Effects:

Solutions:

EXHIBIT 6.21. "Monsy and Michelle" Writing Prompt

In the story "Monsy and Michelle," Monsy tells of her experience with prejudice and explains what she learned from this experience. In your essay, describe Monsy's views on prejudice. To what extent do you agree with Monsy's opinions? To develop your position, be sure to write specific examples from your own experiences, your observations of others, or any of your reading, including this story.

PROCEDURE

First Day

1. Teacher distributes the "Monsy and Michelle" prereading strategies (Exhibit 6.20). The teacher reads the new vocabulary words and gives students a few minutes to write down what they already know about them. They then share in pairs. Teacher asks students to share their guesses and guides students toward a correct definition of each word. Students revise their guesses as needed and write down the correct meanings. Then students write a response to the prereading question: "Have you or someone you know ever experienced prejudice because of your physical appearance, age, religion, or ethnicity? Explain what happened."

2. Teacher distributes copies of the story "Monsy and Michelle" (Exhibit 6.18). Teacher begins by asking students to write two predictions they have about the story using the prereading strategies and the title of the story.

3. Teacher reads the story aloud, stopping after each paragraph and asking students to use one reading strategy of their choice by writing a question, a prediction, a connection, a summary statement, or the like in the margin.

Students can also write their comments on sticky notes and stick them on the page. (After they have finished the lesson, students can attach all these responses to a piece of paper and turn them in for the teacher to review.)

4. Students work in pairs for ten minutes to complete the summarization sheet (Exhibit 6.20). Teacher asks students to share and records their ideas on a copy of the chart posted on the overhead or document camera. Teacher and students discuss differences in student responses, and teacher guides students toward correct responses.

5. Teacher distributes copies of the writing prompt (Exhibit 6.21) and reads it aloud to students. Teacher asks students to reflect on what they've learned about reading and responding to prompts. Teacher asks students to share and then reviews how to "attack" a prompt:

- Read the prompt once all the way through
- Underline words that are unfamiliar and use context clues to make a guess about what the word means
- Reread the prompt and circle key words (words that are telling you to do something and/or key words that are repeated more than once)
- Write a number next to each place you are asked to do something (like numbering the steps in directions)
- Draw boxes around each number so you can brainstorm your ideas for each step of the prompt
- Students write these down on a sheet of paper and staple the sheet to their writing prompt.

Second Day

1. The teacher asks students to think about the previous day's lesson and to work in partners to write down all the steps of "attacking" a prompt. Teacher circulates, and when most students have finished, the teacher calls on several pairs to share what they remembered. Teacher asks students to take out all their materials from the previous day, including the writing prompt and the steps for attacking a prompt. The teacher tells students that now that they have reviewed how to attack a prompt, they will use this strategy with the "Monsy and Michelle" writing prompt (Exhibit 6.21). Teacher gives students five or ten minutes to attack the prompt. If students need more support, this activity can be done together, with the teacher modeling and then students trying it out. Teacher circulates, checking for understanding and offering assistance.

2. The teacher then models drawing three boxes numbered 1, 2, and 3 underneath the prompt, and explains that students will use the boxes to brainstorm ideas for responding to each section of the prompt. The teacher models this process and provides a sentence starter in each box (see the sample in

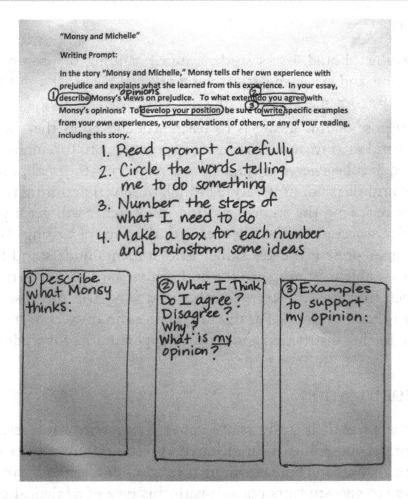

Figure 6.3. Teacher Sample of Attacking the Prompt

Figure 6.3). Students use the sentence frames as springboards to add ideas to each box. Teacher circulates and chooses a few good examples to quickly post on the document camera or reads them aloud.

3. After students have completed their boxes, the teacher models how to use this prewriting exercise to develop a longer response to the prompt. The teacher models how to cite the title and author when responding to a prompt linked to a piece of text. As a class, the teacher and students develop a few different hooks that can be used to engage the reader. They can also develop a thesis statement that students can use or modify. Then the teacher models how the ideas in each box can be organized into a separate body paragraph with a topic sentence and supporting details. Last, the teacher models how to write a concluding paragraph that summarizes the thesis and includes a reflection.

4. Students then use this graphic organizer to write a multiple-paragraph response. Teacher circulates, offering verbal feedback on organization and content.

ASSESSMENT

1. The teacher should assess student understanding of prompt analysis by circulating and reviewing students' work. This will let the teacher know whether further instruction or practice is required.

2. The purpose of this lesson is to teach students tools they can employ in on-demand writing situations and to expose them to the analytical thinking required in college-level writing. Therefore, scoring the final product using a detailed rubric is not necessary. Through observation during the lesson and quickly reviewing the student writing, the teacher will get a good picture of student successes and challenges with this type of writing. The following questions represent the key skills: "Did students understand the prompt? Were they able to summarize the author's views? Did they write the extent to which they agreed with the author and why? Did they use examples to support their position?" The teacher can use the answers to these questions to plan further instruction and practice opportunities for students.

POSSIBLE MODIFICATION

1. If teachers feel their students are not ready to write a full response to the prompt, having students do all of the precomposing activities (including prompt analysis and brainstorming their ideas on the graphic organizer) can be a way to give students practice with this type of analytical prompt. At a later time, the teacher can take students through the same process, but with a different prompt, and then students can write a full response.

Other Activities

Chapter Five presents research-based instructional strategies that we believe are key to an intermediate-level ESL curriculum and can in fact work well with many classes. While the following activities didn't make the list of key strategies for language instruction, we have found them to be effective with our intermediate-level students.

A-B-C

A-B-C—or Answer, Back it up, and Comment or connect—is a strategy for helping students formulate higher-level responses to questions. This strategy, introduced to us by Kelly Young at Pebble Creek Labs, is a great way to scaffold analytical writing and thinking processes with ELLs. This strategy can be modified in various ways, but generally involves the following sequence: students are presented with a question related to a topic of study, they answer the question, back it up with evidence (from a text or texts, personal experience, or observation), and then they make a comment or connection about the evidence. For an example of using the A-B-C strategy, see the lesson plans in Chapter Twelve.

GALLERY WALKS

Gallery walks are a way for students to get out of their seats and move around the room to view student work or other learning materials (such as images, texts, and maps) posted on the classroom walls and to interact with them in various ways. Students can take notes or use graphic organizers to note observations, questions, and responses. It can also be useful to give students sticky notes and have them leave questions and/or comments on the walls as they walk around the room. If you have a large class, it can be helpful to divide students into small groups. Each group can start in a different part of the room and then move together to the next area after a few minutes to prevent traffic jams.

QUICK-WRITES

Quick-writes are student-generated responses to prompts that are not assessed for grammatical correctness. Instead, students build fluency by responding in any form (sentences, words, paragraphs, or drawings) and generating as many ideas as they can. Quick-writes can be used for many purposes: to open a lesson ("Write what you already know about …"), to review a concept ("If you had to explain the concept of _____ to someone else, what would you say?"), to assess student understanding ("What are you still confused about?"), and to deepen critical thinking ("What is your opinion on _____? Why?"). Quick-writes can be a valuable tool to prepare students for speaking activities and for connecting a unit or theme to students' experiences. Quick-writes can also be used as a formative assessment to check student understanding.

SEQUENCING ACTIVITIES

As mentioned in the previous chapter, sequencing activities work well with songs and dialogues. With intermediates, sequencing activities (also called Make and Breaks by Kelly Young at Pebble Creek Labs) can work with more complex text. The teacher can select a multiple-paragraph text and give it to students with the paragraphs mixed up. Students can then cut out the paragraphs and use reading strategies like predicting and context clues to put the text strips in the correct order. It is important to choose a text that contains enough contextual and chronological clues for students to be able to sequence it. For further explanation of the Make and Break strategy, see http://pebblecreeklabs.com.

SENTENCE MODELING

Having students practice writing more complex sentences is a valuable activity in an intermediate-level class. High school teacher Martin Brandt has developed several sentence structures to help students write more advanced sentences. Brandt has created multiple charts to help teachers scaffold this kind of practice for their students. (He can be contacted at martinbrandt@sbcglobal.net for more information.) See Exhibit 6.22 for a sample that uses a sentence from *Into Thin Air* by John Krakauer[10] to model complex sentence construction.

EXHIBIT 6.22. Sentence Modeling: The North Face

Doing What?	Description	Who	Action	Action	Action	What
Straddling the top of the world	one foot in Tibet and one in Nepal	I	chipped the ice from my oxygen mask,	hunched a shoulder against the wind,	and stared absently	at the vast sweep of earth below.

This table allows students to see the different parts of a sentence along with a model of a well-written and complex sentence before trying out their own sentence. This type of sentence modeling chart can be used for a variety of other sentence structures to help students write in more advanced forms.

An image or photograph can serve as an additional scaffold to a sentence chart. Students can view the image, write about what they see, and then be shown a model sentence related to the image. Then when students take a turn at writing their own sentence, they have some writing and thinking to draw from.

GRAPHIC ORGANIZERS

Numerous graphic organizers are available to help English learners organize their thinking before writing and after reading. Research has shown that the use of graphic organizers and other "nonlinguistic representations ... stimulates and increases activity in the brain."[11] Many graphic organizers, like Venn diagrams, K-W-L charts, and word charts, encourage higher-order thinking. It is helpful to offer students multiple opportunities to use graphic organizers, to teach students the purpose behind them, and to encourage students to develop their own graphic organizers. As students gain practice organizing information and ideas in various ways, they can be encouraged to apply these skills as they read and learn in other content classes.

We have found Foldable graphic organizers to be particularly engaging and useful for our students. Foldables are basically three-dimensional graphic organizers that provide more space for content and are fun for students to make.

Tech Tool
Graphic Organizer Resources

Several web sites offer free, printable graphic organizers and online tools for creating graphic organizers. Following are some of the best we've found:

Holt. This site features a collection of graphic organizers that can be downloaded, modified, and printed out. It also contains teaching notes for each graphic organizer listed. (http://my.hrw.com/nsmedia/intgos/html)

Exploratree. Exploratree has a series of thinking guides that can be adapted by teachers and completed by students. (http://www.exploratree.org.uk)

For various types of Foldables and how-to instructions, see:

Making Books. This site by Susan Kapuscinski Gaylord includes great foldable ideas and instructions, including a demonstration video. (http://www.makingbooks.com/freeprojects.shtml)

ELL Classroom. This site has several blog posts describing how to use Foldables with English language learners. (http://ellclassroom.wordpress.com/tag/foldables)

Foldables. This blog by Melinda Sprinkle and Amy Mallow contains great ideas on using Foldables in the classroom and includes many pictures and slide shows. (http://www.foldables.blogspot.com)

REVISED BLOOM'S TAXONOMY

The Revised Bloom's Taxonomy is a great way to teach students about higher-order thinking. It is important for students to see the different levels of thinking and to see how they can be applied in their lives. One way for students to use the Revised Bloom's levels to make their writing more sophisticated is through question writing. Students can practice writing questions (preferably related to a theme being studied in class) for each level of thinking. Question stems and teacher modeling can serve as scaffolds.

Tech Tool
Online Resources for Bloom's Taxonomy

Lists of sample Revised Bloom's Taxonomy question stems can easily be found online by searching "Revised Bloom's question stems." Links to these question stems, as well as other online resources on Bloom's, including some great video clips to help students understand the different levels of Bloom's, can be found in "The Best Resources for Helping Teachers Use Bloom's Taxonomy in the Classroom" at http://larryferlazzo.edublogs.org.

Additional resources, including ones on rubrics, accessible search engines, places where students can write for an authentic audience, and graphic organizers, can be found on our book's web site at www.josseybass.com/go/eslsurvivalguide.

PART FOUR

Teaching English Language Learners in the Content Areas

CHAPTER SEVEN

English Language Learners in the Mainstream Classroom

*T*he Mulla Nasrudin was crawling around in the dust. A man stopped and asked, "What are you doing?" Mulla answered, "I've lost a key to a treasure and am trying to find it." The man offered to help and joined Mulla on the ground. More and more people saw them and also began to help. Finally, one person asked Mulla if he was sure this was the place where he had lost the key. Mulla answered, "No, I lost it inside my house. But it is too dark there. There is far more light out here."[1]

In this Middle Eastern story, the solution to the problem was in one place, but it was easier to look elsewhere.

Teaching any class can be a challenge, and needing to differentiate for English language learners does not make it any easier. It can sometimes be tempting to use a lesson that has a few crumbs of ELL modifications thrown into it—there is "more light" there. Another option is to consider developing unique learning opportunities that are not only particularly accessible to English language learners, but can also offer a superior experience to *all* students. With this strategy, we can see ELLs through a lens of *assets*, not *deficits*.

We believe that there are certain universal principles for making learning more accessible to ELLs and, in fact, make it more accessible to all learners. Research supports our belief. We can call these universal principles the Organizing Cycle (based upon successful strategies used by community organizers): building student relationships, accessing prior knowledge (particularly through student stories), developing student leadership potential, learning by doing, and reflection. We think it is also a particularly helpful framework to use when talking about modifications that mainstream teachers who have ELLs in their classroom can use to create a more fruitful learning environment for all their students, including ELLs. All of the strategies discussed in the preceding chapters fall into these five categories, and using this Organizing Cycle can work as a simple outline for a conversation with any content subject teacher.

This chapter will first provide a short summary of the different elements of the Organizing Cycle, along with the supporting research (and a much more complete discussion can be found in *English Language Learners: Teaching Strategies That Work*, by Larry Ferlazzo).[2] In this summary, we will also include a few specific suggestions on how to apply it in a mainstream English classroom that includes ELLs. Then we'll provide specific suggestions for applying these modifications in social studies, science, and math classes in Chapters Eight, Nine, and Ten.

This book is primarily for ESL teachers and not mainstream teachers with ELLs in their classrooms. We are not suggesting that this chapter will function as a complete guide for mainstream classroom teachers who seek to differentiate instruction. There are many other books dedicated to this topic, including *Differentiating Instruction and Assessment for English Language Learners: A Guide for K–12 Teachers* (by Fairbairn and Jones-Vo) and *Teaching English Language Learners: Across the Content Areas* (by Haynes and Zacarian).[3]

The ideas in this chapter, however, can function as a beginning point for suggestions that ESL teachers might offer to their colleagues. You may notice that we repeat a few points that have already been made earlier in this book. We do so intentionally, since we see this section as more of a stand-alone chapter that an ESL teacher can either use as a quasi-script for a conversation or actually give to a content teacher to read.

What Is the Organizing Cycle?

The framework for the Organizing Cycle is similar to one used by successful community organizers to encourage people to participate in public life, particularly those who have not previously participated in community improvement efforts. It is used to help people learn a new language and new thinking about how to engage with each other and with the world. The concepts behind it can apply equally well to English language learners who are developing competence and confidence in a new language, a new academic environment, and a new culture.

Next we will briefly discuss each of the five steps and how to apply them in a mainstream class that includes English language learners—and why.

BUILDING STRONG RELATIONSHIPS WITH STUDENTS

Creating a supportive environment in a "low-anxiety" classroom is critical in order for ELLs to get "comprehensible input."[4] In Chapter Two, we shared other research highlighting the importance of this kind of atmosphere for ELLs developing self-confidence and intrinsic motivation.

In addition to the specific suggestions in Chapter Two about ways to develop and maintain positive teacher-student and student-student connections, Robert Marzano recommends four simple strategies teachers can keep in mind and implement:[5]

- Showing interest in students' lives by asking them questions about events in the world and in their lives
- Advocating for students by making time for individual conversations and communicating that teachers want to go the extra mile to help students succeed
- Not giving up on students, and positively reinforcing student effort
- Being friendly through smiles, a light and quick supportive touch on the shoulder, and/or sharing an appropriate joke

ACCESSING PRIOR KNOWLEDGE (ESPECIALLY THROUGH STORIES)

We all learn best by connecting new information to what we already know. This personal linkage makes it more likely that new content will be moved into our brain's long-term memory.[6] Research shows that this process is just as important with English language learners as with any other learner.[7]

ELLs may not have extensive prior knowledge about what exactly is going to be covered in a lesson in a mainstream class, such as one studying *Romeo and Juliet* in English. But ELLs do have years of life experience and have likely either been in a relationship, seen a family member or friend in one, or watched one on television or in the movies. Some ELLs may also have knowledge of gangs that they can apply to the study of *Romeo and Juliet*. Making those connections, either through the use of a K-W-L chart or embedded in other ways in the lesson, can spark student curiosity and interest and make the entire lesson more accessible.

In the *Romeo and Juliet* example, it's one thing to have students share that yes, they know about gangs, and leave it at that, and another to have them share a brief narrative about the experience. Cultivating the expression of our students' prior knowledge through their sharing of personal stories can have a particularly strong learning impact. Neuroscientists like Renate Nummela Caine and Geoffrey Caine have found that the brain is particularly receptive to learning in the context of stories,[8] and Jerome Bruner writes that this can be especially important in the context of language acquisition.[9]

We are not suggesting that teachers need to spend hours upon hours eliciting student stories to activate their background knowledge. We are suggesting, however, that teachers consider broadening their perspective about what qualifies as prior knowledge whenever possible. We also encourage teachers to tease out a few more words and sentences from students when they are sharing background knowledge that can be linked to lessons.

The importance of activating student prior knowledge is summed up by long-time second-language researcher, author, and professor Jim Cummins, who wrote: "Activating prior knowledge is like preparing the soil before sowing the seeds of knowledge."[10]

IDENTIFYING AND MENTORING STUDENTS' LEADERSHIP POTENTIAL

As we've mentioned, the Organizing Cycle concept is adapted from the work of successful community organizers. In this type of organizing for social change, some of the key elements of a good leader include being intrinsically motivated, a sense of self-efficacy (or self-confidence or self-esteem), a willingness to take risks and learn from mistakes, and a desire to teach others. Researchers, coincidentally, have found that successful language learners share similar attributes.[11] The Qualities of a Successful Language Learner Lesson Plan in Chapter Twelve is designed to help students learn about this research and evaluate their own progress toward developing these qualities.

There are several ways that content teachers can foster these characteristics among their English language learner students (and their non-ELL students, too) and, through their development, make their class content more accessible to them. Intrinsic motivation can be enhanced through student autonomy, which in turn can be increased through student choice[12] whenever possible—through homework options or a voice in seating arrangements, for example. Having the ability to choose is particularly important to ELLs who likely had little or no voice in the process of moving to a new country.

Teachers can help ELLs develop self-confidence and a willingness to take risks by developing a supportive classroom community—and using the previously suggested relationship-building activities can play a key role in making that happen. Another way to strengthen student belief in their own competence is by regularly assisting them to develop learning strategies they can use to handle challenges. This assistance could include encouraging student use of previously mentioned reflective activities to help them monitor when they have been successful or unsuccessful and why, reinforcing reading comprehension strategies, including summarizing and "monitor and repair," and using inductive learning techniques to help refine student skills at detecting patterns—all tools they can use more and more on their own.[13] Finally, Carol Dweck has done extensive research and writing on the long-term positive impact on student self-confidence of praising effort ("That was impressive today, Zhao, when you really worked hard on understanding that passage—highlighting key words, summarizing, and asking classmates for help"), as opposed to praising intelligence ("You are a really smart kid, Zhao").[14]

The Roman philosopher Seneca reportedly said: "While we teach, we learn." Creating opportunities for all students to teach—especially for ELLs, who might feel that they are in constant learning mode (both language *and* content), with less to contribute than their classmates—is another way teachers can help develop leadership skills. Using the jigsaw method—where small groups of students prepare presentations on different aspects of a chapter or topic—is one way for ELLs to work in a supportive group and gain self-confidence.[15]

The origin of the word *leadership* means "to go, to travel." By mentoring our students' leadership potential, we are better equipping them to choose their own life destinations and how they will get there. Since we are not going to be there for the rest of their journey, we have the responsibility to do this intentionally and strategically.

LEARNING BY DOING

Learning by doing is a phrase popularized by education theorist John Dewey. He believed that we learn better by actually participating in an experience rather than by just being told about it, particularly if we do the work with others.[16] Much subsequent research has borne him out, finding that interactive teaching methods, including various forms of cooperative learning, tend to generate far more effective learning results than lectures.[17]

Well-structured cooperative learning activities (ones that have clear instructions and goals) are especially effective for English language learners, whether they use the jigsaw (mentioned in the previous section), project-based or problem-based learning, think-pair-share, or partner assignments. Grouping, especially with proficient English-speaking classmates, creates countless opportunities for ELLs to be naturally encouraged to speak and participate, as well as creating an atmosphere where they will feel more comfortable asking questions in order to understand content.[18]

In other parts of this book, we have shared numerous examples of another kind of learning by doing—inductive teaching and learning. Providing students examples from which they can create a pattern and form a concept or rule can work in any content class. Text data sets are a key tool to use in this kind of inductive methodology. In addition, many of the scaffolded writing strategies discussed in Chapter Six will also fit into this stage of the Organizing Cycle.

Keeping the perspective of learning by doing in mind when planning class lessons can be an asset to ELLs and non-ELLs alike.

REFLECTION

In Chapter Four we discussed in detail five different categories of reflection: summarize, self-assess, assess the class and teacher, relevance, and higher-order thinking.

All of these can be useful in a content class, especially for the metacognitive value of self-assessing successful learning strategies and for memory reinforcement.

ORGANIZING CYCLE ADD-ONS

Content teachers can use several other instructional strategies that are particularly helpful to ELLs. These may not fit precisely into the Organizing Cycle, but are nonetheless important.

Giving Instructions. The simple act of giving verbal *and* written instructions can help all learners, especially ELLs. In addition, it is far easier for a teacher to point to the board in response to the inevitable repeated question, "What are we supposed to do?"[19]

Preview-View-Review. This is an effective instructional strategy that involves the teacher giving a brief overview of the lesson in the student's native language prior to the lesson, followed by the lesson in English, which is then followed by a review in the native language again.[20]

Even though it is probably unrealistic for most content teachers to directly use this technique, the Web offers an alternative. Many textbooks now offer online multilingual translations or summaries of covered topics. If the text you are using does not, the ones that do probably offer coverage of comparable study units. Students can be given a heads-up about upcoming topics and asked to visit the online native language summaries either at home (if they have Web access) or at school (either during class or at other times in the school day).

Tech Tool
Online Multilingual Support

If your own textbook does not offer multilingual summaries and glossaries, you can find others that do in "The Best Multilingual and Bilingual Sites for Math, Social Studies, and Science" at http://larryferlazzo.edublogs.org.

In addition, there are extensive interactive online resources for all content classes. Many of these sites are very accessible to English language learners, though they are in English, because of the audio and visual support they provide. We will provide specific recommendations on teaching social studies, science, and math in Chapters Eight, Nine, and Ten.

Wait Time, Speaking Rate, and Gestures. Though this has been mentioned several times already throughout the book, it can never be stated too often—after asking a question, wait for a few seconds before calling on someone to respond; don't talk fast, do use gestures, and, if an ELL student tells you she didn't understand what you said, never, ever repeat the same thing in a louder voice!

Word Charts. ELLs are more likely to learn vocabulary if it is directly taught and then reinforced in various contexts.[21] Using the kind of word charts recommended in Chapter Six could be useful for preteaching key vocabulary prior to some lessons.

Visuals. Teaching with pictures and other visuals (such as short video clips) can be huge assets to ELLs.[22] Specific suggestions for teaching social studies, science, and math appear in Chapters Eight, Nine, and Ten.

Bilingual Dictionaries. An ESL classroom should not be the only place where a bilingual dictionary can be found. Identify the native languages of your ELL students and make sure you have the appropriate dictionaries around.

Transfer from ESL. If English language learner students in some content classes are also taking an ESL class during the day, the ESL teacher can create related student homework assignments. For example, the ESL teacher can ask the student to create a word chart of new social studies terms.

More of these kinds of "transfer" assignments, where the ESL teacher helps to explicitly transfer what is being taught in his class to a content class, can also be developed in coordination with content area teachers.

Note-Taking Strategies. For ELLs in content classes, academic listening is a critical skill that places the heaviest processing demands on students.[23] Providing note-taking scaffolds is a key accommodation teachers can offer their ELLs to help students process new vocabulary. A note-taking scaffold can look similar to a cloze passage and include the most important content with blanks for students to fill in as they listen throughout the lesson. For example, a social studies scaffold sheet might have several lines similar to "_____ was the primary cause of the Civil War." As students gain more experience with academic listening and note taking, teachers can gradually remove the scaffold or adjust it to include only a few key words.

Graphic Organizers. Graphic organizers can help all students[24] and particularly help ELLs[25] organize what they are learning and/or help them make connections between new pieces of information. See the Tech Tool under Graphic Organizers in Chapter Six for online resources.

The Content Areas. We believe that the Organizing Cycle—building strong relationships with students, accessing prior knowledge through stories, identifying and mentoring students' leadership potential, learning by doing, and reflection—provides an effective framework for effectively differentiating instruction for *all* learners, including ELLs. We feel that using this kind of research-based model can help maximize student achievement for everyone in the classroom.

In Chapters, Eight, Nine, and Ten we will share specific lesson ideas that teachers can use in social studies, science, and math classes. As we've already mentioned, the brief overview in this chapter is not meant to be a definitive guide for the content teacher. Instead, we hope that the lessons will put a little "meat on the bone" of the Organizing Cycle and help get the creative juices flowing so that teachers can adapt these instructional strategies in ways that work best for their students and for them. We see this chapter as a source of recommendations that ESL teachers can offer their colleagues.

Before we begin discussing each of these three content areas, though, we want to make a point about the first and last elements of the Organizing Cycle: relationship building and reflection.

We discussed in Chapter Two the importance of building a trusting atmosphere in the classroom where students feel safe to take learning risks. This is a critical quality for any successful classroom and is even more critical in a class with English language learners whose risks are often magnified by the questions circulating in their mind: Am I correctly understanding what she is saying? Am I making sense? Are people making fun of me? Why is everything so hard?

Relationship building is a critical element of developing this sense of trust, both when school begins in the fall and through the rest of the year. The basics—a teacher making a point of taking a minute to check in with three or four students each day, not just on the subject that is being studied, but on what is happening in the student's life—can hold true for any teacher in any class. There is often a little time to chat with students arriving in the classroom early and as they are leaving, and while students are working at their desks.

In addition, as we mentioned, well-designed cooperative learning projects where students have been strategically divided by the teacher (often, though not always, with student input) can offer excellent opportunities for strengthening student-to-student relationships.

There are additional relationship-building activities that can be organized periodically in class. Chapter Two shared a number of introductory exercises (such as the Introducing Me activity, an I Am project, or a class scavenger hunt) that can be used throughout the year as student interests change and as they gain new life experiences. If you are teaching in a large school where few students share the same classes, then all classes can do these same exercises, since there will be little student overlap. However, if your students are staying with each other most of the day, doing the same introduction projects in several classes might not be the most energizing experience for them.

An option is to add elements to the standard introductory exercises to customize them for your course of study. We will be making some of those suggestions.

For reflection, the five categories and their representative examples that were shared in Chapter Four can be used in all classes.

This chapter opened with a Middle Eastern folktale about a person looking for a key outside his house, even though he had lost it inside. He was doing this because the light made it easier to look outside. In the chapters that follow, you'll find some ideas on how to find the key inside the house.

Additional resources, including strategies for giving effective feedback to students and more ideas for teaching ELLs in mainstream classes, can be found on our book's web site at www.josseybass.com/go/eslsurvivalguide.

CHAPTER EIGHT

Teaching Social Studies

*N*asreddin Hodja was traveling with a companion. They came to a place that had extremely tall minarets—much taller than the Hodja's friend had ever seen. He asked the Hodja, "How do you think they could have built them so tall?"

"Simple," he explained. "They just go to a well and turn it inside out."[1]

In many ways, Nasreddin Hodja's explanation is similar to the teaching practice that we're suggesting in this chapter and in this book—we are "turning inside out" many traditional teaching assumptions. We are suggesting that, instead of educators using the "sage-on-stage" model, a focus on the relationships, stories, and leadership abilities of our English language learners can result in huge learning strides.

This chapter will discuss how to build these "tall minarets" in social studies classes using The Organizing Cycle.

Building Relationships with Students

Along with, or instead of, some of the questions included in previously mentioned introductory activities, social studies teachers can ask ones like these periodically during the year (of course, as with most assignments, teacher modeling is important):

Describe a geographic feature (such as a hill, mountain, river, jungle, or forest) that you have a fond memory of from your younger days. Draw it and explain why it is such a nice memory.

Think of times when you have been on a hill or mountain, in a forest or jungle, in an ocean or river, on a different continent, or in a different time zone (teachers can add more here if they wish). Draw and describe in writing what it was like and why you were there.

What is the most historic moment you remember? In other words, which moment do you think will be in history books for a long time to come? Draw it and answer these questions: Where were you, what happened, what did you think, and how did you feel? And why do you think it will be remembered in the history books? Ask your parents the same questions, and write down their responses.

We will be learning about the biographies of many historic figures and the most important moments in their lives—in other words, what shaped them into the kind of people they are. Think of two or three key moments in your life that made you the person you are today. Draw them, write about them, and explain why and how you think they have shaped you.

We will be studying economics—money—in this class. Write about and draw three important times in your life when money mattered.

The only limitation to these kinds of questions is your own imagination!

Tech Tool
Making Online Maps and Timelines

Though these kinds of introductory questions can easily be answered with pen, markers, and paper, there are also plenty of free and easy online tools where students can make their own individual multimedia presentations describing important moments and showing them by grabbing images from the Web. These presentations can include making personalized maps and timelines. Following are some of our favorite online map-making and timeline tools.

Maps

Tripline. Tripline is a great map-making application. You just list the various places you want to go in a journey, or a famous trip that has happened in history or literature, or a class field trip itinerary, and an embeddable map is created showing the trip on which you can add written descriptions and photos. You can use your own photos or just search through Flickr. Plus you can pick a soundtrack to go with it as it automatically plays through the travels. (http://www.tripline.net)

GeoTrio. GeoTrio lets you create a virtual tour of just about any place on a map. You type in addresses or locations and easily create multiple stops that show the Google Street View snapshots of the area. You can also upload your own images. What really makes GeoTrio stand out is the ability to easily make an audio recording for each stop on the map. (http://www.geotrio.com/home)

Google Maps: http://maps.google.com.

Scribble Maps. Scribble Maps is a great application that lets you create maps—with markers and images that can be grabbed from the Internet—and you can draw on it, too. Plus no registration is required. (http://www.scribblemaps.com)

Timelines

X Timeline: http://www.xtimeline.com

Dipity: http://www.dipity.com

When in Time: http://whenintime.com

ACCESSING PRIOR KNOWLEDGE THROUGH STORIES

The importance of connecting new information to existing student prior knowledge was explained earlier in Chapter Seven.

The questions in the relationship-building section of Chapter Seven, in addition to providing opportunities to build personal connections, can also help students access related prior knowledge. Following are a few more ways of integrating this idea into the social studies classroom.

K-W-L Charts and Presentations

K-W-L charts (what do you *know,* what do you *want* to learn, and what have you *learned)* were discussed in earlier chapters. Using these charts can be an excellent way to introduce new lessons and in ongoing classroom use, as students organize newly learned information and connect it to what they already know. K-W-L charts also informally assess the quality and quantity of student background knowledge, which in turn can help inform a teacher's instructional plan.

It is very possible that ELL student prior knowledge about many social studies topics will be more limited than that of other students. So how do you turn that challenge into an opportunity? Their knowledge about particular United States–related topics may be narrow, but their overall knowledge of social studies topics may be broad.

For example, before beginning a unit on the American Civil War, in addition to having all students list what they know about that war, the teacher can also invite them to share what they know about *any* civil war. There are few countries in the world that have not experienced these tragedies, and the stories from immigrant students can add to the learning experience of *all* students.

There are other opportunities, too. Before discussing the Mexican-American War, for example, immigrant students from Mexico can be asked to report the very different perspective on that conflict that is taught in their native country (this kind of activity can also help develop the important language learner quality of teaching others). When a world history class is going to start a unit on Chinese history, who better for the class to hear from than a student from that country? And when discussing natural disasters in geography class, the long history of these tragedies extends across all borders.

It doesn't have to stop with K-W-L charts, either. ELL presentations on these topics can be an excellent language-development experience for them and a fruitful learning opportunity for the entire class.

Connecting Personal Stories in Other Ways

Student stories can also be used to engage additional higher-order levels of thinking. All students, including ELLs, can share stories of how and why their families moved to the local community, the risks they took, and how it changed their lives. This information, along with the stories of explorers and immigrants throughout history, can easily be used to develop Venn diagrams, followed by compare-and-contrast essays.

Another example might take place prior to discussing the Protestant Reformation (or other rebellions and revolutions). Students can be asked to think about a change they would like to see happen in the school, why they would like to see it happen, who they might need to help them make that change, why they think they need that help, and what might happen if they do not get that assistance. This activity can be followed by a discussion of Luther's plan of not moving ahead publicly with his Ninety-Five Theses until after he had support from the public and among German princes. Making the connection between the student's thinking process and Luther's strategy can make the lesson more accessible *and*, perhaps even more importantly, teach broader concepts of change and the dangers of recklessness that can be related to many other historical—and personal—events. In other words, good ideas are great, but you want to do what you can to increase their odds of success before you move forward with them.

IDENTIFYING AND MENTORING STUDENTS' LEADERSHIP POTENTIAL

The increasingly difficult tandem of learning a second language and learning content knowledge can grow frustrating for English language learners as they move from the beginning level to higher levels.[2] As the levels of intrinsic motivation decrease during this time, it is important for teachers to use the methods discussed previously that have been shown to assist students to "motivate themselves," including encouraging student autonomy, praising effort, creating opportunities for students to teach, and helping students master learning strategies they can use when facing obstacles.

LEARNING BY DOING

We have discussed the value and effectiveness of inductive learning with students—both with English language learners and with those proficient in the language. The roots of the word *inductive* mean "to lead into" and "to lead." This section describes a scenario for leading students through this kind of guided discovery process in a social studies classroom.

K-W-L charts were mentioned earlier in this chapter, under Accessing Prior Knowledge. However, there are a number of historical eras where it is obvious to the teacher that prior knowledge on a topic may be very limited. In those situations, a teacher may want to use an introductory lesson like this one.

A few days prior to starting a unit on ancient China, a teacher can display three pictures on the classroom wall (ideally they should be oversized, but 8–1/2-by-11-inch images will work and can later be shown on a document camera or overhead projector for students to see an enlarged image): one showing the ancient Chinese use of gunpowder, another an image of Confucius teaching, and the third an image of the recently discovered terra cotta warriors (an Internet search will turn up many photos of all these items, which can be reproduced for an educational setting).

On the day the unit is to begin, students are given a K-W-L chart and asked to write down what they saw in each picture, when they thought it took place or was produced, and what clues led them to that conclusion. Then students write questions they think of for each picture. Students can work individually or, better yet, in pairs.

Next the teacher should explicitly teach a few key vocabulary words, such as *archeology, philosophy,* and *terra cotta,* which students can use to make a small word chart. In addition, a teacher can give a short read-aloud using some of the newly taught words.

Then students can be given a text data set like the one in Exhibit 8.1 (which can easily be expanded if desired). They can read them in pairs and categorize them. Afterward, they can revisit their K-W-L chart about the photos to write down answers to some of the questions they might have found from the data set. Students can later be asked to add new information to the categories as they learn more about the topics. And, as demonstrated in both Chapters Four and Six, data set categories can be extended into essays.

EXHIBIT 8.1. Ancient China Data Set

Categories: Inventions, Archeological Sites, Philosophers

1. Chinese scientists invented gunpowder in the eighth century and began using it in weapons.

2. The Great Wall of China is four thousand miles long and protected the Chinese border.

3. Nearly two thousand years ago, the Chinese invented paper by combining tree bark, rope, old rags, and fish nets.

4. Confucius was a philosopher who believed that there should be strict rules in society and that people should follow those rules.

5. It took one million workers to build hundreds of buildings in the Forbidden City. It was the center of government, and construction on it started over five hundred years ago.

6. The Chinese invented the abacus, which was an ancient calculator. It is still used in some places.

7. Even though Buddhism started in India, it became very popular in China. It was started by an Indian prince named Siddhartha Gautama Buddha.

8. Even though many Chinese eat using chopsticks, they also invented the fork over four thousand years ago.

9. The remains of Peking Man, a creature that lived 750,000 years ago, before humans, have been found in China.

10. Thousands of large clay soldiers made over two thousand years ago were found in 1974.

11. Lao Tsu was a philosopher who believed that the government should not make a lot of rules. He also believed that everything had a dark side and a light side, which he called *yin* and *yang*. His philosophy was called Taoism.

12. The Chinese invented the compass thousands of years ago to show in what direction they were traveling.

A lesson like this incorporates visual clues, cooperative learning, inductive teaching, read-alouds, and explicit vocabulary instruction, including word charts—all instructional methods that have been found to help both ELLs and non-ELLs. We are not suggesting that a teacher needs to incorporate all these elements in every introductory lesson—at times, just doing a K-W-L chart with the photos is workable, as is using visuals (including a video clip) in some other way. Cooperative learning can be used in any number of circumstances. And a text data set (and its optional extension into essays) can be used at any time. We lay out this teaching and learning sequence, though, to offer a practical idea of how these instructional strategies can be effectively used in a social studies class.

REFLECTION

Any of the reflection activities discussed in Chapters Four and Six can be incorporated in a social studies class.

OTHER SUPPORT

Chapter Seven listed a number of useful instructional strategies that can be used by content area teachers to help their ELL students (and other students), including wait time, talking speed, the use of gestures, word charts to assist vocabulary acquisition, bilingual dictionaries, preview-view-review, providing instructions verbally and in writing, and "transfer" assignments from ESL classes. These are all applicable to social studies classes, and in the next subsections we highlight a few more.

Graphic Organizers. In our description of the Organizing Cycle, we provided information and resources on graphic organizers. One organizer we have found particularly useful in social studies is called the Historical Head. This sheet, which is just a simple outline of a large empty head, can be labeled as a specific historical figure or a group of people the class is studying (for example, students can try to imagine themselves as Native Americans enslaved by Spanish conquistadors or as the conquistadors themselves). Students can draw or paste five images inside the head representing the "thoughts, ideas, visions, and motivations" of the person or people. Each image is numbered and then a brief written description explaining how the image connects to the person can be written on the back.[3]

Reviews and Summaries. Holding a brief review at the beginning of class and a brief summary at the end (with students actively participating in both) can be particularly helpful to ELLs in a social studies class.[4]

Tech Tool
Interactive Content Class Resources

In addition to the many primary language online resources available to help ELLs mentioned in Chapter Seven, there are numerous free sites offering engaging social studies resources in English that are accessible to all students, and especially to English language learners. Sites for all content-area classes can be found in "My Best of Series" at http://larryferlazzo.edublogs.org.

Additional resources, including links to interactive online social studies and English exercises, can be found on our book's web site at www .josseybass.com/go/eslsurvivalguide.

CHAPTER NINE

Teaching Science

A father took his son out in the forest one day to teach him the sights and sounds of nature. When the father spotted an interesting sight—a squirrel, a bird's nest, or a beautiful flower—he would not point it out to his son. Instead, he would nonchalantly position his son where he could see the sights himself. The *son* could then point out the discoveries to his father.

This type of guided discovery is the kind of instructional strategy emphasized in this book, and in this chapter written by our colleague Lorie Hammond.

One Size Does Not Fit All

In a time of "scripted," "standardized," and even "teacher-proof" curricula, the ability of teachers to adapt their curricula to the populations they serve has become severely limited in many situations. While there is always a question of how well standardized curricula serve students' needs, the gap between the needs of English language learners and one-size-fits-all texts and activities is often too large for students to bridge. The norm when adapting science curricula for ELL students is to start with a standard science textbook and then to make it accessible through a variety of techniques that simplify the curriculum. The ideas we recommend in this section can be used in that situation, but ideally we prefer a very different approach that does not center on a set curricula, but rather on the needs and strengths of the students involved.

This chapter was written by Lorie Hammond, professor of teacher education at CSU Sacramento and the cofounder and academic director of Peregrine School, a project-based bilingual school for preschool through eighth grade in Davis, California (see PeregrineSchool.org).

The hands-on teaching and learning related to science also offers superior opportunities for language learning in the science classroom and in ESL classes. We have often used science experiments in our English classes to generate vocabulary, speaking, listening, and writing activities, as well as to help prepare students for their mainstream science classes. The science approach discussed here follows the five steps of the Organizing Cycle and is written by our talented colleague, Lorie Hammond.

Building Relationships with Students and Accessing Prior Knowledge

Secondary-level English language learners bring with them two sets of experiences that can make science education relevant to their lives: the way of life they experienced in their home countries, which is often minimally related to schooling; and the adjustment they are currently making to life in the United States. Both of these experiences are founded not only in their linguistic and cultural lives, but also in science, if science is interpreted as the relationship between people and their physical and natural environment. A strong relationship can be built between teachers and students through science as a medium, although this is not generally done.

Immigrant students bring a wealth of knowledge about many things from their home countries, from agriculture to house building to cooking to medicinal herbs. Often this "fund of knowledge" is discredited or simply considered irrelevant in the context of schooling.[1] This is particularly true when students' knowledge does not come from books, but rather from life experience. Students' funds of knowledge link them to their own culture and to the knowledge their families possess. Relating to those funds can help students connect their previous life to their present life, respect their families' traditional knowledge, and feel connected to science, a subject that might have had little or no meaning to them before.[2]

How can a teacher find out what students already know, and what funds of knowledge their prior life experiences contain? One useful tool is *ethnoscience*, an approach used in anthropology in which the relationship of people to a body of knowledge is studied through oral histories. This approach takes students deeper into their prior experience, interviewing family members and community experts about the knowledge their group holds in relation to a particular subject of study. For example, *ethnobotany* is the study of how a group of people relates to plants. It includes all the traditional things one studies about plants, such as how to grow them and their life cycles, as well as more cultural aspects of plants, such as what they mean to people and how they are prepared, stored, and consumed in daily life.

Secondary students are capable of gathering this kind of ethnoscientific information themselves from their own communities and chronicling it. This approach accomplishes two things: (1) the students involved learn to relate to science as active researchers who produce knowledge and (2) their teachers learn about the students and can then find ways to link standards-based school science concepts to what students already know. Perhaps most important, ethnoscience creates a respectful exchange between funds of knowledge in students' cultural communities and new knowledge embodied in western science. After traditional knowledge has been explored, a thoughtful teacher can build curriculum experiences that point out connections and discrepancies between traditional and "scientific" ways of exploring the natural world, and in the process can create meaningful dialogue.[3]

This approach can be used with all students in a variety of activities. These include having a student or community garden using different growing techniques; asking students to use popsicle sticks and other materials to construct model homes from their cultures, placing them outside in the sun with a thermometer for a few hours and then determining which kind of construction is most energy-efficient and why; and having students do a similar experiment with different kinds of boats.

In addition to building on their traditional knowledge, immigrant students face the challenge of understanding science in their new country. Many newcomer ELLs at the secondary level have not experienced standard elementary science curricula and therefore may not know about health, nutrition, hygiene, household chemicals, and other practical matters essential to successful American life. They may also lack the background knowledge that will allow them to be informed citizens for environmental decisions and to assess information about weather, space, transportation systems, and other aspects of modern life. They also might not be familiar with measurement systems used in the United States, such as Fahrenheit thermometers and scales.

Getting to know one's students involves not only knowing their cultural backgrounds, but also talking to them about what they need to know to live their lives with more confidence. Teachers need to establish trust before students will talk to them about their concerns, especially in areas like health. Teachers can help students immeasurably through science classes that provide the basic knowledge students need to cook, predict the weather, and learn about their own bodies. Such basic science information can then be used as a springboard for studying the more abstract and complex science concepts generally taught in high school science classes. It is harder for students to approach it the other way: to apply abstract knowledge to their own lives. Often science can seem remote to ELL and other students, but they may engage in it more readily if science is related to their lives and their daily needs.

Identifying and Mentoring Students' Leadership Potential

Science can be a disempowering or an empowering experience for ELL students. If students are placed in a regular science class without special assistance, they can flounder and feel disempowered. Similarly, if they are not acclimated to western scientific approaches, they can feel culturally alienated by science, as described in the previous section.

To promote an engaging and empowering experience in the science classroom, a teacher will need to apply the many instructional methods already discussed in this book, including the use of visual images, three-dimensional models, kinesthetic interpretations, videos and other nonlinguistic communication approaches, as well as ways of simplifying language (but not concepts) through word banks, speaking slowly, and conscious choices of vocabulary.

It is critical for students to acquire academic language in order to be successful in secondary and postsecondary schools. Elements required include vocabulary development and mastering the ability to use academic language in speaking and writing. Vocabulary development can include both science vocabulary in particular (such as "volume"), and common vocabulary (such as "cloud") that English learners may not know. In addition, it can include two other types of vocabulary usually ignored. One is conceptual vocabulary, such as "density," which can be best understood through inquiry activities. A second type is process vocabulary, such as "predict" and "infer," which applies to various topics in science and other academic subjects. This vocabulary is perhaps most important of all, because it allows students to participate in academic discourse.

Teachers can further help students develop a sense of self-efficacy (or self-confidence), a key quality of leadership, in the following ways:

1. Create study groups of students who speak the same language, so that they can share science concepts with each other in their primary language and then record their work in English.

2. Create a word wall that shows the key concepts in the science unit being studied. It should always be displayed in the classroom and have either clear definitions or pictures to illustrate the words that are listed, or both.

3. Create a chart on the wall listing key words translated into the other languages spoken in the classroom that students can use as a reference.

4. Make handouts that have similar patterns, such as lab sheets that are always the same, so that ELL students catch on to the process of science and can repeat it while studying various topics.

5. Post photos and other visuals illustrating key concepts being studied in science.

When the language and concepts of science are made more accessible to students, they will feel that they are not limited by their still-developing English proficiency. They may then feel more confident about engaging in the class, becoming more intrinsically motivated and more willing to take risks.

Another essential way students can be empowered by science is through a constructivist learning experience, which we will describe as "learning by doing."[4]

Learning by Doing

Constructing knowledge is the central activity in inquiry science instruction, since science educators generally agree that students need to construct their own knowledge through experience and experimentation, rather than learning things directly from teachers or books.[5] The premise of "constructivist" approaches to teaching—which apply to all students—is that science is a culture that must be learned, involving a complex combination of skills, assumptions, and procedures that can only be learned by "acting like a scientist." In short, learning science standards as "facts" to be memorized is like reading only the last page of a mystery novel. The process of science *is* science. Conclusions reached through experimentation are reduced to meaningless factoids unless they are experienced by the learner, who can only understand them through experience.

The constructivist nature of real science instruction is one of the things that can make science a perfect subject for engaging English language learners and other students who might have other challenges with school engagement. However, hands-on activities do not in themselves produce motivation in all students. Many students become motivated only if they know "what science is for" and "who it serves."[6] It is the *connection* of science to daily life, and to issues facing a community, that makes it meaningful to all students, including ELL students.

Science experience can typically be gained in two ways:

1. Science experience can be gained through *guided discovery,* which has similarities to the inductive approach discussed often in this book. The best kind of guided discovery is exemplified by the story that began this chapter of the father positioning his son to be the primary discoverer of new things. **2.** Science experience can be gained through *inquiry,* when students participate in an experimental process using the scientific method. Science experiments provide a great way to empower students, especially if students work in groups to solve a problem together. Students can be encouraged to collaborate, to assume roles as members of a team, and to make decisions about various aspects of their experiment, from the research question to the results. All of these roles help students to develop the executive function, which is the mental process we all use to apply what we have learned in the past to our actions in the present and in the future. Strengthening this ability in our students can lead them to be more capable learners in their future lives.

Reflection

Science is not only a process of doing, but also of dialogue. Too often learning by doing emphasizes activities that motivate students, especially English language learners, but do not necessarily communicate the concepts students need to learn.

The key to making a science lesson not only engaging, but also academically successful, is that discussion follow experience, so that students have a chance to integrate the experiences they have had with key concepts in science.

How can English learners describe their science experiences? Many ELL students cannot write freely about these experiences in English. A structured prompt is essential. Lab sheets that require students to respond to each part of their experiment in drawings and writing, and then require a reflective response at the end, are very useful. If the same lab sheet is used repeatedly, students' progress in writing in English can be monitored along with their understanding of science concepts.[7]

Various tools can be used to measure student success in science. If students are very new to English, they can be asked to make diagrams or drawings with labels, or cartoon-type drawings with story lines, to describe what happened in an experiment or to illustrate something that has been observed. Students can also be placed in small groups or in pairs with others who speak the same primary language to discuss their work, since they can do so fluently in their own language, and then translate their conclusions as a group into English. An inventive teacher will need to figure out alternative ways to elicit students' ideas, even if their English is limited. It is important that students who have worked hard on understanding science be successful at expressing what they have learned, even if they do not yet have enough English proficiency to express it through standard tests or essays.

An Important Final Note

The teaching strategies that make up the Organizing Cycle help all students, not only ELL students, to succeed. Instead of teaching in a deductive style, involving lectures, textbooks, and worksheets, and then working overtime to accommodate ELL students, it is more effective to create an inductive hands-on, minds-on teaching style for all students. All students will be more successful, since constructivism is how people learn best, and science will be accessible for ELL students as well. Tying science to students' lives, incorporating their background experiences, and engaging students as active learners will improve the science program for *all* students, while simultaneously creating a program in which ELL students can shine.

 Additional resources, including links to interactive online science exercises, can be found on our book's web site at www.josseybass.com/go/eslsurvival guide.

CHAPTER TEN

Teaching Math

A mother crab noticed several different animals walking straight one day. She then saw her son moving sideways towards her. The mother decided that he should start walking straight. The little crab tried repeatedly, but failed. He asked his impatient mother to model walking straight for him. She noticed that she made no progress trying to walk straight, but knew she would move quickly walking sideways.

"I give up," she finally admitted. "I just don't think nature intended us all to walk the same way."[1]

This story illustrates that each of us has a unique way of getting from one place to another. Each student brings unique talents from his or her individual strengths and from his or her cultural background. This principle is true for all students, but is particularly valuable when teaching English learners, who come from all over the world. The fund of knowledge that these students bring from their unique experiences can become the basis of a strong math program for English learners.

Our colleague, Lorie Hammond, shares her ideas in this chapter on how to tap this fund of knowledge.

Making Math Relevant

Newcomer students in a middle school English language learners math class pored over the want ads from our local newspaper, attempting to figure out how they

This chapter was written by Lorie Hammond, professor of teacher education at CSU Sacramento and the cofounder and academic director of Peregrine School, a project-based bilingual school for preschool through eighth grade in Davis, California (see PeregrineSchool.org).

would spend their monthly "income," were they to live on their own. Each student had drawn a different job, with its corresponding salary, from a random selection. Their task then became how to meet their monthly needs for housing, food, transportation, and recreation on the salary they received.

Many discussions ensued. Some students from Thailand were surprised that they would have to spend their money on housing and food, since in their country these were things their family produced for themselves. "What did you need money for, then?" a Russian student asked. To our surprise, the Thai student responded that money was for buying a new wife or child. This immediately triggered discussion among all the students about whether women and children should be bought and sold and about how differently money is used here compared to some other countries.

Russian Christian students from very large families (ten to twelve children on average) planned to rent apartments by themselves. They loved the idea of their own individual space. For other students, from more collective cultures, this was a strange and scary idea. They chose to pool their incomes and live together in a big house.

What if the salary a person received was not enough to rent an apartment and buy a car? What kind of education was needed to get jobs that supplied the income needed for a good lifestyle? As newcomers to the United States, having arrived in the last three months, students became engaged in thinking about planning for their futures and began to connect education in this country to obtaining a good job.

Through this exercise, the teacher introduced students to an approach to mathematics that was relevant to their lives, that involved divergent solutions, that encouraged dialogue, and that engaged students as active learners. In this chapter, this example and others will be used to analyze how math might best be taught to English language learners and mainstream students in secondary schools. The five steps of the Organizing Cycle will again be used as a guide.

Building Relationships with Students and Accessing Prior Knowledge

Mathematics is a gatekeeper in many secondary schools. Math proficiency determines not only which math class students will be assigned to, but also whether they can gain access to laboratory science classes and to an academic curriculum in general. For English language learners, the situation is even more complex.

Students' language levels do not necessarily correspond to their levels of proficiency in mathematics. Factors such as whether students come from a developing country, a situation of poverty or war, and whether their experience is rural or urban are often key to understanding their prior knowledge in mathematics. It is particularly important to get to know one's ELL students, because they may be much more competent in mathematics than they at first appear, since they will likely have trouble deciphering word problems and some symbolic codes in English, causing them to score low on standard tests.

On the other hand, some students from rural areas or poverty, or both, may have attended school for a short time or not at all, and may never have learned mathematical conventions common in elementary schools worldwide. To add to the complexity, some students use symbols and algorithms differently because of the conventions in their countries. (In some countries, for example, people use commas where we use periods and vice versa—for example, 1,000.00 would become 1.000,00.) These students will need to be taught to represent numbers in ways that will be understood in the United States.

Students' math skills can also be strongly affected by their competency in English. There is both truth and falsehood in the statement that mathematics is a "universal language." On the one hand, mathematics is its own language, which all students need to learn from scratch in school. Some parts of this language can be manipulated using numbers alone. Thus, when English language learners are mainstreamed into regular classes with English-speaking peers, the first subject they can adjust to is mathematics, since students who are well trained in working with numbers can transfer their skills to the English-speaking context. On the other hand, students at each competency level in English may display different strengths and weaknesses in mathematics. For example, students new to English will do better when yes-or-no responses and responses in their own language are allowed, whereas advanced English learners will be able to participate in conversations about math problems.

All of these factors make clear that teachers must learn about the factors from their students' past experiences, as well as assess their current academic levels, in determining the math placements appropriate to their needs. Activities such as the want ads project described earlier help ELL students, as well as non-ELLs, to do math without severe anxiety and to solve problems in their own way. This in turn allows teachers to analyze (1) students' ability to express ideas about mathematics in English or in some other modality, such as through a graph or diagram and (2) students' background knowledge in formal and informal mathematics.

Learning about students' prior experiences with math can be helpful in determining the instructional strategies to best meet individual student needs. It is not uncommon for teachers of ELLs to experience two extremes in student prior experience, with many students falling in between.

The first extreme is the student who comes from a country that is very strong in mathematics, perhaps stronger than the United States. (Students from Central Asia, East Asia, and the former Soviet Union, for example, often fit this description.) In this case, the central decisions schools must make are equity issues: making sure that English language learners, despite their language ability, can access advanced mathematics classes at their high school or middle school and will receive teaching there that they can comprehend.

The other extreme in student prior experience is the learner who comes from a rural area of a developing country, from a hill tribe or other fourth-world people, or from a war-torn country, and who has had little or no formal schooling before entering school in the United States. This student will not know the basic skills in mathematics typically learned in elementary school, though she may know other ways to solve mathematical problems—ways that are used in her group. This situation, along with a less extreme but common situation of a student who has received a partial mathematics education, can be addressed by the strategies listed next, as we make our way through the Organizing Cycle.

An exciting way to begin is to use the tools of a small but growing field called *ethnomathematics*.[2] This field is a blend of cultural anthropology and mathematics and involves teachers in interviewing students, and students in interviewing family members, about cultural means of solving mathematics problems, followed by the sharing of this information as part of the mathematics classroom curriculum. What is found can be as simple as different conventions of notation or different algorithms, such as other ways of doing long division. In some cases, however, the approach can shed light on deep cultural differences.

In any case, an ethnomathematical approach, in which teachers explore what students and their families already know about mathematics, rather than assuming that they begin with a deficit in relation to conventional American skills, can improve relationships between teachers, parents, and students dramatically, because it shows such respect for and interest in students' cultural knowledge. It can also be very interesting for everyone involved. And again, it can also be an engaging strategy to use with mainstream students who often share a classroom with ELL students.

Identifying and Mentoring Students' Leadership Potential and Learning by Doing

In planning a mathematics curriculum for English language learners, it is important to understand that mathematics is a conceptual subject that can only be understood when students discover answers for themselves. While algorithms play an important role in making mathematics efficient, the real study of mathematics is not the memorization and practice of algorithms, but the understanding of why the algorithms work.

While teachers should give "minilessons" that explain the work that students will do and that target misconceptions or mistakes teachers observe, much of the time in the mathematics class can be spent in active exploration by students individually or, more often, in small groups.

Allowing students to work in groups to solve mathematical problems empowers students and allows them to exert leadership. English language learners need to practice their communication skills, regardless of the subject learned, rather than to work quietly. In fact, language is learned only through communication. Hence, group work enables students to be leaders, organizing how to solve problems, and forwards their general goal of learning English. In some cases, when concepts are hard to understand, students might be grouped with others who speak their own language, so that their discussion of concepts can be more fluid and deep. Students can then translate what they have discovered back into English.

A lesson cycle for a fifty-minute class might go as follows:

- Teacher introducing the problem and/or concept (five minutes)
- Students working in groups to solve a problem or problems, recording their work and solutions on a large piece of paper (thirty minutes)
- Student groups presenting their results to other groups, followed by a reflective discussion among the groups (fifteen minutes)

In this style of constructivist teaching, in which students *construct* their own solutions, problems should be sufficiently challenging, and should have various possible solutions. Manipulatives of various sorts should be available to help students solve their problems. These might include counting cubes, place value cubes, geometric figures, rulers, compasses, triangles, and even common objects, such as beans, that can be arranged and counted.

It is important that students receive scaffolding that helps them to organize their problem solving. Since mathematics involves three languages—visual-geometric, equations, and words—a repeated worksheet such as the one offered here can help students to use all three in the solution of every problem (Exhibit 10.1).

Students new to English will require support in filling out this type of worksheet, which can be completed individually or as a group, depending on teacher goals. This help can come in several forms: a word wall with key terms that students will need to use as a reference, help from other students, allowing phrases rather than sentences or labeled cartoons for students with very little English, or assistance from the teacher. This kind of writing benefits ELLs and non-ELLs alike. Research has found that incorporating writing into mathematics instruction "raises the 'cognitive bar,' challenging students to problem solve and think critically."[3]

Student leadership can also be developed by assigning changing roles during group times, so that students can take turns organizing their group, being the scribe, or taking responsibility for other tasks.

EXHIBIT 10.1. Mathematics Worksheet

Name _____

Date _____

Problem: (already written)

Drawing of how you solved your problem (can be a sequence of drawings):

Equation that explains your problem and solution:

Description of what you did in words:

Reflection

In some countries, mathematics curricula are described as going very deep. Only a few concepts are presented each year, but they are explored in depth. In contrast, United States mathematics textbooks tend to cover many concepts in quick succession, creating an effect that is "an inch deep and a mile wide." This is important for all students, but especially for English language learners who have missed earlier years of schooling and need to catch up in high school. These students will have a less daunting task if teachers can isolate the key concepts that need to be learned, rather than expecting them to wade through extensive materials.

A program in which students solve problems and then pause to share their solutions with each other and reflect upon their new understandings can be powerful in helping students to understand mathematics deeply and therefore gain mastery quickly. Reflective discussions among students are therefore an essential part of good mathematics teaching. The reflective activities recommended in Chapter Four can also be used in the mathematics classroom to promote this kind of thinking and discussion.

Since students' mathematics abilities are not limited by their English levels, it falls to the teacher to figure out how to communicate across language barriers so that students can reach their full mathematics potential. Data shows that English language learners initially test below their peers in mathematics, but once fluent these students are able to accurately demonstrate their higher math skills.[4] Therefore, finding effective ways of teaching mathematics to all students, regardless of English level, is a true equity concern.

Additional resources, including links to interactive online math exercises, can be found on our book's web site at www.josseybass.com/go/eslsurvivalguide.

PART FIVE

Further Strategies to Ensure Success

CHAPTER ELEVEN

Using Learning Games in the ESL Classroom

I n the Middle East long ago, Nasreddin Hodja crossed the border every day with bales of hay carried by a donkey. The guards were sure he was a smuggler, but could never find anything. Years later, one of the guards retired and saw Hodja at a market. "I'm retired, so you can tell me now, what were you smuggling?" Hodja replied, "Donkeys, only donkeys."[1]

It was very obvious to Hodja what was going on every day, but not so obvious to the guards. Teachers can use games in a similar way. "Trick them into thinking they aren't learning and they do," says Roland "Prez" Pryzbylewski, a teacher in the HBO television series *The Wire*. In the show, he gets a very challenging group of kids to learn math by showing them how to determine odds as they play dice for Monopoly money.

Learning another language can be a challenging and often frustrating experience for many of our students. No matter how motivated students are, a good teacher must have many instructional tools at his or her disposal to help students *engage* in the class and not have to *endure* it. Games are one of those tools.

Research Support

Judy Willis, neurologist and teacher, writes that students, especially adolescents, are more likely to store information as part of their long-term memory and make them available for later retrieval by participating in activities they enjoy.[2] Researcher Robert. J. Marzano also endorses learning games as an "engagement activity" that can result in increased student academic achievement.[3]

Games have long been particularly popular in the ESL classroom, and research has borne out their effectiveness. Among their many benefits are creating meaningful and low-anxiety opportunities for learners to use all domains—speaking, listening, reading, and writing[4]—learning to remember things faster and better, and developing greater fluency by "using" the language instead of "thinking" about making sure they use it correctly.[5]

What Are the Qualities of a Good Learning Game?

We use six criteria to judge whether we want to use a game in our classroom:

1. It requires no or extremely minimal preparation on the teacher's part.
2. Any needed materials are developed by the students themselves—the preparation for the games is a language learning experience in itself.
3. In addition to not costing teachers much time, the game can also be done without costing any money.
4. The game is designed in a way to strongly encourage all students in the class to be engaged at all times.
5. The game, after being modeled by the teacher a number of times, can periodically also be led by a student.
6. All students, whether they are winning or losing, should be having fun. Games must be played in the spirit of friendly competition, and not result in those who lost feeling devalued or embarrassed.

CLASSROOM GAMES

The next sections present some games that meet these criteria and can be adapted to all levels of instruction (and to most other subjects in addition to language). Many are old standbys, with a few special modifications. All of these games can be used to reinforce whatever thematic unit is being studied in class at the time. A few of the games are probably most appropriate for beginners—for example, SLAP, Spot the Difference, and the Labeling Game—but all the other games in this chapter can be modified to be useful and enjoyable in a beginning or an intermediate class and, in many instances, any class at all.

GAMES USING SMALL WHITEBOARDS

Having a few small, handheld whiteboards can make a number of games go smoothly, though pieces of scratch paper can act as substitutes.

Divide the class into small groups of two-to-four students. Research shows that the greatest individual gains come in groups of this size.[6] You can change the way groups are formed, sometimes allowing students to choose their own partners and at other times having them "number off." However, always reserve the right to move students around if you feel that one group is obviously too strong or weak in terms of language proficiency.

One game is calling out a question to answer or a word or sentence to spell, giving the groups twenty or thirty seconds to write the answer (telling them not to raise their board until you say time is up), and then having them show the answer. The groups with the correct answer get a point. This way everyone has an opportunity to score a point, not just the first one with the answer. Sometimes you can end this game, and others, with an opportunity for each team to bet all or part of their points on the last question (as in Final Jeopardy). Another option is for the educator to make a list of common writing errors and write them on the board (without indicating which student wrote the mistake) for groups to race to write them correctly. A variation for these games could be assigning a number to each group member. For example, if there are groups of three, each group would have a number one, a number two, and a number three. When it is time for groups to call out the answer or do the response, the teacher could call out "All number ones!" as a way to ensure everyone is participating. As in many of the games in this chapter, students can also develop a list of their own questions and take turns being the game's leader.

A similar game with some different twists is having each group rotate having one person from their group stand up in front with a small whiteboard. All other group members have to remain in their seats. The teacher asks questions that must be answered in writing by the person in front. However, their groups can help them by calling out suggestions. The first person to get the answer correct scores a point for their group. Needless to say, this game can get a little noisy.

Another game where whiteboards come in handy is Hangman. In this version, though, you can dispense with the image of the hanged man—it just adds unneeded complexity and an unnatural ending to the game. The goal is to have students guess entire sentences and not just words. To facilitate this, the teacher should leave an obvious space between the word blanks, and the blanks can be further distinguished by using different colored markers. If you're studying food, for example, instead of having to guess the word *milk*, students have to guess the sentence "I drink milk in the morning." This way, students can learn sentence structure and the game can easily be made harder for students with a greater grasp of the language being taught.

In this version of the Hangman game, students are in groups. Each group gets a turn to guess a letter, and then the teacher either writes a correct letter in the appropriate blank or an incorrect letter below the blanks on the board. Groups get a point deducted if they incorrectly guess the sentence. The first group that writes the correct sentence on their whiteboard scores a point. Groups can guess the sentence at any time, even if it is not their turn.

Playing sound effects and having student groups guess the source of the sound is another game that can be played with whiteboards. It is especially suitable for thematic units like animals and home. A CD containing sound effects can easily be purchased.

Tech Tool
Online Sound Effects

There are many web sites that offer free sound effects. In fact, students can use them to create their own game to share with other students. The best sites include

Sound Snap: http://www.soundsnap.com

Soungle: http://www.soungle.com

Free Sound: http://www.freesound.org

Sound Bible: http://soundbible.com

Tech Tool
Using Online Video Sites in the Classroom

Having Internet access and a computer projector in your classroom is another great way to integrate games in your curriculum. There are free music sites—mentioned in Chapter Three—that show a performer singing a line, immediately followed with that particular line converted into a cloze where students have to provide the correct word (these sites can be adjusted for various proficiency levels). Students—either on their own or in small groups—can complete answers on small whiteboards.

Showing short online videos and asking comprehension questions afterward, with student groups again answering on whiteboards, can be a fun activity. In addition to the countless videos available on YouTube and the video sites mentioned in Chapter Three, there are numerous other sites that host videos unlikely to be blocked by school Internet content filters. They include major media web sites like CNN, The New York Times, National Geographic, and How Stuff Works. And don't forget English Central (http://www.englishcentral.com), which has also been mentioned in previous chapters.

In addition, many of the online games mentioned later in this chapter can also be projected on a screen and answered by small groups in a competitive game.

GAMES THAT FOCUS ON SPEAKING PRACTICE

One game that students enjoy has sometimes been called Telephone. In this version, divide the class into two or three groups, depending on class size. Make sure they are all seated, whisper a sentence into the first person's ear, and then, after the teacher whispers it into the ear of the first person in each group, they each have to whisper it to the next person in their group who in turn has to whisper it to the person next to them. The last person in the group has to come up and whisper to the teacher what the sentence is. The first group who gets it correct gets a point. If their sentence is incorrect, they have to begin again, with the teacher whispering in the first person's ear. After each turn the second person becomes the one who starts off the next whisper, and the person who had begun the previous turn becomes the last.

I Spy is another old but good game. The teacher writes "Yes" and "No" on the board and mentally picks an object in the classroom. Students again are in small groups, and each group has a small whiteboard. Students have to formulate questions that call for yes-or-no answers. For example, "Is it brown?" or "Is it in the front of the class?" Groups take turns asking a question, and the teacher records it under "yes" or "no." For example, the teacher might record "Brown" under "Yes" and "In front" under "No." The first group to correctly guess the object wins.

Messenger and Scribe develops both speaking and writing skills.[7] The educator writes four sentences (or, depending on the class level, four short paragraphs) on four pieces of paper and tapes the four sheets in different sections of the room. You want to be careful that the letters are written in regular size so they can't be seen from a distance—and, ideally, they can be kept and used in future years. Students are then divided into pairs—one is the Messenger and one is the Scribe. One remains seated with a paper and pen, and the other has to run to the wall, read the sentence, and return to the Scribe. The Messenger then repeats what he or she read and the Scribe writes it down. The Messenger cannot stand by the sheet and yell to the Scribe, however. The first five or so teams to write all the sentences correctly, including spelling and punctuation, are the winners. The teacher can then remove the sentences from the wall and review them with students.

GAMES THAT REQUIRE STUDENTS TO CREATE MATERIALS

Students can create the classic game of bingo by making a board on a piece of paper with four squares down and four squares across (they can draw the squares or be given a preprinted bingo sheet). They can write sixteen words out of perhaps twenty-five or thirty the class has been studying and write one in each square. Students can use various items as bingo chips—from little pieces of paper to inexpensive tokens to dry beans. When one person wins, everyone clears their board and plays another game.

Students can also create their own word searches using graph paper. They can exchange their creations with other students and then see who can find the most words in five minutes.

Sentence Scrambles are another popular game. Students are given blank index cards, or they can just cut up pieces of paper. Each student picks one sentence from a book they have been reading and writes the words and punctuation marks on the cards (one word or one punctuation mark per card). They mix up the cards and then paper-clip them together. (Depending on the class level, the teacher may want to check each card stack before they are paper-clipped together). They then do the same for another sentence. Each student can create five of them. The teacher collects them all, divides the class into small groups, and gives each group a stack of the sentence scrambles to put into the correct order. The group that has the largest number of correct sentences in ten or fifteen minutes wins. After a group feels they have one sentence correct the teacher can check it and take the sentence scramble away after giving them a point.

In the game of Slap, students are divided into groups of four with their desks facing each other. Each group has to make cards with one word each written on them from the week's vocabulary list. They are all put face up throughout the four desks. The teacher calls out the word, and the first person to slap the card with their hand gets a point (one person in each group, who also plays the game, is designated the scorekeeper).

Only Connect is a BBC game show that also has a web site (http://www.bbc.co .uk/onlyconnect/quiz). There are sixteen squares with words on each one. The player needs to use the words to create four categories of four words each. It's a great game that helps develop the higher-order thinking skill of categorization. The online game is too difficult for all but advanced English language learners, plus you get only three minutes to complete it. However, the idea is a wonderful one for the ESL classroom (and even mainstream ones, too). Students first think of four different categories—for example, transportation, animals, fruits, and vegetables. Next, they create their own game sheets with sixteen boxes. They think of four words for each of the four categories and write them in the boxes. Finally, they cut out the squares, mix them up, and then exchange their creations with a classmate. Their challenge is to then correctly group the sixteen boxes into four categories. Of course, depending on the English level of the class, you might want to start with fewer boxes.

Headline Clues from Michigan State University also fits into the category of an online game that might be difficult for less proficient students, but could be adapted for classroom use with paper and pen (http://gel.msu.edu/headlineclues/game). In the game, you're shown the lead paragraph, but letters from two words in the headline are missing. Players have to use clues in the first paragraph to identify what the missing words should be. As you play the online version, you can ask for clues. One of the great things about using this game in the classroom is that students can create their own and have classmates try to figure out the answers, as well as giving them clues if needed. Students and teachers can also have fun inventing their own imaginary stories.

OTHER CLASSROOM GAMES

Most ESL classrooms have many word lists and pictures with words posted on the walls. Teachers can divide the class into small groups and give a yardstick to one person from each group (students can take turns). The yardstick-holders start from the same point in the room and wait for the teacher to call out a word. The first person to correctly touch the word with their yardstick gets a point for their group. Other group members have to remain seated, but they can offer verbal assistance. This is also a noisy game. Another alternative is writing words on the board and giving students fly swatters instead of yardsticks.

Two other simple games are Pictionary, where either students or the educator draw something on the board and the first small group to write on their whiteboard the correct word symbolized by the drawing gets a point; and charades, where other students or the teacher act out verbs, again needing to be guessed by student groups.

Dividing students into groups, giving them a sheet of easel paper and a marker, and then calling out the name of a category (such as vegetables or sports) is another simple game. Give students a short period of time to see which groups can write down the biggest number of related words, and have groups check each other. They can call in the teacher when there's a question.

Having a student write a word on the whiteboard, and then having groups compete to see how many words they can write down that begin with the last letter of the word on the board, can be a fun activity.

In the Alphabet Game, students first write the alphabet down the side of their paper. The teacher, or student leader, then calls out the name of a category (such as animals or food) and small groups try to write at least one related word beginning with as many different letters as they can.

Another game for student review can be called Stations. Make five copies of five different worksheets related to the theme the class has been studying (this is one of the few good uses for worksheets). The class can then be divided into five groups of four or so students. One stack of each of the five worksheets will be placed in different sections of the room. Each student group is given a group number and begins at one of the five stations. They will be given three or four minutes (or longer) at each station to complete as many questions on the worksheet as they can and then told to stop. They write their group number on the worksheet, give it to the teacher, and then each group moves to the next station. After students have gone through all the Stations, each group is given another group's papers to correct and the answers are reviewed as a class. The number of correct answers is added up, and the group with the highest number wins.

Tech Tool
Online Worksheets

There are many online sources where free worksheets on many topics can be printed out for use in the Stations game. The best ones include:

Lanternfish: http://bogglesworldesl.com

MES English: http://www.mes-english.com

ESL Kids: http://www.esl-kids.com

One activity that requires a little teacher preparation time is called the Labeling Game. The teacher can write words describing various classroom objects on sticky notes, divide the classroom into four or five groups, and then each day during the week one group will see how fast they can correctly label the classroom objects. The groups are timed, and the one with the fastest time wins. Additional labels are added each week.

Spot the Difference pictures can be a fun way to review vocabulary. Having students identify the differences and, more important, write a word that describes the difference, can provide an engaging competitive activity (in this game, and in all the ones listed in this chapter, you want to have multiple winners). You can find many Spot the Difference sheets to print out for free on the Web, but it's worth a few dollars to purchase Judy W. Olsen's *Look Again Pictures: For Language*

Development and Lifeskills (Alta Book Center, 1998). This is a book of thematically organized Spot the Difference pictures that are specifically designed for English language learners.

ONLINE LEARNING GAMES

There are countless learning games on the Web that are accessible to English language learners. If you have microphones, in fact, these games can reinforce all the domains: speaking, listening, reading, and writing (though there are few good online writing games). They include building vocabulary development with I Spy hidden object games, generating excitement through games where you can create private online virtual rooms where students compete against each other and the score of all players is shown on the screen after each question and response, to—believe it or not—extraordinarily engaging games to practice grammar.

You can find lists of these kinds of games in "A Collection of the Best Lists on Games" at http://larryferlazzo.edublogs.org.

"Creating" is at the top of the Revised Bloom's Taxonomy, and the Web makes it easy for students to create their own online learning games. After they're made, they can be posted on a class blog (see Chapter Two) and other students can play them. You'll find a list of free game creation sites that are accessible to ELLs at the previously mentioned games list.

There are many "adventure," "escape the room," and "hidden object" online video games that at first glance might not appear to have much educational value. However, if you look a little closer, a number of them can be a gold mine for engaging language-development activities. Many gamers on the web create "walkthroughs" for these games—written step-by-step instructions on how to beat them. For example, here's an excerpt from the walkthrough for Phantasy Quest, a student favorite:

- Enter the cave. Go left, and take the skull.
- Go back once and go right, through the single door, through the top door, and through another single door to exit the cave.

Teachers can divide students into pairs and give them copies of walkthroughs—you're unlikely to find another English reading and speaking activity that inspires more engagement. Though class winners might be the first five pairs to get through the entire game, you'll find that students will love getting ahead of others and then will stop to help their classmates so they can show off their video game-playing prowess.

Links to many of these online games and their walkthroughs can be found on the previously mentioned "Collections" list on games.

BOARD GAMES

Board games like Scrabble and Taboo have long been used in the ESL classroom. While these are good games, we prefer having students create their own board games. Not only does that process develop higher-order thinking skills, but it also lets students personalize, with teacher encouragement, the language learning areas where they might need the most reinforcement. There are many online sites that offer free ESL board game templates that students can use to create their own board games, or that teachers can use as models to show the class. Links to these sites can also be found in the "Collections" list mentioned earlier in this chapter.

Though it isn't an actual board game, one game tool that we have found particularly engaging in the ESL classroom is a felt dartboard used with small Velcro balls. There are different dartboards—some with the consonants, some with vowels, some with phonic blends. Incorporating these with some of the previously mentioned games—for example, having a student throw a ball at the consonant board, and then having groups write as many words as they can that begin with that letter—can be a nice game addition.

A company named ESL Education Games used to manufacture these boards, which they called Phonicball. Unfortunately, they are no longer in business, but you can still see examples of their products at http://www .alibaba.com/member/phonicball.html. It is, however, relatively simple to make your own, and you can search the Web for "Velcro Ball Dartboard."

Along with games comes the issue of rewards for the winners and, often, the runner-ups. The rewards can cost the teacher little or nothing—an extra point on that week's test allows students to go to lunch two minutes early, or they don't have to do the required work of copying the plan for the day in their notebook. Sometimes it's a piece of candy or the right to eat food during class.

But generally after a short period of time you'll find that students forget about getting a reward and don't even ask about it. The game itself becomes the reward, and the enjoyment of the experience and the knowledge learned through playing it becomes the intrinsic motivator.

Additional resources, including links to useful video sites, online sources of sound effects, and more information on using online games, can be found on our book's web site at www.josseybass.com/go/eslsurvivalguide.

CHAPTER TWELVE

Handling Potential Challenges

A king had a big tree near his palace, and he wanted it chopped down. The palace was built, and he also wanted a well dug near it. He offered great wealth to whomever could cut down the tree and dig a well.

Many people tried, but no one could make a dent in either the tree or the rock where the king wanted his well.

One day, a man named Boots and his brothers decided they would travel to the palace and try their luck at the tasks.

As they were walking, they heard something that sounded like hacking on top of a hill. "I wonder what is making that noise?" Boots said. "I think I'll go see what it is." His brothers scoffed at him, but Boots went and saw an axe that was chopping wood on its own and took it.

As the brothers continued to walk, they heard another sound in the forest. Boots said, "I wonder what the sound is?" And though his brothers were impatient again, Boots went and found a shovel that was digging on its own. He took it, too.

The brothers then came upon a stream, and Boots said, "I wonder where the water comes from?" Even though his brothers complained, he walked until he found the source of the water—it was a big walnut. He plugged it up with some grass and took it with him.

When they arrived at the palace, Boots' brothers tried chopping and digging first, but got nowhere. Then Boots set his axe to chopping and the tree came down. Then his shovel began digging, and when it reached a good depth he unplugged the walnut, put it in the ground, and the water came out.

Boots was given great wealth, and his brothers afterwards always said to themselves, "Boots sure is smart—he kept wondering about questions and then went and found their answers."[1]

In this Norwegian folktale, Boots is facing the problems of how to cut down an "unchoppable" tree and to dig an "undiggable" well. He figures out solutions to these challenges by taking time to wonder about them, and his reflections lead him to think outside the box for answers. His thinking led him to solutions that made the work easier for him and got the king what he wanted, too.

Though we're not suggesting that thinking about problems will result in finding magical solutions that will do all the work for you, we do believe that schools don't have to be places where "young people go to watch older people work." We'll be offering a few suggestions here about how to approach common classroom challenges—student motivation, textbook integration, error correction, limited access to technology, multilevel classes, students' use of their native language in the classroom, student book selection, and classroom management—in ways that we hope will be energizing to both you and your students.

Student Motivation

Neither of us has ever motivated a student. As Edward Deci, the renowned researcher on motivation issues, wrote: "The proper question is not, 'how can people motivate others?' but rather, 'how can people create the conditions within which others will motivate themselves?'"[2]

There are many strategies ESL teachers can use to help foster students' sense of *intrinsic* motivation, which comes from within themselves, as opposed to *extrinsic* motivation, which comes from outside factors (such as grades).

Teachers and researchers have found that positive teacher-student relationships, a supportive classroom atmosphere, enhancing students' sense of autonomy through providing choices (such as homework options and seating arrangements), and praising effort ("You pronounced the dialogue very clearly, Jose—all that time you spent practicing it paid off") instead of ability ("Your English is great, Jose") are a few strategies teachers can use to strengthen ELL student intrinsic motivation.[3]

ELL students setting their own goals has also been found to be an effective motivating strategy.[4] In addition to the goal-setting exercise in the second lesson plan in this section, Chapter Thirteen provides ideas and tools that can also be used to assist in this process.

Once students have identified their goals, substantial research has been done showing that student use of imagery[5]—particularly with those learning a second language—can result in both increased learning and increased student motivation.[6] We have certainly found that to be true in our own classrooms by having students take thirty seconds at the beginning of each class to visualize in their mind successfully working toward achieving their specific language learning goals.

We use the two following lessons in our classes to help students see how and why it is in their self-interest to do their best learning English inside and outside the classroom. The first lesson is on the economic, health, and neurological advantages of being bilingual. The other lesson discusses the qualities researchers have found important to being a successful language learner (a version of this list can also be found in Chapter Seven).

These lessons provide excellent language opportunities in themselves, and we are able to refer back to them constantly during the school year—both with the entire class and with individual students. We use pieces as mini refresher lessons and are on the lookout for student actions and world news that can be used to reinforce their messages. In class evaluations, students regularly highlight these lessons as some of their most important learning activities during the year.

The Advantages of Being Bilingual or Multilingual Lesson Plan

INSTRUCTIONAL OBJECTIVES

Students will:

1. Learn academic vocabulary, including the words *flexibility, gained, increased, bilingual, disease, bilingual, multilingual,* and others of the teacher's choice.
2. Practice English reading, writing, speaking, and listening skills.
3. Develop critical thinking skills.
4. Strengthen their ability to write grammatically correct sentences.

DURATION

Three sixty-minute class periods, including one double-block on the first day. The third sixty-minute class period should occur one week later. In between these periods, though, the teacher should be checking in with students to see how they are doing in completing the assignment.

ENGLISH LANGUAGE DEVELOPMENT STANDARDS: CALIFORNIA ENGLISH LANGUAGE DEVELOPMENT (ELD) DOMAINS

1. Students use English for everyday communication in socially and culturally appropriate ways and apply listening and speaking skills and strategies in the classroom.
2. Students apply word analysis skills and knowledge of vocabulary to read fluently.
3. Students will read and understand a range of challenging narrative and expository text materials.
5. Students will write well-organized, clear, and coherent text in a variety of academic genres.

6. Students will apply the conventions of standard English usage orally and in writing.

MATERIALS

1. A computer, projector, and Internet access to YouTube (if YouTube is blocked, please see "The Best Ways to Access Educational YouTube Videos in School" at http://larryferlazzo.edublogs.org)

2. Document camera or overhead projector

3. Student copies of the bilingual or multilingual advantages read-aloud (Exhibit 12.1)

4. Student copies of bilingual or multilingual surveys (Exhibit 12.2)—five copies for each student

5. Poster sheets of at least eleven by fourteen inches—two for each student

6. Colored markers

EXHIBIT 12.1. Bilingual or Multilingual Advantages Read-Aloud

Scientists and others have recently found that people get many benefits from learning English (and other languages):

Learning English can increase your income by 20 percent to 25 percent. It's a skill that employers want.

Learning another language "exercises" the brain as if it were a muscle. Because of that increased flexibility, bilingual people are better learners, have a better memory, and can do more things at once better than people who only speak one language. They are also better at solving problems.

People who are bilingual can delay the beginning of Alzheimer's disease by an average of four years over people who only speak one language. Being bilingual strengthens the part of the brain that gets attacked first by the disease.

Sources: M. de Lotbiniere, "Research Backs English as Key to Development," *The Guardian,* July 5, 2011; "Why It Pays to Be Bilingual," *Voxy,* Feb. 15, 2011, retrieved from http://voxy.com/blog; D. Marsh, "Languages Smarten up Your Brain," *The Guardian,* Jan. 25, 2010; C. Dreifus, "The Bilingual Advantage," *New York Times,* May 30, 2011; S. S. Wang, "Building a More Resilient Brain," *Wall Street Journal,* Oct. 12, 2010.

EXHIBIT 12.2. Bilingual or Multilingual Survey

Your name _____

Name of the person you're interviewing _____

1. How has speaking English and another language helped you? Please be specific and, if you can, share personal stories showing how it helped you. (Getting a better job? Easier to get a date? More friends?) Please share at least two ways.

2. How does speaking English and another language make you feel, and why? (More confident? Happier?)

3. What was the hardest thing about learning English, and how did you overcome it?

4. I'm learning English now. What advice would you give me?

PROCEDURE

First Day

1. The teacher tells students he is going to show a series of short video clips (the teacher can choose which ones and how many from "The Best Videos Showing the Importance of Being Bilingual" at http://larryferlazzo.edublogs.org). He explains that he wants students to write down what happens in each one.

2. After he shows the first video, he gives students a few minutes to write down their description and has them share what they wrote with a partner. The teacher then asks one or two students to share with the entire class. Depending on the English level of the class, the teacher may or may not want to write down a description on a document camera or transparency.

3. After this process has been repeated a few times (with students sharing with a different partner after each clip), the teacher asks students to think about what the video clips might have in common. He tells the class he doesn't want anyone to say anything and instead just write it down. After a minute or two, he asks students to share what they wrote. Ideally, students say that the clips all show that it is important to speak more than one language. If not, the teacher can guide students to that conclusion.

4. The teacher then asks students to write down on a piece of paper all the reasons they can think of why it is important for them to learn English, if they think it is important. After a few minutes, students are asked to share with a partner. Then students share with the entire class, and the teacher compiles a list on easel paper or a document camera.

5. The teacher says that students have come up with some great reasons. He also wants to share what scientists and others have found are good reasons for people to speak two or more languages. But first, he wants to introduce a few words that might be new to students. He asks students to create a simple word chart (see Exhibit 6.5 in Chapter Six) and writes the words on his own version on the document camera: *flexibility, gained, increased, bilingual, disease, bilingual, multilingual,* and any other words from the read-aloud that he thinks might be new to his students. The teacher works with students to understand each word and quickly completes the chart.

6. The teacher then passes out copies of the read-aloud (Exhibit 12.1) and asks students to look at his copy on the overhead. He explains he wants people to use their copy to make any notes that they want. The teacher reads the read-aloud.

7. The teacher then tells students he would like them to choose which reason (from the class list and from the read-aloud list) they think is the most

important one for learning English. He gives them a minute or two to think about it and then asks them to write it down.

8. Next the teacher writes these questions on the board: "Is it important to learn English? Why or why not?" He explains he wants students to respond to that question using the ABC format: <u>a</u>nswer the question, <u>b</u>ack it up, and make a <u>c</u>onnection or a <u>c</u>omment. The teacher writes an example on the board:

> Yes, I think it is important to learn English. One reason is because it will help me get a date. If I speak English, then there is a bigger number of people who might want to go out with me. (A little levity in the classroom can be helpful.)

9. Students write their ABC response with the teacher circulating around the classroom to help. Periodically he will ask students with good examples to share their paragraphs on the document camera with the rest of the class.

10. The teacher asks students to turn their response into a poster, writing it in larger letters and drawing a representative picture.

11. Students share their completed poster—either through the "speed dating" method described in Chapter Five or in small groups. The teacher might also want to tell students they need to ask a question of each person after they share. The teacher collects the posters and will place them on the classroom walls later that day.

12. The teacher explains that students are going to talk to five bilingual or multilingual people they know (English needs to be one of the languages), and no more than two of them can be high school students. They are going to ask them the questions on the Bilingual or Multilingual Survey in Exhibit 12.2. The teacher reviews the form, models an interview, gives each student five copies, and tells them they have one week to complete the assignment. The teacher can also give students time to practice with a partner in class.

13. Class ends with a reflection activity of the teacher's choice (see Chapter Four).

Second Day

(One week later, but in-between these classes, the teacher should be checking in with students to see how the interviews are going.)

1. The teacher asks students to take out all their completed survey forms. He explains that he wants them to put a star next to the one answer to each question they think is most helpful. The answers can be on different forms.

2. The teacher explains that students are going to share with their classmates the responses they thought were most helpful. The teacher can either have students share in the speed dating style or in small groups. Students should make a note if they hear a response from another student they particularly like.

3. The teacher asks selected students to share their best response with the entire class.

4. The teacher announces that students are going to make another poster with the best response to the first question on the survey: "How has speaking English helped you?" The poster will include the response and a representative picture.

5. The teacher explains that students will be using the answers to the last few questions on the survey in another lesson (see the next lesson plan in this chapter). He then collects both the posters (which will be displayed on the wall) and the surveys, which he will hold onto for the upcoming lesson on the qualities of a successful language learner.

ASSESSMENT

The teacher can use the ABC assignment and the two posters as a formative assessment to identify student strengths and weaknesses, and as a source for examples to use in a grammar lesson using concept attainment (see Chapter Three). If they wish, teachers can develop a more detailed rubric to evaluate student work. Please see the problem-solution unit plan in Chapter Six for links to rubric sites on the Web.

POSSIBLE EXTENSIONS AND MODIFICATIONS

1. Depending on the English level of the class, expectations and models for the ABC assignment can be simplified or made more challenging.

2. Students can convert their ABC responses or poster ideas to a digital format using a tool like Fotobabble (http://www.fotobabble.com) and any of the other numerous Web 2.0 sites that are free and available (see the Tech Tool on digital storytelling in Chapter Three).

3. Students can prepare a simple teaching lesson on the advantages of being bilingual to present to another class.

4. Small groups of students can create a skit demonstrating the importance of knowing more than one language, using the video clips that were shown as models. They can even be videotaped and uploaded to the Web.

The Qualities of a Successful Language Learner Lesson Plan

INSTRUCTIONAL OBJECTIVES

Students will:

1. Learn academic vocabulary, including the words *qualities, risk, perseverance, assessment,* and other words of the teacher's choice.
2. Practice English reading, writing, speaking, and listening skills.
3. Develop critical thinking skills.
4. Strengthen their ability to write grammatically correct sentences.

DURATION

Two sixty-minute class periods, plus periodic check-ins on how students are doing toward achieving their goals.

ENGLISH LANGUAGE DEVELOPMENT STANDARDS: CALIFORNIA ENGLISH LANGUAGE DEVELOPMENT (ELD) DOMAINS

1. Students use English for everyday communication in socially and culturally appropriate ways and apply listening and speaking skills and strategies in the classroom.
2. Students apply word analysis skills and knowledge of vocabulary to read fluently.
5. Students will write well-organized, clear, and coherent text in a variety of academic genres.
6. Students will apply the conventions of standard English usage orally and in writing.

MATERIALS

1. A computer, projector, and Internet access to YouTube (if YouTube is blocked, please see "The Best Ways to Access Educational YouTube Videos in School" at http://larryferlazzo.edublogs.org)
2. Document camera or overhead projector
3. Student copies of Exhibit 12.3: Successful Language Learner Assessment and Exhibit 12.4: Successful Language Learner Goal Sheet

4. Poster sheets of at least eleven by fourteen inches, one for each student

5. Colored markers

6. Copies of the transcript to the Michael Jordan Nike commercial for all students and selected videos (available at "The Best Videos Illustrating Qualities of a Successful Language Learner" http://larryferlazzo.edublogs.org)

7. Copies of the previous lesson's completed surveys

PROCEDURE

First Day

1. The teacher explains that she is going to show a short video to the class and that she wants students to write a sentence or two afterward describing what they saw. The teacher then shows a video of a penguin getting courage to jump over a gap on a hill. This video, and all others used in this lesson plan, can be found at "The Best Videos Illustrating Qualities of a Successful Language Learner" (see preceding Materials section for URL address). The teacher gives students a minute to write and then asks them to share with a partner. The teacher circulates around the room and identifies good examples of sentences. She tells certain students she is going to ask them to come up to the document camera and share their work.

2. The teacher asks certain students to come up front and share their sentences. She explains that the penguin took a risk by making that leap (the teacher explains more fully what the word *risk* means) and asks "What would have happened to that penguin if it didn't take the risk of leaping?" Students might answer that it would have been stuck on the other side.

3. The teacher explains that they are going to spend some time today learning what researchers have discovered about the qualities of a successful language learner: "What does it take to be a successful learner?" (The teacher also explains more fully what the word *qualities* means.) She explains that a willingness to take risks is one of those qualities. She asks students to take a minute and write and/or draw about a time they took a risk—any kind of risk—and what happened. She says it's okay if the outcome was not positive. She gives an example from her own life.

Note: Research citations on the qualities described in this lesson plan can be found in Chapter Seven.

4. Students share what they wrote with a new partner. The teacher circulates around the room identifying students she will call on to share. After certain

students share with the class, the teacher explains that sometimes risks don't work out, and sometimes we make mistakes. She says she is going to show a short video clip of Michael Jordan (she checks to see if students know who he is, and if not, she explains that he was a famous basketball player and maybe the best to ever play the game). She asks students to watch it once and then watch it again with copies of what he is saying in front of them. The teacher then shows the video to students.

5. The teacher asks students to write down what they think Jordan meant when he said: "I've failed over and over and over again in my life. And that is why I succeed." Students share with a partner, and then the teacher asks certain students to share with the class. She explains that when you make mistakes, it's important that you learn from them, and the same thing is true if you take risks and they don't work out. She asks students to write down and/or draw about a time when they made a mistake and learned from it. She gives an example from her own life.

6. While students are working on their paper, she writes "Qualities of a Successful Language Learner" on the board and underneath it she writes "Taking Risks" and "Learning from Mistakes."

7. The teacher asks students to form groups of three and share what they wrote or drew. She then asks certain students to come up front and share with the class.

8. Next the teacher says she is going to show another video (she can choose from several on the Edublogs web site (see "Materials") that demonstrate perseverance and an appetite for learning). She shows the video and asks students to think about what quality the person or animal in the video is showing. She asks students to share with a person they haven't talked with yet in class that day and then asks certain students to share with the entire class. Students might say that the video shows a person not giving up. The teacher explains what *perseverance* means, and what an *appetite for learning* means. She then writes both on the board.

9. The teacher asks students to think of a time they wanted to give up on doing something, but they didn't. She asks them to write what it was and why they didn't give up. She gives an example from her life. Students share with a partner and then with the class.

10. Next the teacher shows a video of someone teaching another person. She asks students to write down what they saw in the video and share with a partner. She asks certain students to share with the class and points out that being willing to teach others is another important quality of a successful language

learner—we learn best what we teach. She asks students to write down or draw about a time they taught someone else (such as a little brother). She gives an example from her own life and writes "Teaching Others" on the board.

11. The teacher distributes the completed Bilingual or Multilingual Surveys (Exhibit 12.2) from the previous lesson. She asks students to review the answers from the last three questions and decide whether any of them illustrate or represent the qualities of a successful language learner. Students circle and label examples of these qualities and share them with a partner.

Note: This is the midpoint of the lesson. If the teacher wants to divide the lesson into two days, this would be a good place to stop.

12. The teacher then quickly reviews the qualities of a successful language learner that she wrote on the board. She reminds students that they have all demonstrated these qualities already and asks them to review their stories from the previous day. Now, she tells them, the class will focus on applying these qualities to learning English.

13. She explains that she is going to pass out a sheet that they are going to use to assess (she explains that *assessing* is like grading) themselves on if they are applying these qualities to learning English. She emphasizes that their grade is not going to count in the grade book—the important thing is that they are honest.

14. The teacher places a copy of the sheet (Exhibit 12.3: Successful Language Learner Assessment) on the document camera and reads it aloud, reviewing any new vocabulary. She stops at each of the four questions and asks students to answer each one before she moves on to the next.

15. The teacher then passes out the Successful Language Learner Goal Sheet (Exhibit 12.4). She explains that now that students know which areas they need to work harder on, they can make a plan on how to better develop those qualities. She says that students will review their goals and their progress toward accomplishing them each Friday. She reviews the sheet and asks students to complete the first question. She then asks students to share in groups of four, saying that students can change their answers if they hear ideas they like better. She encourages students to ask questions of their classmates to find out why they listed the plans they wrote.

16. The teacher repeats this same sequence for the rest of the sheet and has students share what they wrote in groups of four, but they must be four

different (or mostly different) students each time. When they are in the groups, students can also take the opportunity to share what they wrote for the earlier questions, too.

17. After the sheet is completed, the teacher asks students to identify which goal they think is the most important one to them. She asks students to make a poster describing this goal, their plan to reach it, and why they chose it. This could be in the form of an ABC paragraph (described in the preceding lesson plan).

18. Students work on the poster and then share them in small groups or in "speed dating" style.

19. The teacher collects the sheets and posters from the students, explaining that she is going to make copies of the sheets (so both teacher and students have a copy) and return them the next day. She puts the posters on the classroom walls.

EVERY FRIDAY AFTERWARDS

The teacher asks students to review their goal sheet and write about their progress in their learning log. At the end of a month, students can complete a new goal sheet.

ASSESSMENT

The teacher can use the student writings and the poster as a formative assessment to identify student strengths and weaknesses, and as a source of examples to use in a grammar lesson using concept attainment. If desired, teachers can develop a more detailed rubric to evaluate student work. Please see the problem-solution unit plan in Chapter Six for links to rubric sites on the Web.

POSSIBLE EXTENSIONS AND MODIFICATIONS

1. Students can write and perform short skits demonstrating their plans to accomplish their goals; the skits can be videotaped and uploaded to the Web for student and family review.

2. Students can watch and sing along with the motivation music videos found on "The Best Videos Illustrating Qualities of a Successful Language Learner" (see preceding Materials section for URL address).

EXHIBIT 12.3. Successful Language Learner Assessment

Your name _____

Date _____

Circle the most accurate number: 1 means you don't try at all, and 10 means you try all the time.

1. I take a lot of risks to improve my English: I try speaking to people I don't know, I try to put myself in situations where I have to speak English, and I don't spend all my time with people who speak my native language.

        1   2   3   4   5   6   7   8   9   10

2. I am willing to make a lot of mistakes to improve my English, and I focus on learning from them—not feeling bad about making them. I figure if I don't make mistakes, then I'm not trying hard enough.

        1   2   3   4   5   6   7   8   9   10

3. I feel very motivated to learn English, and I will work and work until I get it right. I remember what we learned about the advantages of being bilingual or multilingual, and I want to make sure I gain all of those advantages.

        1   2   3   4   5   6   7   8   9   10

4. I always try to help my classmates and my family members learn English better. When I understand something better than they do, I try to help them because I know they will help me when I need it.

        1   2   3   4   5   6   7   8   9   10

EXHIBIT 12.4. Successful Language Learner Goal Sheet

Your name _____
Date _____

1. What are two risks I can take over the next month to improve my English? (for example, trying to talk to a native English speaker once each day or asking the teacher if I can read what I wrote to the class once a week)

- _____
- _____

2. What are two things I can do to learn from my mistakes? (for example, writing more in my weekly journal and not being so concerned about my grammar, or writing more in my daily learning log about what I learn from my mistakes)

- _____
- _____

3. What are two things I can do to try harder to learn English over the next month? (for example, reading a more challenging book or reading ten minutes longer each night at home)

- _____
- _____

4. What are two things I can do to help teach what I know about English to someone else? (for example, reading a book to my little brother or sister once a week or asking the teacher if I can lead a small group in class)

- _____
- _____

Textbook Integration

Textbooks can be a double-edged sword—they can be efficient, provide order, and save teachers time; they can provide good models; and they can provide a guide for effective language learning. There can be a danger, however, in teachers (and administrators and school districts) viewing them as being written in stone and insisting they be followed precisely.

We suggest that it is better to see textbooks as a sort of cookbook from which teachers can pick the right dishes for the appropriate occasions. The Latin root of the word *cook* means "to turn over in the mind." We believe that teachers using their experience, judgment, and skills to constantly turn things over in their mind is one of the main job requirements of effective educators.

The level of textbook flexibility provided to teachers varies, however. Because of that potential challenge, we offer a few ideas on how to use a textbook most effectively in the context of the learning and teaching strategies that we have suggested throughout this book.

Textbooks for beginning and early intermediate English language learners are often divided into themes similar to the ones we discussed in Chapter Three on teaching beginning ELLs. In that case, it can be relatively simple to implement the suggestions we'll be making in this section. However, there tends to be a wider variance among textbooks for more advanced ELLs. For those classes, using our suggested instructional strategies is still eminently doable, but may require a little more work.

If you are obligated to follow the textbook closely, our recommendation is to try to use it as a framework for your class. In other words, first examine what the leaning goals are for each chapter and identify the places where you can most easily include more engaging teaching strategies. As Jason Renshaw, a longtime ESL/EFL teacher, puts it, "to innovate within concrete, start with the cracks."[7]

Incorporating more engaging teaching strategies could include any of the following:

- Convert textbook passages or dialogues into text data sets, clozes, or sequencing activities to be completed by students (see Chapters Three through Six for more information on these strategies).

- If there are a lot of questions to answer in a textbook assignment, turn them into a jigsaw exercise (see Chapter Seven), with each partner having a few questions to answer and being prepared to support their answer with reasons.

- Personalize textbook dialogues—and we're not talking about just the names! Often these dialogues have little relationship to the everyday lives of students in a particular class.

- Convert dialogues and grammar lessons into jazz chants. See Chapter Three for more information.

- Turn textbook passages into read-alouds and think-alouds (see Chapters Three and Five for more information).

- Use pictures from the textbook for Picture Word Inductive Model or critical pedagogy lessons (see Chapter Three for more details).

- Most textbooks offer a large number of downloadable supplemental materials. These can be a great source of materials for use in the Stations Game, which is discussed in Chapter Eleven.

- Many textbook publishers offer companion web sites for students with reinforcing interactive exercises. In our experience, often the online activities are superior to what's actually in the print version! If that's the case, by all means bring students to the computer lab or use some of the activities on a computer projector for the entire class.

- Phonics instruction in beginning textbooks can easily be modified into an inductive learning activity similar to the one described in Chapter Three.

- In our opinion, many textbooks lack sufficient scaffolding for teaching writing. Adding many of the writing strategies we suggest throughout the book can be particularly useful to students.

- Don't feel that you have to do all this on your own: you'd be surprised at the huge number of teachers from around the world who are facing similar challenges. By connecting with them as suggested in "The Best Ways ESL/EFL/ELL Teachers Can Develop Personal Learning Networks" (at http://larryferlazzo.edublogs.org), teachers can share useful materials with others.

Error Correction

The issue of error correction, particularly focused on grammar, can be a controversial topic in ESL circles.[8] A number of studies suggest that correction—either through prompts that point out the error to a student and require an immediate attempt at a repair or through "recasts," when teachers rephrase correctly what the student said—can be a useful tool to assist language acquisition.[9]

Other research, however, suggests the opposite—that overt grammar correction can actually be harmful to English language learners. Some researchers suggest that oral grammar correction interrupts communicative activities and can generate a negative reaction from students when they are publicly corrected.[10] These studies point to similar hindrances resulting from correcting written grammatical errors, saying that it contributes to stress, which can inhibit language learning.[11]

These two points of view partially rely on varying perspectives on the difference between language "acquisition" and language "learning," which was described in Chapter One. To "acquire" language, according to many who question the use of error correction, it is important to have a greater emphasis on communication, rather than the correct form.[12] Researchers like Stephen Krashen would suggest that "learning" a language in schools can instead focus too much on the correct forms through grammar instruction and worksheets and not result in students actually being able to communicate effectively in the real world.

We share the concerns of those who question the advantages of error correction. However, we do believe that error correction does have a place in the ESL classroom.

Regular use of concept attainment using both correct and incorrect grammar usage (which can include examples of oral and written language in the classroom and does not identify the student who committed the error); use of games that have students correct common grammar errors (this is discussed specifically in Chapter Eleven); and the use of "recasts" in dialogue journals, as described in Chapter Three, are all teaching strategies we use frequently in our ESL classrooms. Dave Dodgson, an English teacher in Turkey, also suggests that the teacher write a paragraph incorporating several common mistakes made by students and then have them make corrections in small groups.[13]

In addition, instead of returning student-written papers where we point out numerous errors, we might emphasize several positive aspects of an essay and only focus on one type of error. We never just hand back papers with comments. Instead, we always have a private conversation—albeit a brief one during the daily silent reading time—with the student. At times, instead of using this process or in addition to doing it, if we see a common error trend in the class (for example, subject-verb agreement), we might also do a short minilesson that provides more explicit instruction.

Limited Access to Educational Technology

We've discussed using a number of technology tools—document cameras, computer labs, computer projectors, Internet access, and so forth. Most, but not all, readers of this book will probably have access to many of those resources. Some will not. What do you do if you're one of those without access?

First, it's important to remember that technology is just a tool. It can be an important tool that can have a major positive impact on language learning,[14] but great teaching and learning can certainly happen without it. In fact, like any tool, its effect depends on how it's used. Tech used in the ways we suggest throughout this book—as a way to reinforce what has already been learned, as a strategic vehicle through which to heighten student engagement, as a way to help students develop and deepen face-to-face relationships—can result, and has resulted, in significant student learning gains. If it is viewed as a babysitting device, as a time for teachers to do prep work instead of circulating throughout the room, or as an opportunity to get by without thinking through a lesson plan, then it can actually result in a *negative* learning impact.

If you have limited access to tech, but want to maximize what you do have for student language learning, here are a few ideas:

- If you have access to only one computer and a projector, many of the web sites we recommend can still be used very effectively. Whether it is an online karaoke site designed for ELLs to fill in blank words from a song (see Chapter Three), online grammar games and activities, or an animated story, they can all be projected on the screen (and make sure you have good speakers). Students can be divided into partners or groups and can write the correct answers on shared small whiteboards, or even pieces of paper, that they then hold up. These kinds of activities can be used as a game. We have regular access to a computer lab and still use these whole-class activities often.

- If you have a few computers in your classroom, have Internet access, and if you are using a lot of cooperative learning activities (as we hope you are), then regularly assigning small groups or pairs to work on assignments using technology can be an option. It is important, though, to keep track of which students are using the computers to avoid hearing "Johnny has used the computer twice this week and I haven't!" They can also be used in the Stations Game (see Chapter Eleven) as one or two of the stations.

- Again, if you have only a few computers, having students take turns using them during daily Free Voluntary Reading time to access the countless accessible reading opportunities on the Web is another option (see Chapter Three for recommended sites). Having headphones available is important.

- If you do not have a document camera that lets you project book pages, documents, and examples of student work, then, of course, there is the old standby of transparencies and the overhead projector. If that's what you have now, one way to use it to promote student engagement is to give blank transparencies to students for presentation preparation. Then *they* get to be up front as the teacher.

- If you and your students don't have much access to educational technology, money may very well be a major reason behind it. If that is the case, you can find a growing list of inexpensive tech tools, where to get them, and places to seek grant funds for their purchase in "The Best Good, Inexpensive, and Simple Classroom Technology Tools" at http://larryferlazzo.edublogs.org.

Multilevel Classes

Some schools, especially those with small ELL populations, do not create separate classes for beginners and intermediates. Though there are obviously different levels within those two categories of learners, the differences are much more pronounced when you combine both together. Those differences create opportunities and challenges.

One major opportunity relates to a challenge already discussed in this chapter: textbooks. Since few, if any, textbooks cover such a wide range of English levels, it is highly unlikely that teachers will feel pressured to use one. Of course, a teacher might choose an overall strategy of dividing the class in two and, in effect, just using two entirely separate curriculums (and perhaps two different textbooks) in a multilevel class.

At times in our careers, we have done exactly that in multilevel classes. Because of the particular students in those situations, most of the time the two groups work on different assignments with us moving back and forth between groups.

That kind of choice, however, can limit the potential teaching and learning benefits to all the beginner and intermediate students through a more unified combination. In addition, at least in our eyes, such a complete separation is more likely to drive an ESL teacher batty! An overt and constant division of tracks within a class also does little to enhance student morale.

We think a better approach in such a class, and one that we have used on other occasions, is using more unified themes that have easily modifiable assignments across the beginner and intermediate spectrum. This approach also creates exceptional opportunities for all students, and particularly the higher-level students, to become more authentic teachers, one of the key qualities of an effective language learner and one of the best ways to learn (see the Qualities of a Successful Language Learner Lesson Plan earlier in this chapter). It is important for the teacher to ensure that these authentic peer teaching opportunities are beneficial to all students and not just to those being tutored. Another advantage to a unified approach is that it exposes progressing beginners to more challenging learning tasks more quickly.

A key part of making this kind of setting work is effective assessment—formative and summative. Chapter Thirteen covers how this might look in the ESL classroom, and ongoing assessment by both the teacher and the student will be critical in ensuring that a multilevel classroom meets the needs of everyone. Not only does it help teachers determine initial placement, but it also particularly helps to fine-tune placement throughout the year—it creates opportunities, for example, for someone who is a high early intermediate in writing but may be more advanced in speaking to participate in beginner-level writing and intermediate speaking partner work.

Next we discuss how a more coherent double-period multilevel class might look, using many of the key elements of the curriculum discussed in Chapters Three and Five on teaching beginners and intermediates. Please remember that we are not proposing this plan as a scripted curriculum. Instead, this example is just one way a multilevel class could work effectively:

Whole Class. Begin the day with fifteen minutes of Free Voluntary Reading. With a good classroom library, or through copies of free printable books from the Web (see the Free Voluntary Reading section in Chapter Three), this time can be equally effective for both beginners and intermediates. A teacher can easily model increasingly sophisticated uses of reading strategies for all levels. Book Talks—both face to face and online—can be shared with similar ability groups or pairs. In other words, group beginners with other beginners and intermediates with other intermediates.

Whole Class. A photo, video, or cartoon can be used to introduce a Picture Word Inductive Model or critical pedagogy lesson, with beginners writing descriptive words and simple sentences and intermediates developing more sophisticated sentences and paragraphs.

Similar Ability Groups or Partners. Beginners can be using the Picture Word Inductive Model described in Chapter Three. Intermediates can use the elements of the inductive writing process described in Chapter Five to write a persuasive, problem-solution, or autobiographical essay using the class visual as a prompt. For example, if the visual was about school, the intermediates' assignment could connect to a school-related problem or previous incident in the student's life. At times the teacher might want to bring all the intermediates or all the beginners together for a brief specific lesson while the other group works on their assignment.

Whole Class. The entire class is brought together, and the teacher explains that students will work in similar-ability groups or with similar-ability partners to complete one of the following assignments:

- Dialogue or role-play, where beginners are assigned to practice it as written or with small changes, and intermediates use it as a model to develop their own.

- Cloze (fill in the gap) of a short passage, where beginners would have the correct words shown at the bottom of the page and intermediates would not. The teacher could be more strategic about using clozes that are models for academic writing that intermediates are doing.

- Song, where beginners would again have a cloze with the correct words shown at the bottom and intermediates would not have those clues.

- Jigsaw, where beginner groups review more simple text to prepare their presentations and intermediates use more challenging passages.

Similar Groups or Partners. Students do the assigned work related to the dialogue, cloze, song, or jigsaw and make presentations, if appropriate, to the entire class or to just another similar-ability partner. Or presentations can be made to all students at that same level with the teacher monitoring while the other group is working on their assignment or other self-access materials.

Mixed-Ability Partner Groups. This could be a game, a time when intermediate students "teach" a prepared lesson to beginner groups, a picture dictation exercise (again where the intermediate student might be more of the teacher), or one of the other information gap activities described in Chapter Three where one student needs to get information from the other student by questioning him or her. In such a gap exercise, each partner's sheet could have the necessary information, but it could be made more difficult to find in the intermediate student's paper.

Whole Class. Student reflection (see Chapter Four).

In addition, here are other strategies that can be used to differentiate in a multilevel class:

Computer Lab Work. Of course, computer work can be easily differentiated and actually personalized. In addition to the hundreds of thousands of different free activities on the Web, there are many free sites that enable student registration and let students and the teacher monitor progress. We have listed several of them in the Homework section of Chapter Four.

Homework. Homework can certainly be modified for both beginners and intermediates to make it appropriate to their English level.

Peer Tutors. If, as we suggest in Chapter Two, you are able to get volunteer peer tutors from other school classes, they can be used to further assist in differentiated instruction. For example, some days they can be assigned to work with the beginners during similar-ability group work while the teacher can concentrate on the intermediates. The reverse can also be true. Of course, a peer tutor can never be a replacement for a teacher, but can certainly be a positive force in helping students learn English.

Dialogue Journals. In Chapter Three we discussed the use of dialogue journals with "sister classes" composed of students who are fluent in English—either in your school or online with another school. Beginners and intermediates can readily be given different assignments for that task.

Graphic Organizers. Graphic organizers, discussed in many chapters of this book, can be easily modified to provide more support for beginning students and increased complexity for intermediates. For example, a K-W-L chart might contain pictures and words written by beginners, while intermediates can write in sentences.

Primary Language Use in the ESL Classroom

Use of students' primary language (called L1, native language, or heritage language) in the ESL classroom has been a controversial topic. Some claim that its use can hinder learning English and can result in students getting accustomed to using it as a crutch.[15] And researchers appear to confirm that overreliance on a primary language can indeed result in less effective language learning.[16]

However, more and more research has also found that careful and strategic use of a student's primary language—whether through a translation by a teacher, peer tutor, bilingual aide, or assistance from students themselves—can in fact help English language learning, particularly in understanding grammar concepts, vocabulary, instructions, and in developing teacher-student and student-student relationships.[17]

There will be times, however, when limiting primary language use could be important. For example, during information gap activities or Back to the Screen exercises, we will often say that the next fifteen minutes is an English-only time. The chances of this request being generally respected are high in our classroom because students know that we do not typically restrict their own use of L1 at any point (and in fact often use it in the strategic ways mentioned in the last paragraph). We also periodically share with students what research says about L1 overreliance and request that most L1 student use be related to helping each other understand English. Their commitment is more of the honor code variety, since we do not speak all the languages present in our classrooms, but from what we have seen and from what students have written, we believe it is relatively respected.

In summary, we believe that most instruction in an ESL class should be carried out in English. But as researchers William Saunders and Claude Goldenberg have written: "we can imagine using the primary language in a limited but strategic manner during ELD [ESL] instruction in order to ensure that students understand task directions, pay attention to cognates [words that are similar in two languages and have the same—or different—meanings], and master language learning and metacognitive strategies."[18]

Classroom Management

Many teachers, including us, would say that there are likely to be fewer classroom management problems in an ESL class than in a mainstream classroom for a number of reasons, including the fact that many ELLs have a high level of intrinsic motivation. If a good curriculum and engaging instructional strategies are used—like the ones we discuss in this book—few students will question the relevance or usefulness of what is happening in the classroom.

However, that does not mean an ESL classroom is immune from these challenges.

Besides good teaching, solid relationship building, and the suggestions we shared in the Motivation section earlier in this chapter, here are a few research-based tips to keep in mind. They are taken from the book *Helping Students Motivate Themselves: Practical Answers to Classroom Challenges,* by Larry Ferlazzo:[19]

Don't Use Incentives and Rewards. Plenty of research shows that the use of incentives and rewards ("If you do that, I will give you this") can, in the short term, increase compliance in tasks that require lower-level thinking skills. That same research, however, also shows that both in the short term and the long term their use discourages and harms the development of higher-order thinking skills. We included the section on motivation in this chapter to provide practical ways to promote intrinsic desire among students.

This is not to say that, practically speaking, it is bad for a teacher to ever use incentives or rewards. Both of us have been teaching too long to have such an unrealistic perspective. Sometimes you just need compliance *now,* and nothing else seems to be working. We are suggesting that it be used only when absolutely necessary.

Positive-Framed Messages. By knowing students' goals through relationship building and introductory activities, teachers can use more "positive-framed" messages ("Think of all the great things that can happen if you learn English—you can get the job you want as a nurse") than "loss-framed" messages ("If you don't do this, then I am sending you to the office and they'll call your parents").

Emphasizing What Students Can Do. Instead of regularly saying "Don't chew gum" or "You can't go to the bathroom," instead say "You can chew gum after class and you can drink water now" or "Yes, you can go the bathroom. Could you wait for a few minutes for a break in the lesson?"

Being Courteous. Saying "Please," "Thank you," and "I'm sorry" not only provides excellent role modeling, but is also far more likely to result in quicker compliance. Requests are always preferable to commands. This teacher attitude supports a student's need for autonomy, one of the key human needs identified by William Glasser.

Calmness. Teachers reacting out of frustration or anger seldom leads to positive results—believe us, we can speak from plenty of experience! Taking a few deep breaths and speaking softly and respectfully—ideally privately to a student—will generally have far more success than losing one's temper.

Book Selection

Chapter Two discussed issues related to a classroom library. Access to books can be one challenge, and students selecting appropriate books can be another.

As we wrote earlier, we believe it makes things easier for students to have books divided into broadly leveled categories and at the same time encourage students not to be constrained by them. Challenging, high-interest books can be powerful intrinsic motivators to students.

There is a danger, however, in the ESL classroom of students regularly choosing very easy books to read and being hesitant to take the risk in challenging themselves. There is also the potential problem of students choosing books that are far beyond their English level because they want to show off or because they are very interested in the topic but don't have a realistic view of their reading abilities. In either case, teachers will want to help students come to their own conclusions about what kinds of books best serve their needs.

Teachers can approach this challenge by offering suggested guidelines: the book should be on a topic of genuine personal interest to the student, students should look through a book first to ensure that the vocabulary is not too hard or too easy, and if they decide they don't want to continue reading it, they should return it and find a replacement. Our first point can't be emphasized too much—*students must be interested in the book's content.*

One way that we illustrate how students can determine which "challenging" book might be right for them is with a simple teacher dramatization. We first ask students if they think we can reach the top of something easy in the classroom—for example, the top of a medium-tall bookcase or even the floor. They say "Yes," we go touch it, and then explain that it was easy. Then we ask them if they think we can touch something that is out of our reach in class—for example, the ceiling. They say "No," we try (to student laughter), and fail. We then explain that it was too hard. Finally, we identify something that we can reach with some effort—the top of the whiteboard, perhaps. We prepare with much drama, get a running start, touch its top, and explain that this is what we mean by choosing a "challenging" book—one that students are interested in and can understand with some effort. Teachers can explain this point further by asking students if they would always want to play sports opponents who were not as good or equal to them or only perform easy songs on musical instruments. This is another way to help students see the advantages to taking risks.

In addition, for highly motivated students who have a very strong desire to read certain popular books, we have loaned them two copies—one in English and one in their primary language. However, before we provide the students with those copies, we discuss the purpose of the class—to learn English—and ask for their commitment to focus on reading the English version and use the translated copy only sparingly to help them on occasion.

Many years ago, a man who worked with Mahatma Gandhi in India told one of us that the key to Gandhi's success was that he looked at every problem as an opportunity, not as a pain. That perspective has served us well over the years, and we hope that this chapter has provided some tools that might similarly help you.

Additional resources, including more ideas on incorporating mental imagery, teaching multilevel classes, using technology in the classroom, and dealing with error correction, can be found on our book's web site at www.josseybass.com/go/eslsurvivalguide.

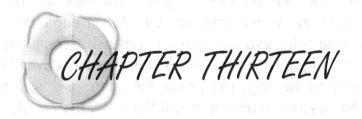

CHAPTER THIRTEEN

Assessing English Language Learners

Long ago a prince set off on his horse seeking adventure. He came upon four animals in a forest—a tiger, a dog, an eagle, and an ant—who were arguing over the carcass of a deer. The lion asked the prince to help settle their argument by dividing the deer's carcass into four parts in exchange for a reward.

The prince gladly obliged and divided the carcass into four even sections. The animals were pleased and offered the prince a reward. The lion and the dog each gave him a piece of their hair, the eagle gave him a feather, and the ant gave him one of his antennae. They told the prince he could use each of these items to transform his human body into animal form by saying "tiger," "dog," and so on. When he wanted to return to human form he simply needed to say "man."

The prince continued on his way until he came to a large castle surrounded by a high wall. Thinking it would be impossible to gain entrance to the castle because of the high wall, he began to turn around until he remembered the feather in his pocket. He then used the feather to turn into an eagle and flew over the wall up to the highest tower, where he discovered a beautiful princess. He flew in the window and said "man" and turned back into a prince. The princess lamented that she was being held prisoner by an evil giant who would kill anyone who tried to rescue her. She further explained the only way to kill the giant was to find the secret egg that contained the giant's life within it and to destroy it.

At that moment, a booming voice sounded in the hall as the giant approached the tower. Just as he was about to barge into the room, the prince used the antenna and transformed into a tiny ant. The giant was confused as he had heard two voices, but searched the room and found no one but the princess.

The giant left the room, turned into a pigeon, and flew off. The prince, who was watching the giant the whole time, turned into an eagle and followed the pigeon to a cave, where he saw the pigeon with a box containing the secret egg. As soon as the pigeon saw the eagle land in the cave, he turned into a coyote and swallowed the egg. The prince then changed from an eagle to a tiger and chased the coyote. Unable to avoid the tiger, the coyote changed into a hare and hid under some bushes. The prince changed from a tiger to a dog and was able to dive under the bushes and capture the hare. The prince then broke the egg and the giant was destroyed.

He transformed into an eagle and flew to the castle. He then turned back into human form and freed the princess. They were married and lived happily together in the castle from that day forth.[1]

The prince in this folktale must constantly adapt and make adjustments to the rapidly changing circumstances he faces as he tries to slay the giant. Teachers and students face a similar challenge in today's world, where educational policies and assessments are constantly changing. ESL teachers face the additional challenge of assessing ELLs in an effective and equitable way in their own classrooms. They must also support their students as they face standardized tests that are not always equitable or designed with their needs in mind.

The prince in the story felt confident in his ability to slay the giant because of the tools at his disposal. It is our hope that this chapter will provide both knowledge and tools that teachers can use to navigate the challenge of assessing English language learners.

Assessing ELLs: Key Principles

Before sharing information on different types of assessments and ideas for implementing assessment in the ESL classroom, we feel it is first important to share a few key principles that can serve as a foundation for equitable and effective assessment of ELLs. We know many teachers may feel overwhelmed by the assessments at the state, district, and site level that they are required to implement, but were created without their input. We also know how it feels to bombard students with multiple assessments that aren't directly connected to what they are learning and don't yield timely or valuable information on their progress. It is our hope that the following principles and assessment ideas will help teachers assess their ELL students in a meaningful way, one that yields value for both the student and the teacher.

- *Be data-informed, not data-driven.* When schools are *data-informed,* they use assessment data to make thoughtful decisions that directly benefit students.[2] When schools are *data-driven,* they may make decisions that do not help students, like keeping students who are "borderline" between algebra and a higher level of math in algebra so that they do well on the algebra state test. Or, in English, teachers might focus a lot of energy on teaching a strand that is heavy on the tests, even though it might not help the student become a lifelong reader. In other words, the school may tend to focus on its institutional self-interest instead of what's best for the students. However, in schools that are *data-informed*, test results are just one more piece of information that can be helpful in determining future directions. Teachers who are data-informed will use assessment data to reflect on their practice, identify areas to modify and adjust, and seek out the resources and knowledge needed to enact those changes.

• *Assess knowledge and language separately.* Many ELL students may not be able to fully demonstrate what they know and what they can do because of their limited levels of proficiency in English. It is not effective to measure a student's content knowledge by using an assessment that requires them to produce language beyond their level of proficiency. For example, asking beginning-level students to demonstrate their knowledge of a plant's life cycle by writing an essay is more a test of their English skills than their actual content knowledge. Researchers have recommended that teachers implement test modifications for their ELLs, such as simplifying test questions or allowing the use of bilingual dictionaries, in order "to prevent language limitations from unnecessarily sacrificing ELLs' test performance."[3]

• *Assess students according to their* current *proficiency level.* As discussed in earlier chapters, it is important to get to know your students, identify their academic strengths and challenges, and know their current levels of English proficiency in speaking, reading, and writing. Having this information allows teachers to assess students according to their current level of English proficiency—not by the results of the last standardized test they took.

• *Involve students in self-assessment.* Involving students in the assessment process can be powerful and can result in increased motivation and learning. When students are asked to evaluate their own progress, they feel more ownership of the learning process and are better able to identify specific learning goals for themselves. Research suggests that "when students are expected to evaluate themselves and when they view their input in the learning progress as meaningful, their self-assessment can be very helpful, if not integral, to their learning."[4] For examples of student self-evaluation, see the section on Reflection in Chapter Four and in the Student Self-Assessment discussion later in this chapter.

INITIAL, FORMATIVE, AND SUMMATIVE ASSESSMENT WITH ELLS

The following subsections describe three common assessment processes—initial, formative, and summative—that may be used to assess the progress of ELLs.

Initial or Diagnostic Assessments

When students enter a class, it can be helpful to assess their reading, writing, and speaking skills to get an idea of their current proficiency level. The purpose of these initial assessments is to gain information about students' levels of English in order to tailor future instruction to meet students' specific language needs. These types of assessments can also indicate whether a student has been placed in the appropriate class for their level of proficiency. Most schools and/or districts have protocols for assessing ELLs as they enter school. However, ESL teachers are the ones who interact with these students on a daily basis in a comfortable and safe environment, and therefore may be more capable of making accurate judgments about students' language abilities. Teachers can initially assess students' English abilities in a variety of ways, but here are a few we have found effective:

- *Writing.* Having students produce a piece of writing either in response to a prompt or on a certain topic is a way to get an idea of students' writing abilities. The teacher should think carefully about the prompt or topic and ensure that it is accessible. For example, after showing students a letter from the teacher (see Exhibit 2.1), students could be asked to write a letter to the teacher about themselves.

Having students read a short piece of text and then write to a prompt can offer the teacher valuable information about students' reading comprehension skills and writing skills. Exhibit 13.1 is an example of an initial assessment we have used with our intermediate ELLs to gather information on students' reading, writing, and thinking skills. The teacher can select a piece of text that fits the level of the students and adjust the language of the prompt as needed.

Of course, one piece of writing is not going to fully illustrate a student's English abilities, but it can be a quick snapshot that the teacher can use to plan further assessments and conversations with students as he or she gets to know them at the beginning of the year.

- *Cloze assessments.* Giving students cloze passages with fill-in-the-blanks (or gap-fill) can give the teacher useful information about students' vocabulary levels and reading comprehension skills. As students read a passage and make guesses about which words might go in the blanks, they must employ comprehension strategies like using context clues, as well as drawing on their own vocabulary knowledge.

This type of initial cloze assessment can be used to plan future reading instruction and can be done several times during the year to measure student progress. Clozes are a form of assessment that also serve to develop students' language skills each time they are assessed. In fact, research has shown that using clozes with students "led to significant gains in ESL students' receptive and productive vocabulary, and an increased ability to use the vocabulary in other contexts."[5]

EXHIBIT 13.1. Initial Assessment

Name _____

Date _____

Excerpt

> The older you are, the younger you get when you move to the United
> States. Two years after my father and I moved here from Guatemala I could
> speak English. I learned it on the playground and by watching lots of TV.
> Don't believe what people say—cartoons make you *smart*. But my father,
> he worked all day in a kitchen with Mexicans and Salvadorans. His English
> was worse than a kindergartener's. He would only buy food at the *bodega*
> down the block. Outside of there he lowered his eyes and tried to get by on
> mumbles and smiles. He didn't want strangers to hear his mistakes. So he
> used me to make phone calls and to talk to the landlady and to buy things
> in stores where you had to use English. He got younger. I got older.

Source: P. Fleishman, ''Gonzalo,'' in *Seedfolks* (New York: Harper Trophy, 1997), 17–18.

Writing Prompt

Read the paragraph above and write an essay responding to the following questions.
Describe Gonzalo's experience of moving to the United States. Write your opinion
about Gonzalo's experience: What do you think about *his* experience? How is his
experience similar to or different from your own? Be sure to use specific examples
from the paragraph above, anything else you've read, and/or your own life.

When creating a cloze, it is important to carefully select the text and which words are omitted so that students can use contextual clues to make their guesses. The level of the passage can be adjusted according to the overall proficiency level of the class. For more on creating and using cloze passages, including where to find online cloze activities, see the Clozes section in Chapter Five.

- *Fluency assessments.* Sitting down with each student and listening to them read aloud in English can be a useful practice at the beginning of the year to get an idea of students' reading abilities in English. This is also a valuable opportunity for the teacher to have a brief one-on-one conversation with each student, which also serves as an informal assessment of students' speaking and listening skills (and the teacher can ask a few questions about students' lives and interests).

It is important that teachers choose an appropriate level of text for students to read aloud and that it is done in a sensitive, safe way so that students do not feel they are being tested. The teacher can casually ask students to read a little bit either from the teacher-selected text or from a student's free, voluntary reading book. If you wish, you can have students read for about a minute and discreetly keep track of the time, mark the errors made, and make notations about the students' reading behaviors (such as tracking with finger, sounding out words, or skipping word endings).

As with cloze assessments, this type of initial fluency assessment can be used to plan future reading instruction and can also be used throughout the year to measure student progress. It is important to use the same level of text or the same reading book in order to get an accurate measure of progress. Students can also record a beginning-of-the-year reading fluency sample on a web site such as Fotobabble, which can be maintained online indefinitely and used later on as a formative assessment.

- *Speaking and listening assessments.* Teachers can initially assess their students' speaking and listening skills in a very simple way—by having brief, one-on-one conversations with students. As stated earlier, these can be part of the reading fluency assessment, as the teacher sits individually with each student. The teacher can informally ask students a similar set of questions (about their family, interests, or favorites). The teacher may want to wait to record her observations until after they have finished talking with the student, so she is able to give her full attention to the student. It can also be helpful for the teacher to briefly share a couple of things about her family, interests, and the like, in order for the conversation to feel natural and to promote relationship building and trust.

Formative Assessment Process

Formative assessment is not a type of test or assessment, but is a *process* that combines teaching, learning, and assessment. It is an ongoing process where teachers and students evaluate assessment evidence in order to make adjustments to their teaching and learning. Gathering this assessment evidence can be done in multiple ways—including more formal measures, such as written tests, and informal practices, such as student self-evaluation or observation.[6] The formative assessment process is an effective way for teachers to check students' understanding throughout the learning process and then use this information to guide instruction.

This type of ongoing assessment process is critically important when teaching ELL students in order to identify when and how students need extra support. As WestEd researcher Robert Linquanti points out, "Formative assessment practices have enormous potential to strengthen teachers' capacities to developmentally stage or 'scaffold' ELLs' language and content learning."[7] Many other researchers have affirmed the value of formative assessment as a powerful tool for teachers and students when used as a natural part of teaching and learning: "There should be a seamless transition between instruction and formative assessment. If its feedback truly shapes instruction, formative assessments do not need to be forced or complex to administer, but instead are a natural check for understanding that will be useful for planning the next lesson."[8]

The formative assessment process serves to strengthen students' abilities to assess their own progress, to set and evaluate their own learning goals, and to make adjustments accordingly. Formative assessment also elicits valuable feedback from students about what teachers are doing effectively and what they could do better.

The following activities can be used by teachers and students to collect evidence of student learning and progress. It is important to remember that *how* the teacher chooses to use this information ultimately determines whether it is "formative" in nature. Effective teaching and assessment involve using this evidence to make decisions about what students need and how best to meet those needs and encourage students to use this information in the same way.

- *Weekly "tests."* Assessing students on a weekly basis on what has been taught over the week can help the teacher check for student understanding. This information can help the teacher identify which students need more help and which concepts need to be further practiced. Both the teacher and the students can gain valuable information from these tests about what they need to do differently. In order for these "tests" to be helpful to students and the teacher, they need to be short and low stakes (not used as a "gotcha" or in a punitive way). It is also important that these assessments reflect what has already been taught and not be new concepts. When administered in a positive learning environment, these types of weekly tests can build students' confidence as they are able to demonstrate what they have learned. They can also be used as a teaching opportunity, as the teacher identifies questions or parts of the test that students struggled with and reteaches those concepts. Weekly tests can take various forms—labeling pictures, multiple choice, writing to a prompt, performing a role-play—depending on the level of the class and the concepts being assessed. For an example of a weekly assessment used with beginners, see the Sample Friday Test in Exhibit 4.4.

Using frequent low-stakes assessments—where students and teachers reflect on the results and make changes—is a key part of the formative assessment process and produces powerful results. As W. James Popham explains, "recent reviews of more than 4,000 research investigations show clearly that when this [formative] process is well implemented in the classroom, it can essentially double the speed of student learning."[9]

- *Writing prompts.* Teachers can assess student learning by having students write to a prompt. These prompts can take many forms, such as a question to answer, a statement with which to agree or disagree, a picture to describe, or a response to a text or video clip. It is important that writing prompts for ELLs contain clear directions and take into account the cultural and linguistic knowledge that students currently possess.[10] Asking students to write about content they have not yet learned or about cultural situations they are not familiar with will not yield valuable information about students' true abilities. For example, giving students a prompt asking them to describe their favorite carnival or fair ride might be confusing for students who haven't attended this type of event or aren't familiar with the term *carnival*.

- *Student self-assessment and reflection.* Activities that promote metacognitive thinking and ask students to reflect on their learning processes are key to the formative assessment process. When students are asked to think about *what* they have learned and *how* they have learned it (the learning strategies they've used), they are better able to understand their own learning processes and can set new goals for themselves. Students can reflect on their learning in many ways: answering a set of questions, drawing a picture or set of pictures to represent their learning process, talking with a partner, or keeping a learning log or journal, for example. Students can be prompted to reflect on their learnings of academic concepts as well as life lessons and personal growth. The teacher can use these responses to check for student understanding, but also to check the pulse of the class in terms of student motivation, confidence levels, and levels of metacognition.

For more examples of student reflection, see the lesson plans in Chapter Twelve and the Reflection section in Chapter Four.

- *Goal sheets.* As we explained in Chapter Five, having students set their own goals and evaluate progress toward achieving them is an effective part of the formative assessment process. It is important to help students distinguish between learning goals and performance goals. Research has shown the advantages of emphasizing learning goals ("I want to take more leadership in small groups") over performance goals ("I want to get an A in this class"). Both are important, but the issue is which one is given greater weight. Goal sheets are an effective way to help students set goals and track their progress. It can be helpful to identify specific goals. For example, "I will read in English for 20 minutes each night" is more specific than "I will read more." Also, goals need to be achievable in a short period of time and not impossibly difficult. The teacher can model how to set effective goals and also how to evaluate one's progress toward achieving them by asking students to periodically write or talk about what they have achieved, what they still would like to achieve, and *how* they will do it. An example of a goal sheet we use with our classes can be found in the lesson plan on the Qualities of a Successful Language Learner in Chapter Twelve. The goal sheet for that lesson plan (Exhibit 12.4) can be modified in a variety of ways to promote student goal setting and evaluation.

- *Cloze or fluency.* As described previously, cloze and fluency assessments can be used to initially assess students' reading skills. They can also be used throughout the year as formative assessments that the teacher can use to design instruction and target areas students are struggling with. For example, a teacher who frequently listens to students read aloud on an individual basis might notice that her students are not pausing when they see a comma. She could then decide to model reading a passage aloud and pausing slightly at the commas, and then give her students time to practice in pairs. A teacher can continue this same process with different elements of reading fluency such as intonation, pronunciation, and appropriate reading rate.

- *Online audio recording.* Using an online audio recording site like Fotobabble is a way for students and the teacher to assess student progress in speaking and reading fluency. Students can periodically record themselves (speaking or reading a text) and then can reflect on their improvement over time.

- *Observation.* A huge part of formative assessment takes place on a daily basis as the teacher observes his students. Teachers are constantly observing both the progress their students are making and the struggles they are encountering. This informal type of assessment should be formative, as the teacher changes and adapts both curriculum and instruction to meet students' current needs.

We have found it helpful to jot down our observations during a lesson either on sticky notes or in a journal so that we can return to them later as we plan the next lesson. We also find it useful to create a folder for each of our students where we store their initial assessments and any written observational data. These can be easily accessed for parent meetings and at the end of a grading period. Teachers can also make a sheet for each student that contains a checklist of behaviors or skills they will be observing and space for additional comments.

• *Student conferences.* Meeting with students on an individual basis to discuss their learning progress can be hugely beneficial and informative. Asking students to share their goal sheets is one way to structure a conversation about student progress. During a conference, it can be helpful for the teacher to give students specific feedback such as "I've noticed that you are using more sensory details in your writing," as opposed to general comments like "Your writing is getting better." Robert Marzano explains that a key to formative assessment is providing students with "sound feedback," which means "it should be frequent, give students a clear picture of their progress and how they might improve, and provide encouragement."[11] It is also important to praise students' effort and not their intelligence. As mentioned earlier, research has shown that students who were praised for their effort instead of their intelligence worked harder, were more persistent, and scored higher on IQ tests compared to those who were praised for their intelligence.[12]

A student conference obviously isn't the only time to give feedback to students. There are many opportunities each day when teachers can provide this kind of "sound feedback." For more research and ideas on giving students feedback, see "The Best Resources for Learning How to Best Give Feedback to Students" at http://larryferlazzo.edublogs.org.

• *Rubrics.* Rubrics can be used as part of the formative assessment process and also can be used as a summative assessment after students have completed an essay or project. Teachers can develop rubrics for many types of assignments and projects and then create lessons that align with the assessment. It can be helpful to share the rubric with students before they even start a project. When students are shown a rubric at the beginning, they have the opportunity to better understand the criteria they must meet in order to be successful. It can also be useful to involve students in the creation of rubrics by asking them to select several criteria that they feel should be included on the rubric. This allows students to put the rubric criteria into their own words and to take more ownership of the assessment process.

Rubrics can be used as a guide for students to assess their work over the course of a project. Each time our students start an essay, we first go over the rubric together and then refer back to it often as they produce their drafts. Having a set of criteria also helps the students and the teacher focus on the specific areas that will be assessed, so that the revising process can be more targeted and effective.

Well-designed rubrics can be useful for students to understand the criteria of an assignment and to use as a tool for self-evaluation. However, not all rubrics are helpful all of the time. Rubrics with highly technical language or that don't align with the concepts students are being taught can be confusing and defeating for students. Creating different rubrics for every assignment can be confusing for students and time-consuming for the teacher. Also, using only one general rubric for different assignments and types of writing isn't beneficial because the criteria may be too vague. It can also be frustrating when rubrics are imposed on teachers and their students without their input, especially when they are being used as an assessment measure and are not aligned to the curriculum.

See Chapter Six for a list of online rubric sites.

Summative Assessment

Summative assessment differs from the formative assessment process in that it is mainly used at the end of an instructional sequence or grading period to measure student learning. Summative assessments often include midterm and final exams, benchmark tests, and state standardized tests. The typical goal of these types of assessments is to collect information about what students have and have not learned. Of course, many argue that most standardized tests do not accurately depict what ELLs have learned because many of the tests, at least the ones up to now, have not taken language proficiency into account. Developers of the next generation of high-stakes tests claim these new ones will be different. (High-stakes tests will be discussed in more detail later in this chapter.)

We question the usefulness of many large, high-stakes tests as they currently exist because they aren't always the best indicators of students' growth. However, some forms of summative assessment used in the classroom can be useful in measuring student progress. We use summative assessments with our ELL students at both the end of the semester and at the end of the year. The following are summative assessments we have used with our ELL students that we have found valuable.

- *Portfolios*. Portfolios can be an effective way for students to demonstrate their growth in reading, writing, and thinking throughout the semester or school year. Keeping portfolios "assists students in evaluating themselves and assists you in evaluating your own program."[13] We have found it beneficial for our students to create their own portfolios at the end of a semester. We give each student a folder and a set of directions for what kinds of "evidence" they must include to document their learning in writing, reading, speaking, and thinking (see Exhibit 13.2). Students then take time to look through their binders and pull out work samples that demonstrate their learning. They also write an explanation of how each piece of work shows their learning. This process can be modified depending upon the level of the class. For example, beginners can choose a "before" work sample from the beginning of the semester and an "after" work sample from the end of the semester to show their progress.

EXHIBIT 13.2. Portfolio Directions

Semester Portfolio Project

Please answer these questions on a piece of lined paper. Write complete sentences.

1. Look through your portfolio at your evidence of reading. How many books did you finish this semester? How many pages are you reading each day? How have you improved as a reader this semester?

2. Look at your text logs. Choose two examples of your best text logs. Cut them out and glue them on your paper. Underneath each text log, explain *why* it is an example of your best work. Which reading strategies did you use? How does it show your understanding of the book?

3. What were the two books that you liked the most this semester? Please write at least two reasons why you liked each book.

4. Look at the writing you did this semester, especially your essays and longer writing pieces. Choose your best example and explain *why* it is your best. What did you learn by doing this piece of writing? What process did you use to complete this piece of writing? Please attach this writing piece to the back of your answers.

5. What would you like to improve (get better at) next semester and *why*?

6. Think about the kind of person, student, reader, and writer you were on the first day of school in September. Draw a picture of yourself *then* on one half of this paper. Then think about the kind of person, student, reader, and writer you are now. Draw a picture of yourself *now* on the other half of your paper. Write at least one sentence describing what your picture represents and why: I was _____ in September and now I'm _____ because _____.

Please attach your picture to the back of your answers.

- *End-of-semester or end-of-year exam.* Many of the formative assessments explained earlier can be used at the end of a semester or grading period to demonstrate learning over time. At the end of each semester, we give our students fluency and cloze assessments so we can compare the scores to their initial reading assessments from the beginning of the year. Students can also respond to a writing prompt similar to the initial prompt they wrote at the beginning of the year. Speaking and reading fluency progress can be measured using online audio recording web sites, or students can respond orally to a set of questions in a one-on-one conversation with the teacher (as described in the Initial Assessment section in this chapter).

ELLs and Standardized Testing

Currently many ELLs take two types of summative assessments each year: a standardized state test that measures content knowledge and skills and an English language proficiency test that measures proficiency in English listening, speaking, reading, and writing. These state standardized tests are being revised to reflect the new Common Core standards. The Common Core State Standards Initiative is an effort to establish a shared set of educational English language arts and mathematics standards focused on college and career readiness that states can adopt (http://www.corestandards.org/frequently-asked-questions). There are currently no ELL-specific Common Core standards; however, the process to develop a new English language proficiency test is already under way. The development of this "next generation" of state testing is currently in process and being funded by federal grant money.[14] Two state consortiums are working on new state standardized tests to align with the Common Core standards. Two other consortiums have emerged to focus on the development of a new English language proficiency test. At the time of this book's publication, all of this is still in development.

Even though a level of uncertainty exists with these new tests, one thing is certain: our students will take standardized tests each year. One way for educators to help students feel less anxiety and to do their best on these tests is to make sure ELLs have access to testing accommodations. Depending upon the state, different accommodations are allowed to help ELLs access these tests. The most common accommodations include simplified instructions, providing instructions in the native language, extra time, small-group administration, and use of bilingual dictionaries or glossaries.[15] Research has indicated that "appropriate accommodations enable English learners to show what they know and can do on content tests administered in English (such as a math test) by reducing interference of English language demands on the test." Research has also found that for accommodations to be successful, they must also be used frequently during regular instructional time so students have experience with them.[16] Most important, accommodations must be matched to individual student needs, which can change over time as they gain proficiency. (For a list of ELL accommodations by state, see http://ells.ceee.gwu.edu.)

Another way teachers can help make the testing process more comfortable and accessible for their students is by sharing some basic test-taking tips with them. Of course, we don't recommend that test prep ever take the place of language development instruction. Ultimately the best way for students to raise their test scores is through the development of academic English literacy with the support of engaging classroom instruction. In other words, all the activities we have recommended in this book. However, the following ideas represent a few ways to help students feel more comfortable and do their best on standardized tests:[17]

- Familiarize students with the test format and types of questions. Most states provide sample tests online.

- Remind students that it is okay to skip hard questions and come back to them later (this helps avoid ELLs getting stuck on one question for a long period of time).

- Teach intermediate and advanced ELLs the difference between literal and inferential questions. This can help students identify when they should be able to find the answer on the page and when they must infer the answer in their mind.

Of course, these are not the only strategies to help ELLs feel more comfortable and prepared for standardized tests. Basic elements, like providing students with healthy snacks and explaining the importance of getting enough sleep the night before testing, can also decrease anxiety and boost energy.

Grading in the ESL Classroom

Figuring out how to apply assessment information in the ESL classroom to the official grading process required by most schools can be challenging. It is important for grades of ELLs to reflect the effort put forth by the student and the growth each individual student has made throughout the grading period. The various assessments described earlier can all be used within an ESL classroom to determine how a student is progressing in the different areas of language development.

In content-area classes, where a student's level of English proficiency can directly affect his or her ability to learn the content, it is critical that the teacher not penalize students based on their language proficiency. Of course, this assumes that the student has been correctly placed in a mainstream class. It is not appropriate for a beginner or early intermediate ELL to be placed in a mainstream content class. For students who are properly placed and who are working to the best of their ability in the time given, it can be quite discouraging to receive low or failing grades.

Content teachers can grade ELLs more equitably by offering alternative forms of assessment and providing modifications such as more time, bilingual dictionaries, and simplification of directions and questions. Some schools also offer a more accurate picture of ELL student achievement in content classes by adding a comment on the student's grade report or transcript explaining the grade was for an "adjusted curriculum." This can allow for grading practices that "do not encourage students to give up or coast but rather hold them to the standards that they as individual learners are capable of reaching."[18]

We have emphasized the importance of student self-assessment and reflection throughout this book, and in both ESL and content area classes we strongly recommend that this concept be applied to grading as well. Students can be asked to suggest their own grades—and back their suggestions up with evidence—so that teachers can consider those recommendations. We have found that 90 percent of the time we agree with their suggested grade, 5 percent of the time we increase it, and 5 percent of the time we reduce it.

While we certainly don't claim to know the perfect way to assign grades in the ESL classroom, the following suggestions may be helpful for teachers as they work their way through this process. We have adapted and modified the following guidelines from the Sacramento City Unified School District to reflect our own classroom practice:[19]

> Sacramento City Unified recommends that in order to assign grades for ELLs that are "valid, reliable, and fair," they should be based on indicators that address three criteria: product, process, and progress. It is also recommended that students are made aware of what the grading process will be right from the start. Teachers could use both summative and formative assessments in order to measure students' progress in the following three areas.

1. Product Criteria (quality of student work) 40 percent.
   - Tests and Quizzes
   - Prompted Writing
   - Performance Activities and Tasks
   - Ongoing Requirements (daily reading, journals, learning logs, etc.)
   - Projects and Essays
2. Process Criteria (how students do their work) 20 percent
   - Collaboration
   - Daily work habits and homework

3. Progress Criteria (evidence that students are progressing) 40 percent
   - Acquisition of social language
   - Academic language development

Navigating the world of assessment of English language learners can be challenging for both teachers and students. It is easy to get caught up in the nuts and bolts of grading, but ultimately in everything we do—whether it's grading, teaching lessons, or interacting with students—we need to ask ourselves, What will help this student move forward? In other words, what strategies will help this student develop intrinsic motivation and gain proficiency?

We hope you have gained (or been reminded of) some effective assessment practices and strategies that will promote learning and equitable assessment in the ESL classroom. We also hope you will use these ideas to reflect on your own assessment practices. Ultimately ESL teachers must use their own judgment to determine what types of assessment techniques will work best with their students.

Additional resources, including ones on rubrics, formative assessment, test-taking strategies for students, up-to-date information on the new English Proficiency and Common Core standardized tests, and links to work being done connecting Common Core to ELLs can be found on our book's web site at www.josseybass.com/go/eslsurvivalguide.

Afterword

*A*nansi the spider had all the world's wisdom in one pot and went to hide it at the top of a tree. He was having a hard time climbing with it, though, and his son suggested he tie it to his back. Anansi was tired and frustrated at hearing a young person trying to give him advice, so he threw the pot down. It hit the ground and all the wisdom spilt into a stream and washed out to sea. So now, no one person has all the wisdom in the world — everyone has some to share.[1]

This West African folktale emphasizes the message we would like to leave you with — though we feel that our book is an excellent resource for teachers of English language learners, we certainly don't feel we have a monopoly on the truth.

In this book, we have offered the best suggestions and advice we can about teaching English language learners. These recommendations come out of our classroom experience and well-documented research from multiple sources.

However, as we said in our Introduction, we also believe that it is important for schools to develop long-term relationships with high-quality professional development organizations that can provide on-site assistance for educators. While we have discussed the great advantages that professional connections developed through social media can provide, they are no substitute for hands-on support from experienced educators committed to developing long term and positive professional relationships with teachers and their schools.

Our school works closely with three groups that we highly recommend:

Pebble Creek Labs and its director, Kelly Young, offer some of the nation's premier training on instructional strategies. Though Young's work is not specifically geared for ESL teachers and students, his assistance has probably been the most influential on the way we teach. (http://pebblecreeklabs.com)

The WRITE Institute is based at the San Diego County Office of Education and provides exceptional teacher training and curriculum for English language learners. (http://www.sdcoe.net/lret2/els/?loc=write&m=3)

The California Writing Project and its national group, the National Writing Project, have provided important support to all our teachers, including those working with English language learners, on developing effective strategies to teach writing. (http://www.californiawritingproject.org; http://www.nwp.org)

This kind of ongoing support is especially important as states are now adopting Common Core standards. As we are writing this book, there are no Common Core standards for ESL. However, major efforts are under way both to develop parallel ESL standards aligned with the Common Core and to develop related standardized student language proficiency assessments.

Finally, it is important to remember that online resources related to English language learners are constantly being changed and developed. Ferlazzo writes the most popular blog on the Web for teachers of ELLs, and we encourage you to read it regularly and contribute your own comments, ideas, and experiences.

Our students are different every year, educators learn from experiences every year, new research is done every year, and new education policies are adopted by governing authorities every year.

For these reasons, we might want to keep in mind this quotation from Winston Churchill: "Now this is not the end. It is not even the beginning of the end. But it is, perhaps, the end of the beginning."[2]

Visit our book's web site at www.josseybass.com/go/eslsurvivalguide for up-to-date information on Common Core standards for ELLs, language proficiency tests, and new teaching resources.

Notes

Introduction

1. "The Hummingbird and the Forest Fire" (n.d.). Retrieved from http://www
.youtube.com/watch?v=1hr3i3LYGU4.

Chapter One

1. "Climbing the Mountain," *World of Tales: Stories for Children, Folktales, Fairy
Tales and Fables from around the World* (n.d.). Retrieved from http://worldoftales
.com/Native_American_folktales/Native_American_Folktale_3.html.

2. M. Csikszentmihalyi, *Flow: The Psychology of Optimal Experience* (New York: Harper
Perennial, 1990).

3. S. Krashen, *The Compelling (Not Just Interesting) Input Hypothesis* (2011). Retrieved
from http://www.tprstorytelling.com/images/The_Compelling_Input_Hypoth
esis.pdf, 1.

4. California Department of Education, *Improving Education for English Learners: Research-Based Approaches* (Sacramento: California Department of Education, 2010). Retrieved from http://www.cal.org/resources/pubs/improving
-education-for-english-learners.html, 1.

5. J. Batalova and M. McHugh, *Number and Growth of Students in U.S. Schools in Need of
English Instruction* (Washington, DC: Migration Policy Institute, 2010). Retrieved
from http://www.migrationinformation.org/ellinfo/FactSheet_ELL1.pdf.

6. C. Goldenberg, "Teaching English Language Learners: What the Research
Does—and Does Not—Say." *American Educator* (Summer 2008): 8–23, 42–4.

7. Goldenberg, "Teaching English Language Learners."

8. J. Batalova and M. McHugh, *Top Languages Spoken by English Language Learners Nationally and by State* (Washington, DC: Migration Policy Institute, 2010). Retrieved from http://www.migrationinformation.org/ellinfo/FactSheet_ELL3 .pdf.

9. National Council of Teachers of English, *English Language Learners* (Urbana, IL: National Council of Teachers of English, 2008). Retrieved from http://www.ncte.org/library/NCTEFiles/Resources/PolicyResearch/ ELLResearchBrief.pdf.

10. National Council of Teachers of English, *English Language Learners.*

11. National Council of Teachers of English, *English Language Learners.*

12. National Council of Teachers of English, *English Language Learners.*

13. M. E. Calderon, "Expediting Language, Literacy, and Learning for Adolescent ELLs." *STARlight* no. 6 (Dec. 2008). Retrieved from http://en.elresearch .org/issues/6.

14. National Education Association, *English Language Learners Face Unique Challenges* (Washington, DC: National Education Association, 2008). Retrieved from http://www.weac.org/Libraries/PDF/ELL.sflb.ashx.

15. Calderon, "Expediting Language, Literacy, and Learning for Adolescent ELLs."

16. L. Olsen, "A Closer Look at Long-Term English Learners: A Focus on New Directions." *STARlight* no. 7 (Dec. 2010). Retrieved from http://en.elresearch .org/issues/7.

17. S. D. Sparks, "Study: Older Students May Learn Language Rules Faster." *Education Week*, July 26, 2011. Retrieved from http://blogs.edweek .org/edweek/inside-school-research/2011/07/study_older_students_may_learn .html.

18. J. Cummins, "Cognitive/Academic Language Proficiency, Linguistic Interdependence, the Optimum Age Question and Some Other Matters." *Working Papers on Bilingualism* no. 19 (1979):121–9.

19. Cummins, "Cognitive/Academic Language Proficiency."

20. L. W. Fillmore and C. Snow, *What Elementary Teachers Need to Know about Language* (Washington, DC: Center for Applied Linguistics, Nov. 2000). Retrieved from http://www.cal.org/resources/digest/0006fillmore.html.

21. R. Scarcella, *Academic English: A Conceptual Framework* (Irvine: University of California Irvine, Linguistic Minority Research Institute, 2003). Retrieved from http://academics.utep.edu/LinkClick.aspx?link=Scarcella.pdf&tabid=63592& mid=143176.

22. Howard Research, *Kindergarten to 12th Grade English as a Second Language Literature Review Update* (Calgary, Canada: Howard Research, Oct. 2009). Retrieved from http://education.alberta.ca/media/1182477/esl_lit_review.pdf.

23. S. D. Krashen, *Second Language Acquisition and Second Language Learning* (Oxford, UK: Pergamon Press, 1981). Retrieved from http://sdkrashen.com/SL_Acquisition_and_Learning/SL_Acquisition_and_Learning.pdf.

24. Goldenberg, "Teaching English Language Learners."

25. S. Krashen and T. Terrell, *The Natural Approach* (Englewood Cliffs, NJ: Alemany Press, 1983).

26. K. Robertson and K. Ford, "Language Acquisition: An Overview," 2008. Retrieved from http://www.colorincolorado.org/article/26751/?utm_source=Twitter&utm_medium=Hootsuite&utm_campaign=CCSocialMedia.

27. Robertson and Ford, "Language Acquisition."

28. Goldenberg, "Teaching English Language Learners."

29. D. H. Schunk, "Self-Efficacy for Reading and Writing: Influence of Modeling, Goal Setting, and Self-Evaluation." *Reading and Writing Quarterly* 19 (2003): 159–72. Retrieved from http://libres.uncg.edu/ir/uncg/f/D_Schunk_Self_2003.pdf, 161.

30. R. J. Marzano, *The Art and Science of Teaching* (Alexandria, VA: ASCD, 2007).

31. M. Y. Szpara and I. Ahmad, *Making Social Studies Meaningful for ELL Students: Content and Pedagogy in Mainstream Secondary School Classrooms* (Brookville, NY: Long Island University, 2006). Retrieved from http://www.usca.edu/essays/vol162006/ahmad.pdf.

32. Goldenberg, "Teaching English Language Learners."

33. Goldenberg, "Teaching English Language Learners."

34. Goldenberg, "Teaching English Language Learners."

35. *Understand Curriculum and Reshape Instruction: Checking for Understanding.* (n.d.). Retrieved from http://www.cds.hawaii.edu/heupena/strategies/understand/strategies/strategy04.php.

36. Howard Research, *Kindergarten to 12th Grade English as a Second Language Literature Review Update*.

Chapter Two

1. Hmong folktale, similar to the Aesop's fable "The Farmer and His Sons" (n.d.). Retrieved from http://mythfolklore.net/aesopica/milowinter/78.htm.

2. L. Ferlazzo, "The Best Resources on the Importance of Building Positive Relationships with Students," March 8, 2011. Retrieved from http://larryferlazzo.edublogs.org.

3. C. Suarez-Orozco, A. Pimental, and M. Martin, "The Significance of Relationships: Academic Engagement and Achievement among Newcomer Immigrant Youth." *Teachers College Record* 111, no. 3 (2009): 712–49, pp. 712–3.

4. A. Gregory and M. B. Ripski, "Adolescent Trust in Teachers: Implications for Behavior in the High School Classroom." *School Psychology Review* 37, no. 3 (2008): 337–353, p. 345.

5. R. J. Marzano, *The Art and Science of Teaching* (Alexandria, VA: ASCD, 2007), 150.

6. L. Ferlazzo, "How I Milked a Lesson for Every Last Ounce of Learning and Why I'm an Idiot for Not Thinking of It Earlier," Jan. 22, 2011. Retrieved from http://larryferlazzo.edublogs.org.

7. J. Yatvin, "Letting Teachers Re-Invent Their Own Wheel." *Washington Post*, July 6, 2011. Retrieved from http://www.washingtonpost.com/blogs/answer-sheet /post/letting-teachers-re-invent-their-own-wheel/2011/07/06/gIQAM9lQ1H _blog.html?wprss=answer-sheet.

8. Yatvin, "Letting Teachers Re-Invent Their Own Wheel."

9. R. J. Marzano and J. S. Marzano, "Building Classroom Relationships: The Key to Classroom Management." *Educational Leadership* 61, no. 1 (2003): 6–13. Retrieved from http://www.ascd.org/publications/educational-leadership /sept03/vol61/num01/The-Key-to-Classroom-Management.aspx.

10. Marzano, *The Art and Science of Teaching*.

11. California Department of Education, *Improving Education for English Learners: Research-Based Approaches* (Sacramento: California Department of Education, 2010). Retrieved from http://www.cal.org/resources/pubs/improving -education-for-english-learners.html, 195.

12. "Are You Happy for Me? How Sharing Positive Events with Others Provides Personal and Interpersonal Benefits." *Journal of Personal and Social Psychology* 99, no. 2 (2010): 311–29.

13. D. W. Johnson, R. T. Johnson, and C. Roseth, "Do Peer Relationships Affect Achievement?" *Newsletter of the Cooperative Learning Institute* 21, no. 1 (2006): 1–4, p. 3.

14. Johnson, Johnson, and Roseth, "Do Peer Relationships Affect Achievement?" 4.

15. Southwest Educational Development Laboratory, *A New Wave of Evidence: The Impact of School, Family, and Community Connections on Achievement* (Austin, TX: Southwest Educational Development Laboratory, 2002).

16. M. Kratochvil, "Urban Tactics: Translating for Parents Means Growing up Fast." *New York Times* archives, 2001. Retrieved from http://www.nytimes .com/2001/08/26/nyregion/urban-tactics-translating-for-parents-means -growing-up-fast.html?pagewanted=1.

17. L. Ferlazzo and L. Hammond, *Building Parent Engagement in Schools* (Santa Barbara, CA: Linworth, 2009).

18. "Why It Pays to Be Bilingual." VOXYblog, Feb. 15, 2011. Retrieved from http://voxy.com/blog/2011/02/why-it-pays-to-be-bilingual-infographic/?view =infographic.

19. The Minneapolis Foundation, *Insights: Immigrant Experiences* (Saint Paul, MN: Wilder Research, May 2010). Retrieved from https://destination2010.tmfportal .org/Repository/D2010/Documents/Insight%20Reports/Destination%202010 %20Immigrant%20Experiences.pdf, 12.

20. L. Ferlazzo, *English Language Learners: Strategies That Work* (Columbus, OH: Linworth, 2010), 8.

21. L. Ferlazzo, "The Best Resources for Learning about Handwriting and Learning," Jan. 24, 2011. Retrieved from http://larryferlazzo.edublogs.org.

22. J. Cummins, *BICS and CALP*. Retrieved from http://iteachilearn.org/cummins /bicscalp.html.

23. J. Cummins, *Computer Assisted Text Scaffolding for Curriculum Access and Language Learning/Acquisition*. Retrieved from http://iteachilearn.org/cummins/comptext .html.

24. G. Goodman, *The Reading Renaissance/Accelerated Reader Program: Pinal County School-to-Work Evaluation Report* (1999). ERIC document no. ED 427299.

25. S. Krashen, "The (Lack of) Experimental Evidence Supporting the Use of Accelerated Reader." *Journal of Children's Literature* 29, no. 2 (2003): 16–30.

26. "For Poor Families, Especially, Books at Home Propel Children to More Years in School." May 26, 2010. Retrieved from http://www.voanews.com/learning english/home/For-Poor-Especially-Books-at-Home-Propel-Children-in -School-94917694.html?refresh=1.

27. L. A. Lyttle, *Do Peer Tutors Help Teach ESL Students to Learn English as a Second Language More Successfully?* April 7, 2011. ERIC document no. ED 518172. Retrieved from http://eric.ed.gov/PDFS/ED518172.pdf, 9.

28. Howard Research, *Kindergarten to 12th Grade English as a Second Language Literature Review Update* (Calgary, Canada: Howard Research, Oct. 2009). Retrieved from http://education.alberta.ca/media/1182477/esl_lit_review.pdf.

29. M. Hubenthal and T. O'Brien, "Revisiting Your Classroom's Walls: The Pedagogical Power of Posters," Dec. 23, 2009. Retrieved from http://www.iris .edu/hq/files/programs/education_and_outreach/poster_pilot/Poster_Guide _v2a.pdf, 4.

30. Ferlazzo and Hammond, *Building Parent Engagement in Schools*; L. Ferlazzo, "The Best Places to Find Research on Technology and Language Teaching/Learning," Feb. 23, 2011. Retrieved from http://larryferlazzo.edublogs.org.

31. Howard Research, *Kindergarten to 12th Grade English as a Second Language Literature Review Update*, 39.

32. Canadian Federation for the Humanities and Social Sciences, "Wikipedia Improves Students' Work: Students Become Much More Concerned with Accuracy When Their Research Is Posted Online, Study Finds." *Science Daily*, May 31, 2011. Retrieved from http://www.sciencedaily.com/releases /2011/05/110531102708.htm.

33. C. Goldenberg, "Teaching English Language Learners: What the Research Does—and Does Not—Say." *American Educator* (Summer 2008): 8–23, 42–4. Retrieved from http://www.aft.org/pdfs/americaneducator/summer2008/gold enberg.pdf, 20.

34. R. J. Marzano, *A Handbook for Classroom Management That Works* (Alexandria, VA: ASCD, 2005), 5–6.

Chapter Three

1. L. Eskicioglu, "Scientific Meeting," 2001. Retrieved from http://www.read literature.com/h010429.htm.

2. B. Joyce, M. Hrycauk, and E. Calhoun, "A Second Chance for Struggling Readers." *Educational Leadership* 58, no. 6 (Mar. 2001); K. D. Wood and J. Tinajero, "Using Pictures to Teach Content to Second Language Learners." *Middle School Journal* 33, no. 5 (2002): 47–51. Retrieved from http://www.amle.org /Publications/MiddleSchoolJournal/Articles/May2002/Article7/tabid/423 /Default.aspx.

3. E. Calhoun, *Teaching Beginning Reading and Writing with the Picture Word Inductive Mode* (Alexandria, VA: Association for Supervision and Curriculum Development, 1999).

4. E. Calhoun, T. Poirier, N. Simon, and L. Mueller, *Teacher (and District) Research: Three Inquiries into the Picture Word Inductive Model.* Paper presented at the Annual Meeting of the American Educational Research Association, Seattle, WA, April 2001. Retrieved from http://www.eric.ed.gov/PDFS/ED456107.pdf.

5. D. Wilson and M. Conyers, *60 Strategies for Increasing Student Learning* (Orlando, FL: BrainSmart, 2011).

6. J. D. Ozubko and C. M. Macleod, "The Production Effect in Memory: Evidence That Distinctiveness Underlies the Benefit." *Journal of Experimental Psychology: Learning, Memory, and Cognition* 36, no. 6 (2010): 1543–49. Retrieved from http:// www.ncbi.nlm.nih.gov/pubmed/20804284.

7. M. K. Kabilan, "Developing the Critical ESL Learner: The Freire's Way." *ELT Newsletter,* June 2000. Retrieved from http://www.eltnewsletter.com/back /June2000/art192000.shtml.

8. I. Shor, *Freire for the Classroom* (Portsmouth, NH: Heinemann, 1987), 164.

9. L. Ferlazzo, "Freire's Learning Sequence." *Library Media Connection*, Jan./Feb. 2011. Retrieved from http://linworth.com/pdf/lmc/hot_stuff/LMC_JanFeb11_MediaMaven.pdf, 5

10. J. Mathews-Aydinli, *Problem-Based Learning and Adult English Language Learners.* CAELA Brief (Washington, DC: Center for Adult English Language Acquisition, Apr. 2007). Retrieved from http://www.cal.org/caela/esl_resources/briefs/Problem-based.pdf.

11. C. C. Block, S. R. Parris, K. L. Reed, C. S. Whiteley, and M. D. Cleveland, "Instructional Approaches That Significantly Increase Reading Comprehension." *Journal of Educational Psychology* 101, no. 2 (2009): 262–81. Retrieved from http://bestpracticesweekly.com/wp-content/uploads/2011/07/Best-uses-of-independent-reading-time-Article.pdf.

12. L. Ferlazzo, "The Best Resources Documenting the Effectiveness of Free Voluntary Reading," Feb. 26, 2011. Retrieved from http://larryferlazzo.edublogs.org.

13. S. Krashen, *81 Generalizations about Free Voluntary Reading.* IATEFL Young Learner and Teenager Special Interest Group Publication, 2009. Retrieved from http://successfulenglish.com/wp-content/uploads/2010/01/81-Generalizations-about-FVR-2009.pdf.

14. J. Cummins, *Computer Assisted Text Scaffolding for Curriculum Access and Language Learning/Acquisition.* Retrieved from http://iteachilearn.org/cummins/comptext.html.

15. C. O. Kit, "Report on the Action Research Project on English Dictation in a Local Primary School." *Hong Kong Teachers' Centre Journal* 2 (2004): 1–10. Retrieved from http://edb.org.hk/hktc/download/journal/j2/P1–10.pdf.

16. G. R. Kiany and E. Shiramiry, "The Effect of Frequent Dictation on the Listening Comprehension Ability of Elementary EFL Learners." *TESL Canada Journal* 20, no. 1 (2002): 57–63.

17. R. Kidd, "Teaching ESL Grammar through Dictation." *TESL Canada Journal* 10, no. 1 (1992): 49–61.

18. J. Bruner, J. J. Goodnow, and G. A. Austin, *A Study of Thinking* (New York: Science Editions, 1967).

19. J. Willis, *Research-Based Strategies to Ignite Student Learning* (Alexandria, VA: ASCD, 2006), 15.

20. N. Shamnad, *Effectiveness of Concept Attainment Model on Achievement in Arabic Grammar of Standard IX Students.* Unpublished thesis, Mahatma Ghandi University, Kottayam, India, 2005.

21. L. Alfieri, P. J. Brooks, N. J. Aldrich, and H. R. Tenenbaum, "Does discovery-based instruction enhance learning?" [Abstract.] *Journal of Educational Psychology*

103, no. 1 (2011): 1–18. Retrieved from http://psycnet.apa.org/index.cfm?fa=buy.optionToBuy&id=2010-23599-001; R. J. Marzano, "The Perils and Promises of Discovery Learning." *Educational Leadership* 69, no. 1 (2011): 86–7. Retrieved from http://www.ascd.org/publications/educational-leadership/sept11/vol69/num01/The-Perils-and-Promises-of-Discovery-Learning.aspx.

22. S. F. Peregoy and O. Boyle, *Reading, Writing, and Learning in ESL* (Boston: Pearson Education, 2008), 279.

23. X. Liang, B. A. Mohan, and M. Early, "Issues of Cooperative Learning in ESL Classes: A Literature Review." *TESL Canada Journal* 15, no. 2 (1998): 13–23. Retrieved from http://www.teslcanadajournal.ca/index.php/tesl/article/viewFile/698/529; E. K. Polley, *Learner Perceptions of Small Group and Pair Work in the ESL Classroom: Implications for Conditions in Second Language Acquisition.* Unpublished thesis, University of Texas, Arlington, 2007. Retrieved from http://dspace.uta.edu/bitstream/handle/10106/315/umi-uta-1643.pdf?sequence=1.

24. S. Krashen, "Basic Phonics." *TexTESOL III Newsletter* (Nov. 2004): 2–4.

25. S. Bassano, *Sounds Easy! Phonics, Spelling, and Pronunciation Practice* (Provo, UT: Alta Book Center, 2002). Retrieved from http://altaesl.com/Detail.cfm?CatalogID=1543.

26. L. Ferlazzo, *English Language Learners: Teaching Strategies That Work* (Santa Barbara, CA: Linworth, an imprint of ABC-CLIO, 2010), 86.

27. Krashen, "Basic Phonics"; S. Krashen, *81 Generalizations about Free Voluntary Reading*, IATEFL Young Learner and Teenager Special Interest Group Publication, 2009. Retrieved from http://successfulenglish.com/wp-content/uploads/2010/01/81-Generalizations-about-FVR-2009.pdf.

28. B. Cambourne, *The Drum Opinion* (Oct. 13, 2009). Retrieved from http://www.abc.net.au/unleashed/29262.html.

29. L. Ferlazzo, *English Language Learners: Teaching Strategies That Work*, 78.

30. H. D. Brown, *Principles of Language Learning and Teaching*, 5th ed. (White Plains, NY: Pearson Longman, 2007), 105.

31. A. M. Dettenrieder, *Total Physical Response Storytelling and the Teaching of Grammar Rules in Second Language Instruction.* Unpublished research project, Regis University, 2006. Retrieved from http://adr.coalliance.org/codr/fez/eserv/codr:559/RUETD00307.pdf.

32. J. J. Asher, *The Total Physical Response* (TPR): *Review of the Evidence*, May 2009. Retrieved from http://www.tpr-world.com/review_evidence.pdf.

33. K. Schoepp, "Reasons for Using Songs in the ESL/EFL classroom." *The Internet TESL Journal* VII, no. 2 (2001). Retrieved from http://iteslj.org/Articles/Schoepp-Songs.html.

34. X. Li and M. Brand, "Effectiveness of Music on Vocabulary Acquisition, Language Usage, and Meaning for Mainland Chinese ESL Learners." *Contributions to Music Education* 36, no. 1 (2009): 73–84. Retrieved from http://krpb.pbworks.com/f/music-esl.pdf.

35. E. Jensen, "Music Tickles the Reward Centers in the Brain." *Brain-Based Jensen Learning*, June 1, 2001. Retrieved from http://www.jensenlearning.com/news/music-tickles-the-reward-centers-in-the-brain/brain-based-learning.

36. C. Graham, "How to Create a Jazz Chant." *Teaching Village*, May 23, 2010. Retrieved from http://www.teachingvillage.org/2010/05/23/how-to-create-a-jazz-chant-by-carolyn-graham.

37. L. Ferlazzo, "The Best Sites (and Videos) for Learning about Jazz Chants," July 28, 2011. Retrieved from http://larryferlazzo.edublogs.org.

38. F. Tang and D. Loyet, "Celebrating Twenty-Five Years of Jazz Chants." *Idiom*, Fall 2003. Retrieved from http://www.nystesol.org/pub/idiom_archive/idiom_fall 2003.html.

39. S.-Y. Wu, "Effective Activities for Teaching English Idioms to EFL Learners." *The Internet TESL Journal* XIV, no. 3 (2008). Retrieved from http://iteslj.org/Techniques/Wu-TeachingIdioms.html.

40. L. Ferlazzo, "How We Made an Excellent Speaking Activity Even Better," Apr. 11, 2011. Retrieved from http://larryferlazzo.edublogs.org.

41. P. Nation, "The Four Strands." *Innovation in Language Teaching* 1, no. 1 (2007): 1–12. Retrieved from http://www.victoria.ac.nz/lals/staff/Publications/paul-nation/2007-Four-strands.pdf.

42. L. Pollard, N. Hess, and J. Herron, *Zero Prep for Beginners: Ready-to-Go Activities for the Language Classroom* (Provo, UT: Alta Book Center, 2001).

43. National Center for Technology Innovation and Center for Implementing Technology in Education, "Captioned Media: Literacy Support for Diverse Learners." *Reading Rockets*, 2010. Retrieved from http://www.readingrockets.org/article/35793.

44. C. Canning-Wilson, "Practical Aspects of Using Video in the Foreign Language Classroom." *The Internet TESL Journal* VI, no. 11 (2000). Retrieved from http://iteslj.org/Articles/Canning-Video.html.

45. Canning-Wilson, "Practical Aspects of Using Video in the Foreign Language Classroom"; R. T. Williams and P. Lutes, *Using Video in the ESL Classroom*. (n.d.). Retrieved from http://www.takamatsu-u.ac.jp/library/06_gakunaisyupan/kiyo/no48/001–013_williams.pdf.

46. L. Ferlazzo, "Improvisation in the ESL/EFL Classroom—at Least in Mine," Dec. 2, 2009. Retrieved from http://larryferlazzo.edublogs.org.

47. C. Sherman, *The Neuroscience of Improvisation*. The Dana Foundation, June 13, 2011. Retrieved from http://dana.org/news/features/detail.aspx?id=33254.

Chapter Four

1. B. Lopez de Mariscal, *The Harvest Birds (Los pajaros de la cosecha)* (San Francisco: Children's Book Press, 2001).

2. R. J. Marzano, *The Art and Science of Teaching* (Alexandria, VA: ASCD, 2007), 57.

3. R. Wormeli, *Summarization in Any Subject: 50 Techniques to Improve Student Learning*. (Alexandria, VA: ASCD, 2004), 2.

4. Marzano, *The Art and Science of Teaching*.

5. D. H. Schunk, "Self-Efficacy for Reading and Writing: Influence of Modeling, Goal Setting, and Self-Evaluation." *Reading and Writing Quarterly* 19 (2003): 159–72. Retrieved from http://libres.uncg.edu/ir/uncg/f/D_Schunk_Self _2003.pdf.

6. C. S. Hulleman and J. M. Harackiewicz, "Promoting Interest and Performance in High School Science Classes." *Science* 326, no. 5958 (2009): 1410–2. Retrieved from http://www.sciencemag.org/content/326/5958/1410.full.pdf.

7. P. Pappas, *A Taxonomy of Reflection: Critical Thinking for Students, Teachers, and Principals (Part I)*. Jan. 4, 2010. Retrieved from http://peterpappas.blogs.com/copy _paste/2010/01/taxonomy-reflection-critical-thinking-students-teachers -principals-.html.

8. C. Vatterott, *Rethinking Homework: Best Practices That Support Diverse Needs* (Alexandria, VA: ASCD, 2009); C. Vatterott, "Five Hallmarks of Good Homework." *Educational Leadership* 68, no. 1 (2010): 10–15. Retrieved from http://www.ascd.org/publications/educational-leadership/sept10/vol68 /num01/Five-Hallmarks-of-Good-Homework.aspx.

9. E. Barker, *Barking up the Wrong Tree*. Aug. 2, 2010. Retrieved from http:// www.bakadesuyo.com/whats-an-easy-way-to-strengthen-your-relation?utm _source=feedburner&utm_medium=feed&utm_campaign=Feed:+bakade -suyo+(Barking+up+the+wrong+tree.

10. "A Conversation with FOB: What Works for Adult ESL Students." Focus on Basics 6, no. C (Sept. 2003). Retrieved from http://www.ncsall .net/?id=189.

11. S. F. Peregoy and O. Boyle, *Reading, Writing, and Learning in ESL* (Boston: Pearson Education, 2008), 93.

12. "Acquiring Power Inspires People to Take Risks, Act, According to Stanford Business School Research." Jan. 23, 2009. Retrieved from http://www .reuters.com/article/2009/01/23/idUS128822+23-Jan-2009+BW20090123; N.

J. Fast, D. H. Gruenfeld, N. Sivanathan, and A. D. Galinsky, "The Thought of Acquiring Power Motivates People to Act." Dec. 1, 2008. Retrieved from http://www.hci.org/lib/thought-acquiring-power-motivates-people-act.

13. S. D. Sparks, "Science Grows on Acquiring New Language." *Education Week,* Oct. 22, 2010. Retrieved from http://www.edweek.org/ew/articles/2010/10 /22/09window_ep.h30.html?tkn=TNPFqJBHpqUPsAmtxWv1RHBwsJn%2BT WCr%2BbC9&cmp=clp-edweek.

14. V. L. Holmes and M. R. Moulton, "Dialogue Journals as an ESL Learning Strategy." *Journal of Adolescent and Adult Literacy* 40, no. 8 (1997): 616–21; see also a list at http://www.gallaudet.edu/documents/clerc/dialogue-journal-and -writing-abstracts.pdf.

15. M. S. Summak and others. *Drama Behind the Curtain: Shadow Theatre in EFL/ESL classes.* Paper presented at the Annual Meeting of the Teachers of English to Speakers of Other Languages, Baltimore, MD, Mar. 1994.

16. S.-Y. Wu, "Effective Activities for Teaching English Idioms to EFL Learners. *The Internet TESL Journal* XIV, no. 3 (2008). Retrieved from http://iteslj.org /Techniques/Wu-TeachingIdioms.html.

17. S. D. Sparks, "Studies Find Students Learn More by 'Acting out' Text." *Education Week,* July 12, 2011. Retrieved from http://www.edweek.org/ew/articles/2011 /07/13/36read.h30.html?tkn=NPPFMxdzo%2Bnoreu2xBC70BSm2Vz2KWbb BWlk&cmp=ENL-EU-NEWS1.

18. R. J. Marzano, *Cues and Questions.* Marzano Research Laboratory, 2009. Retrieved from http://www.marzanoresearch.com/research/cues_and_questions.aspx.

Chapter Five

1. "Parable of the Gem in the Robe." (n.d.). Retrieved from http://www.gakkaion line.net/kids/gem.html.

2. G. P. Latham and E. A. Locke, "Enhancing the Benefits and Overcoming the Pitfalls of Goal Setting." *Organizational Dynamics* 35, no. 4 (2006): 332–40.

3. L. Ferlazzo, "The Best Resources on Students Using Gestures and Physical Movement to Help with Learning," June 2, 2011. Retrieved from http://larry ferlazzo.edublogs.org.

4. R. J. Marzano, *Building Background Knowledge for Academic Achievement: Research on What Works in Schools* (Alexandria, VA: ASCD, 2004).

5. Marzano, *Building Background Knowledge for Academic Achievement,* 97.

6. E. Jensen, *Brain-Based Learning* (San Diego: Brain Store, 2000).

7. M. J. Drucker, "What Reading Teachers Should Know about ESL Learners." *The Reading Teacher* 57, no. 1 (2003): 22–9. Retrieved from http://read4343 .pbworks.com/f/Drucker.pdf, 27.

8. R. Farr and J. Conner, "Using Think-Alouds to Improve Reading Comprehension." *Reading Rockets,* 2004. Retrieved from http://www.readingrockets.org /article/102.

9. C. Carrubba, *Round Robin Reading: Is There Justification for Its Use or Are There Better Alternatives Available for Oral Reading Instruction?* Williamsburg, VA: College of William and Mary, College of Education, Curriculum, and Instruction, n.d. Retrieved from http://tvo.wikispaces.com/file/view/justify+RRR.pdf.

10. T. V. Rasinski, *Assessing Reading Fluency.* Honolulu: Pacific Resources for Education and Learning, 2004. Retrieved from http://www.prel.org/products/re _/assessing-fluency.pdf, 4.

11. S. Krashen, "Reach out and Read (Aloud)." *Language Magazine,* Dec. 2011. Retrieved from http://languagemagazine.com/?page_id=2688.

12. D. M. Barone and S. H. Xu, *Literacy Instruction for English Language Learners* (New York: Guilford, 2008), 231–2.

13. J. Willis, *Research-Based Strategies to Ignite Student Learning* (Alexandria, VA: ASCD, 2006), 33.

14. B. Joyce and E. Calhoun, *Learning to Teach Inductively* (Boston: Allyn & Bacon, 1998), 176.

15. G. Graff and C. Birkenstein, *They Say, I Say: The Moves That Matter in Academic Writing* (New York: Norton, 2006), XI.

16. S. Graham and D. Perin, *Writing Next: Effective Strategies to Improve Writing of Adolescents in Middle and High Schools—A Report to the Carnegie Corporation of New York* (Washington, DC: Alliance for Excellent Education, 2007). Retrieved from http://www.all4ed.org/files/WritingNext.pdf.

17. P. Nation, "The Four Strands." *Innovation in Language Teaching* 1, no. 1 (2007): 1–12. Retrieved from http://www.victoria.ac.nz/lals/staff/Publications/paul -nation/2007-Four-strands.pdf.

Chapter Six

1. "The Stag at the Pool" (n.d.). Retrieved from http://aesopfables.com/aesop4 .html.

2. L. Ferlazzo, *Helping Students Motivate Themselves: Practical Answers to Classroom Challenges* (Larchmont, NY: Eye on Education, 2011).

3. D. W. Booth and L. Swartz, *Literacy Techniques for Building Successful Readers and Writers* (Ontario: Pembroke, 2004), 103.

4. S. F. Peregoy and O. Boyle, *Reading, Writing, and Learning in ESL* (Boston: Pearson Education, 2008), 94–5.

5. S. Kujawa and L. Huske, *Critical Issue: Building on Prior Knowledge and Meaningful Student Contexts/Culture* (Naperville, IL: North Central Regional Educational Laboratory, 1995). Retrieved from http://www.ncrel.org/sdrs/areas /issues/students/learning/lr100.htm.

6. N. Dresser, *I Felt Like I Was from Another Planet: Writing from Personal Experience* (Boston: Addison Wesley, 1994).

7. D. DiSalvo, "When You Expect Rapid Feedback, the Fire to Perform Gets Hotter." *Neuronarrative*, Mar. 11, 2010. Retrieved from http://neuronarrative .wordpress.com/2010/03/11/when-you-expect-rapid-feedback-the-fire-to -perform-gets-hotter.

8. A. Rodier, "A Cure for Writer's Block: Writing for Real Audiences." *The Quarterly* 22, no. 2 (2000). Retrieved from http://www.nwp.org/cs/public/print/nwp_au /489.

9. L. Ferlazzo and L. Hammond, *Building Parent Engagement in Schools* (Santa Barbara, CA: Linworth, 2009).

10. J. Krakauer, *Into Thin Air: A Personal Account of the Mt. Everest Disaster* (New York: Anchor Books/Doubleday, 1999).

11. R. J. Marzano, *Classroom Instruction That Works* (Denver: McREL, 2001), 73.

Chapter Seven

1. H. Forest, *Wisdom Tales from around the World* (Little Rock, AK: August House, 1996), 62.

2. L. Ferlazzo, *English Language Learners: Strategies That Work* (Columbus, OH: Linworth, 2010).

3. S. Fairbairn and S. Jones-Vo, *Differentiating Instruction and Assessment for English Language Learners: A Guide for K–12 Teachers* (Philadelphia: Caslon, 2010); J. Haynes and D. Zacarian, *Teaching English Language Learners: Across the Content Areas* (Alexandria, VA: ASCD, 2010).

4. S. D. Krashen, *Principles and Practice in Second Language Acquisition* (Upper Saddle River, NJ: Prentice-Hall, 1981), 6.

5. R. J. Marzano, "Relating to Students: It's What You Do That Counts." *Educational Leadership* 68(6) (2001): 82–3. Retrieved from http://www.ascd.org /publications/educational-leadership/mar11/vol68/num06/Relating-to -Students@-It's-What-You-Do-That-Counts.aspx.

6. J. Willis, *Research-Based Strategies to Ignite Student Learning* (Alexandria, VA: ASCD, 2006).

7. California Department of Education, *Improving Education for English Learners: Research-Based Approaches* (Sacramento, CA: California Department of Education, 2010). Retrieved from http://www.cal.org/resources/pubs/improving-education-for-english-learners.html.

8. G. Caine and R. N. Caine, *Making Connections: Teaching and the Human Brain* (Menlo Park, CA: Addison Wesley, 1994).

9. J. Bruner, *Acts of Meaning* (Cambridge, MA: Harvard College, 1992).

10. *Into the Book: Strategies for Learning* (n.d.). Retrieved from http://reading.ecb.org/teacher/priorknowledge/pk_research.html.

11. Ferlazzo, *English Language Learners.*

12. E. L. Deci, *Why We Do What We Do* (New York: Penguin Books, 1995).

13. A. S. Rausch, "Language Learning Strategies Instruction and Language Use Applied to Foreign Language Reading and Writing: A Simplified 'Menu' Approach." *Literacy Across Cultures* 4, no. 1 (2000). Retrieved from http://www2.aasa.ac.jp/~dcdycus/LAC2000/rausch.htm.

14. D. Glenn, "Carol Dweck's Attitude: It's Not about How Smart You Are." *The Chronicle of Higher Education,* May 9, 2010. Retrieved from http://chronicle.com/article/Carol-Dwecks-Attitude/65405.

15. S. F. Peregoy and O. Boyle, *Reading, Writing, and Learning in ESL* (Boston: Pearson Education, 2008), 357.

16. M. A. Fitzgerald, M. Orey, and R. M. Branch, *Educational Media and Technology Yearbook,* vol. 29 (Westport, CT: Libraries Unlimited, 2004). Retrieved from http://books.google.com, 132.

17. R. J. Marzano, *Cooperative Learning* (n.d.). Retrieved from http://www.marzanoresearch.com/research/strategy_cooperative_learning.aspx?utm_source=twitterfeed&utm_medium=twitter; B. K. Saville, "Using Evidence-Based Teaching Methods to Improve Education," Oct. 21, 2009. Retrieved from https://tle.wisc.edu/node/1045.

18. Peregoy and Boyle, *Reading, Writing, and Learning in ESL.*

19. C. Goldenberg, "Teaching English Language Learners: What the Research Does—and Does Not—Say." *American Educator* (Summer 2008): 8–23, 42–4. Retrieved from http://www.aft.org/pdfs/americaneducator/summer2008/goldenberg.pdf.

20. Goldenberg, "Teaching English Language Learners."

21. Goldenberg, "Teaching English Language Learners."

22. Goldenberg, "Teaching English Language Learners."

23. California Department of Education, *Improving Education for English Learners: Research-Based Approaches* (Sacramento, CA: California Department of Education,

2010). Retrieved from http://www.cal.org/resources/pubs/improving-education-for-english-learners.html.

24. T. Hall and N. Strangman, *Graphic Organizers* (Wakefield, MA: National Center on Accessing the General Curriculum, 2002). Retrieved from http://aim.cast.org/learn/historyarchive/backgroundpapers/graphic_organizers.

25. X. Jiang and W. Grabe, "Graphic Organizers in Reading Instruction: Research Findings and Issues." *Reading in a Foreign Language* 19, no. 1 (2007).

Chapter Eight

1. L. Eskicioglu, "Building a Minaret," 2001. Retrieved from http://www.read literature.com/h010512.htm.

2. C. Griffiths, ed. *Lessons from Good Language Learners.* (Cambridge, UK: Cambridge University Press, 2008).

3. J. Percoco, *A Passion for the Past* (Portsmouth, NH: Heinemann, 1998), 33.

4. M. Y. Szpara and I. Ahmad, *Making Social Studies Meaningful for ELL Students: Content and Pedagogy in Mainstream Secondary School Classrooms* (2006). Retrieved from http://www.usca.edu/essays/vol162006/ahmad.pdf.

Chapter Nine

1. L. C. Moll, C. Amanti, D. Neff, and N. Gonzalez, "Funds of Knowledge for Teaching: Using a Qualitative Approach to Connect Homes and Classrooms." *Theory into Practice xxxi*, no. 2 (1994): 132–41.

2. S. Paloma-McCaleb, *Building Communities of Learners* (New York: St. Martin's Press, 1994).

3. T. L. Barcenal, P. B. Purita, L. N. Morano, S. E. Nichols, and D. L. Tippins, *Just in Case: Encounters in Science and Math Teaching and Learning* (La Paz, Iloilo City, Philippines: West Visayas State University Printing Press, 2002).

4. M. J. Schleppegrell and M. C. Colombi, eds., *Developing Advanced Literacy in First and Second Languages: Meaning and Power* (Mahwah, NJ: Lawrence Erlbaum Associates, 2002).

5. R. Osborne and P. Freyberg, *Learning in Science: The Implications of Children's Science* (Birkenhead, New Zealand: Heinemann Education, 1985).

6. A. C. Barton and M. D. Osborne, *Teaching Science in Diverse Settings: Marginalized Discourses and Classroom Practice* (New York: Peter Lang, 2001).

7. B. J. Merino and L. Hammond, "Writing to Learn: Science in the Upper Elementary Bilingual Classroom," in *Developing Advanced Literacy in First and Second Languages:*

Meaning with Power, M. J. Schleppegrell and M. C. Colombi, eds. (Mahwah, NJ: Lawrence Erlbaum Associates, 2002).

Chapter Ten

1. Adapted from "The Crab and Its Mother," an Aesop fable. Retrieved from http://storywise.com.sg/storytelling/story-the-crab-and-its-mother.

2. F. Favilli, "Ethnomathematics and Mathematics Education." *Proceedings of the 10th International Congress of Mathematics Education,* Copenhagen, n.d. Retrieved from http://www.dm.unipi.it/~favilli/Ethnomathematics_Proceedings_ICME10.pdf; also see International Study Group on Ethnomathematics (ISGEm), "Ethnomathematics on the Web." Retrieved from http://isgem.rpi.edu/pl/ethnomathematics-web.

3. V. Urquhart, *Using Writing in Mathematics to Deepen Student Learning* (Denver, CO: Midcontinent Research for Education and Learning, 2009), 4. Retrieved from http://www.mcrel.org/pdf/mathematics/0121TG_writing_in_mathematics.pdf.

4. R. J. Kopriva, *Assessing the Skills and Abilities in Math and Science of ELLs with Low English Proficiency: A Promising New Method* (Acton: Australian Academy of Science, National Clearinghouse for English Language Acquisition, 2003).

Chapter Eleven

1. "Smuggling" (n.d.). Retrieved from http://www.naqshbandi.ca/pages/print.php?id_article=403&language=English.

2. J. Willis, *Research-Based Strategies to Ignite Student Learning* (Alexandria, VA: ASCD, 2006).

3. R. J. Marzano, *The Art and Science of Teaching* (Alexandria, VA: ASCD, 2007), 103.

4. G. M. Jacobs and K. Cates, "Global Education in Second Language Teaching." *KATA* 1, no. 1 (1999): 44–56. Retrieved from http://www.georgejacobs.net/EE/Global%20Issues%20in%20Second%20Language%20TeachingKATA.doc.

5. A. Uberman, "The Use of Games for Vocabulary Presentation and Revision." *English Teaching Forum* 36, no. 1 (1998). Retrieved from http://eca.state.gov/forum/vols/vol36/no1/p20.htm.

6. Marzano, *The Art and Science of Teaching.*

7. J. Wink, *Critical Pedagogy: Notes from the REAL WORLD,* 3rd ed. (Boston: Allyn & Bacon, 2004).

Chapter Twelve

1. H. A. Heiner, "Boots and His Brothers," SurLaLune Fairy Tales, 2005. Retrieved from http://www.surlalunefairytales.com/books/norway/thornethomsen/boots brothers.html.

2. E. L. Deci, *Why We Do What We Do* (New York: Penguin Books, 1995), 10.

3. D. Thanasoulas, "Motivation and motivating in the foreign language class-room." *The Internet TESL Journal* VIII, no. 11 (Nov. 2002). Retrieved from http://iteslj.org/Articles/Thanasoulas-Motivation.html.

4. T. Koda-Dallow and M. Hobbs, "Personal Goal-Setting and Autonomy in Language Learning." *Supporting Independent English Language Learning in the 21st Century: Proceedings of the Independent Learning Association Conference Inaugural,* 2005. Retrieved from http://independentlearning.org/ILA/ila05/KOD05058.pdf.

5. L. Ferlazzo, "My Best Posts on Helping Students 'Visualize Success,'" Dec. 23, 2010. Retrieved from http://larryferlazzo.edublogs.org.

6. Z. Dörnyei, "Motivation and the Vision of Knowing a Second Language," in *IATEFL 2008: Exeter Conference Selections,* B. Beaven, ed. (Canterbury: IATEFL, 2009).

7. J. Renshaw, "To Innovate within Concrete, Start with the Cracks." May 1, 2010. Retrieved from http://jasonrenshaw.typepad.com/jason_renshaws_web_log /2010/05/to-innovate-within-concrete-start-with-the-cracks.html

8. L. Ferlazzo, "The Best Resources on ESL/EFL/ELL Error Correction," Sept. 4, 2011. Retrieved from http://larryferlazzo.edublogs.org.

9. California Department of Education, *Improving Education for English Learners: Research-Based Approaches* (Sacramento, CA: California Department of Education, 2010). Retrieved from http://www.cal.org/resources/pubs/improving -education-for-english-learners.html.

10. J. Truscott, "The Continuing Problems of Oral Grammar Correcting." *The International Journal of Foreign Language Teaching* 1, no. 2 (Spring 2005): 17–22.

11. J. Truscott, "The Case against Grammar Correction in L2 Writing Classes." *Language Learning* 46, no. 2 (1996): 327–69.

12. S. D. Krashen, *Second Language Acquisition and Second Language Learning* (Oxford, UK: Pergamon Press, 1981). Retrieved from http://sdkrashen.com /SL_Acquisition_and_Learning/SL_Acquisition_and_Learning.pdf.

13. D. Dodgson, *Reflections of a Teacher and Learner: Tracking My Experiences as an EFL Teacher and an MA Student!* August 7, 2011. Retrieved from http://www.davedodgson.com/2011/08/rscon3-feeding-back-and-moving -forward.html.

14. L. Ferlazzo, "The Best Places to Find Research on Technology and Language Teaching/Learning," Feb. 23, 2011. Retrieved from http://larryferlazzo.edublogs.org.

15. M. Jadallah and F. Hasan, *A Review of Some New Trends in Using L1 in the EFL* (n.d.). Retrieved from http://www.qou.edu/english/conferences/firstNational Conference/pdfFiles/drMufeed.pdf.

16. W. Saunders and C. Goldenberg, *Improving Education for English Learners* (Sacramento, CA: California Department of Education, 2010). Retrieved from http://www.cal.org/resources/pubs/improving-education-for-english-learners.html.

17. Jadallah and Hasan, *A Review of Some New Trends in Using L1 in the EFL*.

18. Saunders and Goldenberg, *Improving Education for English Learners*.

19. L. Ferlazzo, *Helping Students Motivate Themselves: Practical Answers to Classroom Challenges* (Larchmont, NY: Eye on Education, 2011).

Chapter Thirteen

1. "El Secreto del Gigante (The Giant's Secret)" (n.d.). Retrieved from http://www.g-world.org/magictales/secreto.html.

2. L. Ferlazzo, "The Best Resources Showing Why We Need to Be 'Data-Informed' and Not 'Data-Driven,'" Jan. 28, 2011. Retrieved from http://larryferlazzo.edublogs.org.

3. C. Goldenberg, "Teaching English Language Learners: What the Research Does—and Does Not—Say." *American Educator* (Summer 2008): 8–23, 42–4. Retrieved from http://www.aft.org/pdfs/americaneducator/summer2008/goldenberg.pdf, 20.

4. WIDA Consortium, *FLARE Formative Assessment Model* (n.d.). Retrieved from http://flareassessment.org/assessTools/selfAssess.aspx.

5. Howard Research, *Kindergarten to 12th Grade English as a Second Language Literature Review Update* (Calgary, Canada: Howard Research, Oct. 2009). Retrieved from http://education.alberta.ca/media/1182477/esl_lit_review.pdf, 41.

6. J. Popham, "Formative Assessment: A Process, Not a Test." *Education Week*, Feb. 22, 2011. Retrieved from http://www.edweek.org/ew/articles/2011/02/23/21popham.h30.html?tkn=PSCCGmSb%2FB5QkuTaRS6t7BoT2I7Q%2FQ9NdgMl&cmp=clp-sb-ascd.

7. R. Linquanti, *The Road Ahead for State Assessments*. May 16, 2011. Retrieved from http://renniecenter.issuelab.org/research/listing/road_ahead_for_state_assessments.

8. Wisconsin Center for Education Research, "IDEAL Formative Assessments Rating Tool." *WIDA Focus on Formative Assessment* 1, no. 2 (2009): 5. Retrieved from www.wida.us/get.aspx?id=215, 5.

9. Popham, "Formative Assessment," para. 7.

10. "Ongoing Assessment of Language, Literacy, and Content Learning." *Teaching Diverse Learners: Equity and Excellence for All* (n.d.). Retrieved from http://www.alliance.brown.edu/tdl/assessment/perfassess.shtml.

11. R. J. Marzano, *Classroom Assessment and Grading That Work* (Alexandria, VA: ASCD, 2006), 11.

12. J. Lehrer, *Learning from Mistakes*. Oct. 22, 2009. Retrieved from http://scienceblogs.com/cortex/2009/10/learning_from_mistakes.php.

13. S. F. Peregoy and O. Boyle, *Reading, Writing, and Learning in ESL* (Boston: Pearson Education, 2008), 265.

14. L. Ferlazzo, "The Best Resources for Learning about the 'Next Generation' of State Testing," June 10, 2011. Retrieved from http://larryferlazzo.edublogs.org.

15. "No Child Left Behind (NCLB) and the Assessment of English Language Learners." Colorín Colorado, 2008. Retrieved from http://www.colorincolorado.org/article/22763/?utm_source=Twitter&utm_medium=Hootsuite&utm_campaign=CCSocialMedia.

16. Center for Public Education, *What Research Says about Testing Accommodations for ELLs* (Alexandria, VA: Center for Public Education, n.d.). Retrieved from http://www.centerforpubliceducation.org/Main-Menu/Instruction/What-research-says-about-English-language-learners-At-a-glance/What-research-says-about-testing-accommodations-for-ELLs.html.

17. "No Child Left Behind (NCLB) and the Assessment of English Language Learners."

18. R. VanDeWeghe, "The Gray Areas of Grading." *English Journal* 96, no. 6 (2007): 74–7. Retrieved from http://www.siprep.org/prodev/documents/Grading.pdf, 77.

19. *Course of Study for English Language Development* (Sacramento, CA: Sacramento City Unified School District, 2005), 5.

Afterword

1. "Anansi." (n.d.). Retrieved from http://en.wikipedia.org/wiki/Anansi.

2. E. M. Knowles, *The Oxford Dictionary of Quotations* (Oxford, UK: Oxford University, 1999).

Index